Horace Liveright

Publisher of the Twenties

By Walker Gilmer

David Lewis   New York

Grateful acknowledgment is made to the following sources:

Quotations from unpublished letters of Sherwood Anderson, copyright © 1970 by Eleanor Copenhaver Anderson, are by permission of Harold Ober Associates, Inc.

Quotations from the *Letters of Sherwood Anderson*, eds. Howard Mumford Jones and Walter B. Rideout, copyright 1953 by Eleanor Anderson, are by permission of Little, Brown and Company.

Quotations from the *New York Times*, © 1922–23–27 by The New York Times Company, are by permission of The New York Times Company.

Quotations from *Sherwood Anderson's Memoirs*, copyright 1942 by Eleanor Anderson, are by permission of the University of North Carolina Press.

Quotations from the *Letters of Theodore Dreiser*, ed. Robert E. Elias, © 1959 by the Trustees of the University of Pennsylvania, are by permission of the University Press, University of Pennsylvania.

Quotations from "Horace Liveright: An Unedited Obituary," by Bennett Cerf, *Publishers' Weekly*, October 7, 1933, © 1933 by the R. R. Bowker Company, are by permission of the R. R. Bowker Company, a Xerox company.

Quotations from "The Man Who Was Unafraid," by Edith Stern, *Saturday Review of Literature*, June 28, 1941, copyright 1941 The Saturday Review Company, Inc.; renewed 1968 Saturday Review, Inc., are by permission of Saturday Review, Inc.

Quotations from *The Letters of Hart Crane, 1916–1932*, ed. Brom Weber, copyright 1952 by Brom Weber, are by permission of Mr. Weber.

For Peggy

Preface

This book is intended to be an account of the publishing career of Horace Brisbin Liveright. It was the professional Liveright who first attracted my attention, and it is his public career that I have attempted to delineate. Since he was one of the most important and colorful publishers of the Twentieth century, an account of his publishing activities seemed long overdue. In the nearly forty years since his death, accounts of Liveright have been scattered here and there in newspapers and magazines, reminiscences and critical biographies, one long forgotten novel—*The Years of Indiscretion* (Maurice Hanline, New York, 1934) —and a scarcely memorable movie, *The Scoundrel* (1935); in short, his portrait has been found in the prejudices of the living and the residues of the dead. Thus it has been my intention to give a history of the house Liveright cofounded and a profile of the man himself as publisher, to show Liveright as a shaping force on contemporary literature through his association with many of the authors who created it and to make clear his vigorous opposition to any form of censorship—to demonstrate the publisher's position, then, as a part of the creative ferment of the Twenties.

Between 1917 and 1930 Liveright issued new works by many different writers: Theodore Dreiser, Sherwood Anderson, William Faulkner, Ernest Hemingway, Hart Crane, E. E. Cummings, Ezra Pound, T. S. Eliot, Eugene O'Neill, and scores of others; simply to list them is to list many of the great names of modern American literature. Add to this roster the Modern Library, works by Sigmund Freud, Bertrand Russell, Wolfgang Kohler, Roger Martin du Gard, and François Mauriac, and the significance of Liveright's achievement grows. The qualities that typify a Liveright book seem to be originality and rebellion. From his reissue of Dreiser's *Sister Carrie* in 1917 to his publication of Russell's *Marriage and Morals* as well as Michael Gold's *Jews Without Money* at the end of the Twenties, Liveright published scores of books which were new in method and content and which questioned or openly criticized the accepted ideals of American society. These are the qualities, more than any others, which characterized both the man and the era—and which found expression in his books. Many an innovative thinker, not yet critically or financially established, found an eager sponsor in Liveright, for he seemed to be a publisher writers could and did exploit.

The firm Liveright headed throughout the Twenties also gave opportunity for training to the young writers and future executives who worked there. They were drawn to Liveright by his unmistakeable mixture of talent and eccentricity, a sense of uniqueness, which, in the words of one, "made the literary sky glow." None ever regretted it. Boni & Liveright employee-alumni included individuals who went on to both trade and national prominence: Louis Auerbach, sales manager of The Dial Press; Edward L. Bernays, author and public relations counsel; Bennett Cerf; Saxe Commins, editor; Donald Friede, cofounder of Covici-Friede; Louis Greene, former president of the R. R. Bowker Company; Maurice Hanline, author; Lillian Hellman; Beatrice Bakrow Kaufman, author; Manuel Komroff, author; Louis Kronenberger, author and drama critic; Julian Messner, founder of Julian Messner, Inc.; Isidor Schneider, author; Thomas Seltzer, founder of Thomas Seltzer, Inc.; Leon Shimkin, president of Simon & Schuster; Richard Simon, cofounder of Simon & Schuster; Manuel Siwek, president of Grosset and Dunlap; T. R. Smith, editor; Edith Stern, author; Aaron Sussman, cofounder of Sussman and Sugar; Edward A. Weeks, author and former editor of the *Atlantic Monthly*; and Leane Zugsmith, author.

Liveright made startling changes in a profession that had once offered a genteel career to gentlemen who could not write themselves. He was an upstart who—through promotion, advertising, and publicity—compelled the same attention for his books that Hearst had compelled for his newspapers. Initially publishing was an adventure for Liveright, though from time to time some other venture like the theater or the stock market replaced it; but the Liveright flair remained nearly to the end. The publisher himself often gave an impression of haste and snap judgment, but he had plenty of common sense. He could be offensive while seeming sensitive to hardship of any kind. He was bored unless he was fighting, and for most of the decade the forces of censorship were his most tenacious opponents. But battling for his books reflected more than Liveright's eagerness for publicity; he was interested in new ideas, and he believed in the works he published.

There was no lukewarm reaction to Liveright. He inspired both an adulation and a hatred that time has not diminished. Interviews and extant sources confirm this view: the ones who admired him thought he was a genius; the ones who didn't like him thought he was a bastard; and the ones who really loathed him are unwilling to acknowledge either his accomplishments or his existence.

Liveright's was a baroque personality. He was a man driven by intense inner conflicts, by contradictions of impulse and outlook. His urge toward nonconformity was opposed by an almost insatiable desire to be accepted by his peers; his flamboyant independence and egotism were counterbalanced by self-doubt and vulnerability. He was an unlikely combination of cruelty and charity, showmanship and integrity. These contradictions are reflected in his achievements and his failures; eventually they destroyed him. Liveright was a Gatsby-like figure who sometimes epitomized the excesses of the Twenties at their most blatant. On the other hand, one has only to consider the books he published, the way he promoted them, and the conviction with which he defended them to discover a man who was ahead of his time. Important writers, playwrights, and artists were doing memorable things during that era—and Horace Liveright recognized the significance of their achievements.

WALKER GILMER

April, 1970

Acknowledgments

Of all the people who helped make this book possible, I am indebted first to Herman Liveright, the publisher's son, who reminisced with me at length about his father and allowed me to quote extensively from his father's papers.

I should like to acknowledge too my appreciation for the invaluable aid given me in correspondence, interviews, and documents by the following: the late Albert Boni, Madeleine Boyd, Bennett Cerf, Louis Cline, Marc Connelly, Malcolm Cowley, Mrs. E. E. Cummings, the late Donald Friede, Lewis Galantière, Louis Greene, Harry Hansen, the late B. W. Huebsch, Horace Kallen, Manuel Komroff, Louis Kronenberg, Margaret Leech (Mrs. Ralph Pulitzer), William C. Lengel, Annette Liveright, Babette Liveright, Anita Loos, Ken McCormick, the late Kathryn Messner, Gorham Munson, Arthur Pell, Gilbert Seldes, Henry Simon, Manuel Siwek, Sigmund Spaeth, Edith Stern, Aaron Sussman, Phillip Wittenberg, and the late Stark Young.

I am also grateful to Mildred C. Smith of *Publishers' Weekly*, Amy Nyholm of the Newberry Library, Anne Freudenberg of the University of Virginia Library, and Audrey Knowlton of the DePauw University Library for assisting me in locating Liveright materal. My specal thanks go to Mrs. Neda M. Westlake, Curator of the Rare Book Collecton at the University of Pennsylvania Library, who was especially helpful and most gracious to me during the hours I spent working with the Liveright Collection.

For permission to quote from letters and other documents relating to Liveright's career, I am indebted to George S. Russell, for the Gertrude Atherton correspondence; the Mercantile-Safe Deposit and Trust Company, Baltimore, Maryland, for the excerpt from Dreiser's letter to Mencken, August 27, 1920; the Charles Patterson Van Pelt Library of the University of Pennsylvania, for material from the Dreiser Collection; the University Press of the same institution, for excerpts from Dreiser's letters; Brom Weber, for excerpts from Crane's letters; Eleanor Anderson, Harold Ober Associates, Inc., and Little, Brown and Company, for the Anderson materials; the University of North Carolina Press, for excerpts from *Sherwood Anderson's Memoirs*; *Publishers' Weekly*, for excerpts from "Horace Liveright: An Unedited Obituary"; and the *Saturday Review*, for excerpts from "The Man Who Was Unafraid."

I am happy to acknowledge that the old Liveright Publishing Comportation is now publishing new books once again.

For reading the manuscript in various forms and for other kinds of assistance, I am grateful to Fred L. Bergmann, Elizabeth Christman, Harold Garriott, and Barbara McClaine, all of DePauw University; Doris H. Platt of the State Historical Society of Wisconsin; Wallace W. Douglas and Ernest Samuels of Northwestern University, Walter B. Rideout of the University of Wisconsin; Cody Barnard, my editor; and Stanley Lewis, my publisher.

Finally, I am grateful to my wife, Peggy Gilmer, my companion in research and discussion, on the road, in boarding houses and hamburger joints. Her contributions are too numerous to list.

Contents

Boni & Liveright

On a fall morning in New York City in 1916 two strangers met over a desk piled with household gadgets and agreed to go into the book business together. One of them, Albert Boni, twenty-four, had only limited experience in this trade; the other, twenty-nine-year-old Horace Liveright had none at all.[1] Their total assets included $16,500—borrowed at that—and a million dollar idea, the reprinting of modern classics by British and Continental writers in cheap editions. They planned to call their publications, somewhat grandly, the Modern Library of the World's Best Books. Although both were unaware of it, time was running out on the old, established houses, which refused to recognize the challenge of a younger generation, and this new firm would respond to that need by issuing new titles in addition to the Modern Library once business was underway. Thus there were two results of this chance meeting: the founding of Boni & Liveright, and the emergence of Liveright, who was energetic, flamboyant, and reckless—as eager to gamble on writers and oppose censorship as he was to be noticed. Together, they signaled the opening of a new era in American publishing and literature.

Born on December 10, 1886, in Osceola Mills, Pennsylvania, Liveright and his parents, Henry and Henrietta Fleisher Liveright, moved to Philadelphia when he was in grammar school. However, his education was concluded a few years later, when, as he explained it: "I became involved in a violent argument with a teacher of history, [and] with the arrogance of youth concluded I knew more than the teacher and left school."[2] At fourteen Liveright secured a job as an office boy with a Philadelphia stockbroker and eventually became a margin clerk. At seventeen he composed the book and lyrics for a comic opera called *John Smith,* which was actually put into rehearsal on Broadway but did not open because its backer, Elmer Rice, ran out of money. Evenings in New York during production of his opera occasionally found Liveright, living on $500 borrowed from his father, seated alone in Peacock Alley at the Waldorf-Astoria Hotel, where he tipped a bellhop to page him as "Lord Roseberry," his carefully staged exits always ending inconspicuously in the men's room. After his abortive experience as a playwright, Liveright settled in New York where, after several years as a securities and bond salesman for Sutro Brothers, he became manager of the bond department of Day, Adams & Company.[3] In 1911, he married Lucile Elsas, the daughter of a vice president of the International Paper Company, and, financed by his father-in-law, he left the bond business to organize his own company for the manufacture and sale of toilet paper. In an early burst of literary enthusiasm, Liveright called his product Pick-Quick Paper and temporarily became a small-time entrepreneur.

While Liveright promoted his business uptown, Albert Boni, in 1913, took the money his father had given him to finish Harvard as well as attend law school and, with his brother Charles, opened the Washington Square Book Shop at 137 MacDougal Street.[4] The Boni brothers began publishing in a very limited way. The first volume to bear their imprint was *Not Guilty* by Robert Blatchford, who later became better known for his works of socialist propaganda. *Not Guilty*, a sociological study of crime, sold over fifty thousand copies and put the neophyte publishers in a financial position to back an entirely different kind of enterprise, Alfred Kreymborg's little magazine, *The Glebe*. Kreymborg arrived one day at the Washington Square Book Shop with a packet from Ezra Pound under his arm; it contained the Imagist anthology.[5] Sharing Kreymborg's pioneering spirit, the Bonis agreed to finance publication of *The Glebe*, even though their resources were limited. The most important issue, the Imagist number, appeared in February 1914. Called *Des Imagistes: An Anthology*, it contained poems by Pound, Hilda Doolittle, John Cournos, Amy Lowell, Ford Madox Ford, William Carlos Williams, and several others, as well as one lyric by the then unknown James Joyce. But *The Glebe* died later that year after ten issues as a result of editorial disputes between Kreymborg and the Bonis.[6] Kreymborg, who preferred to publish the poetry of unknown Americans, often clashed with the Bonis, who wanted to issue the prose translations of Continental writers. Before its demise, however, they did succeed in producing Kreymborg's novelette, *Erna Vitek*, works by Horace Traubel and William English Walling, and translations of plays by Leonid Andreyev and Frank Wedekind in different numbers of the periodical.

Next, the Bonis were briefly involved in a production called the Little Leather Library, thirty pocket-sized volumes of classics and abridgments that sold by mail for $2.98 a set.[7] The Little Leather Library, forerunner of the Modern Library, sold in large quantities on subscription as well as to Woolworth's and other stores. In fact, Woolworth's took a million copies the first year it carried the series.

Next door to the bookshop was the newly reorganized Liberal Club—"A Meeting Place for Those Interested in New Ideas"—and below it was Polly Holladay's basement restaurant.[8] Soon, with the permission of their joint landlady, Jenny Belardi, the Bonis and the Liberal Club members cut a door through the wall between the two brownstones so that the patrons of each could mingle more easily. A club, a restaurant, and a library provided the setting for budding Socialists and unpublished poets to mix with the famous: Emma Goldman, John Reed, Big Bill Heywood, Theodore Dreiser, Margaret Sanger, Henrietta Rodman, and Dr. A. A. Brill.

The founding of the Theatre Guild took place in a casual, uncertain way in the back room of the bookshop.[9] Several members of the Liberal Club, together with a few other Village residents, decided to stage a play using the store as their makeshift theater. They chose to present Lord Dunsany's *The Glittering Gate,* because copies of it were handy on the shelves surrounding them. Under the leadership of Ida Rauh, Robert Edmond Jones, and Lawrence Langner, and with the support of George Cram Cook, Hutchins Hapgood, their wives Susan Glaspell and Neith Boyce, Ida Rauh's husband Max Eastman, Wilbur Daniel Steele, John Reed, and Mary Heaton Vorse, the amateur group called themselves the Washington Square Players and incorporated in the winter of 1914. When the Players moved to Broadway, eventually becoming the Theatre Guild, a splinter faction led by the Cooks and the Hapgoods, wishing to remain amateur and off Broadway, went to Cape Cod to present their own efforts. Calling themselves the Provincetown

Players, they eventually returned to the Village in 1916 and settled at 133 MacDougal Street. There they were joined by other aspiring young writers—among them Djuna Barnes, Alfred Kreymborg, Harry Kemp, Floyd Dell, and the Millay sisters—and during their six seasons in the Village offered many productions, including plays by Dreiser and Eugene O'Neill, in their tiny, uncomfortable playhouse.

Outside financial pressures caused the Bonis to sell their interest in the Little Leather Library, and by the end of 1915 they were out of the publishing business altogether.[10] The brothers sold the Washington Square Book Shop to Frank Shay, a Village friend and a member of the Provincetown Players, and Albert Boni joined an advertising agency uptown owned by Alfred Wallerstein. Boni's motive in taking the job was to gain business experience, but in six months, with as much business training as he could possibly acquire, he was back in publishing again.

Boni's arrival at Wallerstein's agency was preceded by that of Liveright, who had already been there for several weeks. Despite its ingenious trade name, Pick-Quick Papers had failed, and Liveright was using an office at the advertising firm as a temporary headquarters while he explored devices that might be manufactured and marketed more successfully than toilet paper.[11] His father-in-law, discouraged by the Pick-Quick fiasco, had announced that he would back Liveright only once more. No one knows whether this sink-or-swim dictum had any moderating effect on his mercurial son-in-law. At any rate, after prolonged absence from the office, Liveright arrived there one morning burdened with an armload of manufacturing possibilities, in this case various kinds of household gadgets. He immediately fell upon Boni, the other occupant of the office and a total stranger to him, and asked his opinion of the relative merits of each device. Boni, who was surprised but game, matched Liveright's enthusiasm by carefully considering each one and finally choosing a self-sealing jar lid as the best sales prospect. This important decision made, Liveright listened while Boni told him about his publishing ventures and his idea for a series of reprints that would include only modern classics by European writers. Liveright, utterly unprepared in any way for the publishing business, but excited by Boni's idea, immediately offered himself as a partner. Boni was nearly broke, but Liveright proposed to finance their operation with the "last" of his father-in-law's loans. As equal partners—Liveright put up the $12,500 for capitalization, while Boni supplied $4,000 and the idea—the two men began at once to plan their business organization and make up their first list.

By the spring of 1917, when Boni & Liveright announced the first volumes of the Modern Library, the literary and publishing center of the United States had shifted from Boston to New York, but the character of the book industry had not changed at all.[12] During the nineteenth century most American classics were issued in Boston. In fact, at one time "there was a saying current in the book trade that if the books on the list of Houghton, Mifflin & Co., of Boston should vanish, little American literature would remain; for this great house published Emerson, Longfellow, Hawthorne, Whittier, Lowell, Aldrich, and other leaders of the time."[13] Despite their dominant position in the center of literary activity in America, Boston houses looked to England in matters of taste and book handling. Books were issued for a selected audience rather than a large one, and the business of publishing itself was treated with the formality of a sacred rite. Cultivated Christian gentlemen in editorial positions, books often as static in content as the promotion they received, Longfellow and Tennyson as the touchstones of writing—all these conditions were firmly entrenched as parts of the genteel tradition that Boston came to epitomize.

By 1900, however, publishers located in New York were on the way to becoming the unchallenged leaders of the industry, although firms continued to be founded in New England, Philadelphia, and Chicago. The giants of the nineteenth century—such as D. Appleton & Company; Dodd, Mead & Company; Doubleday, Page & Company; E. P. Dutton; Harper & Brothers; Henry Holt; G. P. Putnam's Sons; and Charles Scribner's Sons in New York; and in Boston, Houghton Mifflin and Little, Brown & Company—continued to control what reached the public in book form. Their domination seemed to have become accepted—and, in the opinion of many young men interested in publishing careers, oppressive. Many of these houses remained in the hands of the founders' families well into the twentieth century, so official inbreeding further delayed change. Rebellious young American writers felt the weight of this judicious nepotism when their works, advanced in technique or critical of society, were refused at established firms. In addition, until the Twenties, many old-line houses remained under the controlling influence of the New England Brahmins and their editors, who had set the literary and intellectual standards of the entire country for so many decades. In 1917, a house might have its headquarters in New York, but the prevailing influence upon it remained Bostonian. According to publishing executives of today, practice prior to the Twenties followed a generally British-bred, Eastern-university tradition which had proven both commercially successful and safe from most outside criticism. Literary revolt in substance or style, like outspokenness in sex and politics, met inflexible timidity in established firms.

The reluctance of many older houses to publish the proponents of insurgency or experiment is completely understandable. The authors these firms were accustomed to offering the public reflected their own conservative political, moral, and critical standards. Moreover, these writers had been successful, and prosperity does not induce change. A world at war, large-scale economic depression, and the great challenging of standards were forces of the future. To the rebels of the 1910's—both writers and publishers—conservative houses run by cautious executives appeared to follow a pattern of publishing harmless historical fiction, westerns, uplifting religious tracts, and happy, saccharine tales of contemporary life; indeed, best-seller lists from 1900 to 1915 seem to substantiate their conviction. Of course, some old-guard publishers *did* accept the works of several important authors who were popular writers as well as critics of America. For example, Doubleday, offered *The Jungle* as well as novels by Frank Norris and Ellen Glasgow; the American branch of the London-based firm, the Macmillan Company, published novels by radicals like Jack London, Arthur Bullen, Ernest Poole, and Upton Sinclair; Harper's issued Dreiser's *Jennie Gerhardt* though it balked at *The Titan;* and the novels of Edith Wharton, William Dean Howells, and Robert Herrick, each of them critical of portions of American society and written from a tempered, but disapproving point of view, appeared regularly during the prewar era.

The fact remains, however, that with the exception of Dreiser, none of the preceding authors was a recognized leader of the new literary generation which came to prominence in the Twenties. Although old-line houses issued many reputable books and some very distinguished ones, neophyte publishers believed that they ignored much important Continental literature and rejected the writings of many young Americans. Surely, for established publishers, the most important reason was that the new literature promised to have little popular appeal in an apparently tranquil, conservative United States. Publishing firms are, after all, businesses first, and they cater to the taste of their public.

The American people had made their preferences in literature well known. They wanted poetry to have a clear, sensible message, whether its source was New England or Indiana, "scholarly" or homespun. In fiction, the range of popular taste was somewhat broader. During the first two decades of the twentieth century, Zane Grey began a spectacular career with Harper's. Macmillan's lists included the equally illustrious Owen Wister and Winston Churchill; Dodd, Mead issued the works of George Barr McCutcheon; John Fox, Jr.'s *The Little Shepherd of Kingdom Come* (1903) and *The Trail of the Lonesome Pine* (1908) each sold over a million copies for Scribner's.[14] Doubleday was guaranteed almost a million dollars every other year by the novels of Booth Tarkington and Mrs. Gene Stratton Porter. Houghton Mifflin, Century, Macmillan, and L. C. Page published America's other favorite women novelists: Kate Douglas Wiggin, Alice Hegan Rice, Kathleen Norris, and Eleanor H. Porter. And when readers had had their fill of life in the Cabbage Patch, or those inspiring, indomitable heroines, Rebecca, Pollyanna, and Mother, they could buy new editions of the Brahmins in the latest ornate calf-bindings; the New Englanders were perennial best-sellers.

In 1917, when Harriett Monroe made her annual plea to Chicagoans for financial contributions, most of them were reading their poetry in the recently published *A Heap o' Livin'*, by Edgar A. Guest. The year that saw Ezra Pound become foreign editor of Margaret Anderson's *Little Review,* and *The Masses* suppressed by the United States government because its editors—Max Eastman,

Floyd Dell, John Reed, and Art Young—were too outspoken in their criticism of United States' participation in World War I, found Americans immersed in Harold Bell Wright's *When A Man's A Man* and Eleanor H. Porter's *Just David*. Other little magazines, *The Poetry Review of America, The Soil*, and *The Seven Arts* died in 1917.[15] Their deaths were the natural outcome of the financial and editorial instability that undermined these courageous and enthusiastic periodicals.

Intellectuals who had found publishing firms in the hands of the timid had also met with failure in the editorial offices of their periodical counterparts; *The Atlantic Monthly, The Century Magazine*, and the journals controlled by Harper's and Scribner's were not sympathetic to the rebellion around them. But at least the little magazines supplied a market, as the field of book publishing did not. True, these unsteady ventures could not pay their contributors, but they did offer them a hearing before a limited but vital audience. In their dedication to new voices, the Monroes and the Andersons reflected the very quality all but totally lacking in the publishing field of the day—courage—the courage to promote intellectuals outspoken in their criticism of contemporary sacred cows, in their disdain for the firmly established heritage of an older, still nineteenth-century-oriented society. The men who unconsciously followed the examples of these brave literary ladies did so not only because they were venturesome, but also because they were Jews, to whom the publishing field had been firmly closed.

According to many retired publishing executives anti-Semitism was general among publishers in the 1910's. Young Jews interested in publishing careers either were refused jobs outright when they applied at old-line houses or were told that for *them* there would be no opportunity for advancement. As a result, they established their own houses which lacked any allegiance to the entrenched Anglo-American literary heritage, that foundation of respectable conservatism which had proved so profitable for their older rivals. In most cases untrained by the Copelands or Tinkers of the Eastern universities, they looked with sympathy on the ferment in thought and writing which was now brewing both in the United States and abroad. In the first place, they had nothing to lose; they had neither the contacts nor the contracts with established writers. In the second, protest and rebellion appealed to these neophytes and if it was good writing, so much the better. Finally, the Jewish publishers were aware that the intellectual needs of masses of non–Anglo-Saxons were not being met by the publishing policy of the old-line houses. They were, therefore, eager to reestablish contact with the Continent. The older houses, family-owned or otherwise, maintained their narrow editorial policies and lost young writers to the more enterprising newcomers who welcomed both the insurgency and the insurgent. Long before the late Twenties, when the established houses had somewhat overcome their anti-Semitism, the Jewish pioneers of a new, incandescent age were either established—as in the case of B. W. Huebsch, Alfred A. Knopf, and Horace Liveright—or successfully underway, as witness Random House, Covici-Friede, Simon & Schuster, and The Viking Press.

The first Jew to enter general publishing in the twentieth century was B. W. Huebsch, who, in 1902, issued his first volume, E. H. Griggs' *A History of Meditations*.[16] Huebsch's virtually one-man operation posed no threat to established firms; "take it to Huebsch—he publishes anything," was their unanimous advice to unknowns. Huebsch often found his writers abroad: in Germany, Hauptmann and Sudermann; in Russia, Gorky and Chekhov; in Norway, Strindberg; and in England, H. G. Wells. His publication in 1915 of James Joyce's *Portrait of the Artist as a Young Man* marked the first appearance of fiction by the Irishman in the United States. A few years later Huebsch issued Sherwood Anderson's *Winesburg, Ohio* and the *New Poems* of D. H. Lawrence. From 1920 to 1924, he published the liberal periodical, *The Freeman,* in which the essays of Harold Stearns and H. L. Mencken appeared; Stearns' pieces turned up later in his book *America and the Young Intellectual*, Mencken's in his book *Prejudices*. When B. W. Huebsch merged his list with Harold K. Ginzburg's in 1925, the highly successful Viking Press of today was underway.

After a brief apprenticeship with Doubleday, Alfred A. Knopf went into business for himself in 1915.[17] Dissatisfied with the lack-luster design and cheap bindings which characterized contemporary books, Knopf, together with his wife Blanche, who became the firm's vice president, published his authors in the most physically outstanding volumes that were to be found in American trade editions. He combed Europe for new, exciting works. In 1917, fifty-three of the seventy-two volumes he issued were written by foreigners. More than any other publisher, the Knopfs became identified with the best in Continental literature; Tolstoy, Gogol, Dostoyevsky, Gorky, Nietzsche, Mann, and Gide all appeared under the Borzoi imprint. British writers like Beerbohm, Forster, Elizabeth Bowen, and Katherine Mansfield, along with Americans like H. L. Mencken, George Jean Nathan, Joseph Hergesheimer, and Willa Cather, found their way to the house. The Knopfs made Continental writers their own, while many young American authors gravitated to Boni & Liveright, the third major firm founded by Jews.

A new spirit of adventure and liberalism had entered the genteel occupation of gentlemen. The old line found it could avoid association with the new Jewish executives by unofficially excluding them from the Publishers' Club, but in the marketplace the enterprising upstarts had their own way. A formerly ingrown, static industry began to evolve into an open forum for all types of creative writing and new ideas. "Soon to become the most noisome stench in the nostrils of the established was Horace Liveright."[18]

Liveright, both president and business manager of the firm, planned the advertising campaigns, handled the sales, and made irregular trips to the bank to borrow money and repay it.[19] He went on the theory that the banks would become accustomed to lending the firm money and would then be in the habit of doing so—if and when they really needed it. This is one of the more harmless examples of his business prowess; as a management policy, it was enough to drive Boni wild. Eager to expand, Liveright urged his partner to publish something by his revolutionary friends in the Village. The notable, early success of the Modern Library had provided the firm with a lucrative backlog as well as additional capital, so the infant firm was able to issue new books or reprints almost at once: *A History of Tammany Hall* by Gustavus Myers; *A Family of Noblemen* by M. Y. Saltykov; and *Utopia of Usurers* by G. K. Chesterton. These first works, together with those that Boni and Liveright published from 1917 through 1919, led to their being considered by rival publishers a politically radical house as well as unofficial publishers for all writers living below Fourteenth Street.

At the inception of their venture the publishers added a young salesman, Louis Greene, to their two-man operation.[20] Greene helped them organize their mailing lists and sold the Modern Library; at the same time he was selling books for Alfred Knopf. Soon after the first volumes bearing the B & L imprint appeared, Thomas Seltzer, Boni's uncle, bought a one-third interest in the firm.[21] Seltzer's background in foreign languages and his contacts with young writers from his days as an editor of *The Masses* made his tenure at Boni & Liveright an especially valuable one in building up its list.

Boni's original scheme for the firm was simply the production of a series of reprints that lay between the established classics of the Everyman's Library, published by E. P. Dutton & Company, and the current, popular fiction mechanically ground out by the A. L. Burt and Grosset and Dunlap presses.[22] For the most part, Boni's early selections in 1917 reflected the avant-garde influence of his Washington Square book-borrowing friends: Wilde, *The Picture of Dorian Gray*; Strindberg, *Married*; Kipling, *Soldiers Three*; Stevenson, *Treasure Island*; Wells, *The War in the Air*; Ibsen, *A Doll's House, The Enemy of the People*, and *Ghosts*; France, *The Red Lily;* DeMaupassant, *Mademoiselle Fifi, and Other Stories*; Nietzsche, *Thus Spake Zarathustra*; Dostoyevsky, *Poor People*; Maeterlinck, *A Miracle of Saint Anthony*; and Schopenhauer, *Studies in Pessimism*. Priced at sixty cents each, bound in limp lambskin, and duodecimo in size, most of these books could not be found elsewhere in such a convenient and attractive form; some, moreover, were out of print and others unavailable in this country. The demand for the first volumes in the Modern Library was so great that Boni and Liveright decided to issue six more titles immediately: Butler, *The Way of All Flesh*; Meredith, *Diana of the Crossways*; Shaw, *An Unsocial Socialist*; Moore, *Confessions of a Young Man*; Hardy, *The Mayor of Casterbridge*; and *The Best Russian Short Stories*, edited by Thomas Seltzer.

While the new publishers were filling orders for the Modern Library in July 1917, Frank Shay, who ran the Washington Square

Book Shop after the Bonis' departure, gave the firm an opportunity to become associated with a writer both men admired—Theodore Dreiser.[23] Shay, who in addition to running the bookstore had published a few books—most notably, a series of pamphlets called the Provincetown Plays—had made arrangements with Dreiser to issue a reprint of *Sister Carrie*. Shay had just received his draft notification, and since he was anxious to clear up his business affairs, he offered to transfer his agreement with Dreiser to Boni & Liveright, subject to the author's approval. Liveright went immediately to the Village to get Dreiser's views. He found the writer agreeable to the generous offer he proposed, as long as certain provisions—including the immediate publication of his unproduced play, *The Hand of the Potter*—were met. Whether Dreiser's prima-donna tactics at that time were due to his distrust of all publishers, dating from his first, crushing experience with Doubleday, his dislike of Jews, or simply innate distrust, the strings he attached to his early dealings with Liveright were the first in a long series during their thirteen-year association.

When Liveright found him, Dreiser had earned less than $600 during the preceding months from the combined sales of seven works that were available to the public and nothing, of course, from the one that was not. His publishers, intimidated by the threat of censorship, had cut hundreds of pages of what he called "woman stuff" from the pages of his later novels; he was in debt to a publisher he could not tolerate for an $1800 advance on his next novel, which was to be called *The Bulwark*; on hand he had a philosophical play, *The Hand of the Potter*, which no publisher would accept, and no producer sponsor.[24]

The publication of *Sister Carrie* by Doubleday, Page & Company in 1900, against the wishes of its president, Frank Doubleday, had marked the beginning of Dreiser's battles with publishers.[25] Only 583 copies of the small edition of his first novel were disposed of, including 127 volumes given away to reviewers, leaving the novelist with a profit of $68.40. His "immoral" book was rejected wherever he took it, until B. W. Dodge & Company, in which Dreiser had invested $5,000, reissued it in 1907.[26] Two years later *Sister Carrie* had sold over ten thousand copies in trade and reprint editions.[27] But Dreiser's 10 per cent royalty failed to bring him much income even from this satisfactory sale, for the Dodge Company failed and Dreiser lost both his investment and his sponsor.[28] When *Jennie Gerhardt* was accepted by Harper's in 1911 and proved an even better seller than its predecessor, Dreiser was elated to be offered a $2,000 advance by his new publishers on his next novel.[29] This work, *The Financier*, sold over eight thousand copies during its first three months on the market, but despite its success and Harper's reissue of *Sister Carrie*, Dreiser found himself in debt to his publisher.[30]

Harper's decided to halt publication of Dreiser's next novel, *The Titan*, during its trip through the bindery. Its realism, they said, was too explicit.[31] Moreover, the book was rejected by other American firms, until J. Jefferson Jones, director of the newly established American branch of the British publishing house, John Lane and Company, arranged with Harper's to take it over and finally issued it in 1914.[32] In debt to both firms, Dreiser hoped that *The "Genius,"* issued by Jones in October 1915 would make him solvent. Despite an unfavorable reception, it sold 7,887 copies before its sale was stopped in July 1916 by John Sumner, newly appointed Secretary of the New York Society for the Suppression of Vice.[33] Prior to its removal from circulation, Jones had published Dreiser's *Plays of the Natural and Supernatural* as well as *A Hoosier Holiday*, largely on the basis of the writer's growing reputation. In the fall of 1916 and the following spring Dreiser and Jones were at logger-heads. Dreiser refused to cut *The "Genius"*; Jones refused to risk prison by continuing its sale. Sumner's "warning," to remove all obscene matter or discontinue its sale, followed by a visit from U. S. postal inspectors, even caused the anxious publisher to recall unsold copies from bookstores all over the country.[34] Since the novel had, in fact, been issued, Jones had fulfilled his part of the contract, and Dreiser found no relief in the courts, which never had occasion to determine the status of the work.

The "Genius" remained stored in the Lane stockroom for the next seven years. The earlier revenue from this work, in addition to the continuing royalties from *Sister Carrie* and *The Financier*, each nearing twenty-five thousand copies, and *Jennie Gerhardt*, close to thirty thousand, went to repay his debt at Harper's and for living expenses.[35] In desperation, Dreiser even tried to be his own promoter by mailing out five thousand printed cards listing his books and the firms that handled them. Each read:

> Mr. Dreiser's works have been continuously attacked by Puritans solely because America is not yet used to a vigorous portrayal of itself. If you will examine these books for yourself you will discover the reason for his present high position in American letters. If your local book dealer will not get any of these for you, address the publishers direct, or George C. Baker, 165 West Tenth Street, New York City.[36]

George C. Baker, of course, was Theodore Dreiser.

From Liveright's point of view, Dreiser was an established, controversial figure in American letters, a writer of great commercial promise and the most attractive kind of author for a young firm to promote. Anxious to become the novelist's publisher, Liveright told Dreiser that he wanted to double the number of volumes of *Sister Carrie* that Shay had planned to issue.[37] Next, Liveright proposed to publish whatever Dreiser offered him, to pay for it liberally, to promote it effectively, and to fight for it in the courts should the need arise.[38] The publisher further promised, as soon as he had enough money, to attempt to bring all of Dreiser's earlier works under his imprint so that the author might enjoy a greater, more stable income. Finally, Liveright offered the writer advances of $500 to $1000 for works the author would be willing to submit to Boni & Liveright for publication. A much larger advance, $4000, on a novel, *The Bulwark*, came later. At a time when publishers preferred to give advances to writers whose previous works had proved successful —they gave no money at all to unknowns—and considering Dreiser's current situation, Liveright's generosity was a real gamble.

Dreiser met this proposal with extreme caution. He signed no contract, but permitted the firm to issue *Sister Carrie,* while he retained control of the plates and the rights. He demanded, and got, Liveright's promise to publish *The Hand of the Potter,* which, following the Lane rejection, had been turned down by one magazine after another and remained unproduced. Boni & Liveright then proceeded to reprint *Sister Carrie,* in the fall of 1917—its sixth appearance since 1900—in accordance with the terms of their agreement.[39] Dreiser, who had all but stopped working on *The Bulwark* before Liveright approached him, but didn't tell his publisher, next sent in a volume of short stories which was issued in 1918. This collection, *Free and Other Stories*, was made up of works that had been consistently praised and rejected by magazine editors (who wanted something more cheerful), when Dreiser had submitted these stories separately in the past.[40] In fact, Dreiser received at least seventy-six rejections of his short stories, essays, and plays during 1918, the first full year of his association with Liveright.[41] However, the author was apparently not pleased with the firm's handling of the work, and, in the first demonstration of what was to become a regular practice on his part, Dreiser threatened to sever his connection with the house. *Free* had sold a respectable, but hardly spectacular 2,742 copies from its publication to December 1, 1918; moreover, Liveright was not making any apparent progress in taking over *The "Genius"* from the John Lane Company in order to reissue it, especially after Dreiser had arranged for him to do so.[42]

In what was to become his regular role as Dreiser's publisher, Liveright defended his exploitation of the volume and pleaded with the author to remain with the firm.

> I am completing our Spring list. It would be a great loss to us if you should decide not to have us publish *Twelve Men* or in fact any other books. I felt that when we agreed to publish *The Hand of the Potter*, which I feel that practically every other publisher in the country would have lacked the courage to do, you considered that we were the sort of people to publish and push all your future books. . . . I have no hesitation in saying that I think we have done as well with *Free* as any publisher could have done, and that we will earn as much for you on *Twelve Men* as any other publisher can.[43]

In addition, Liveright explained, Lane had doubled his original asking price for *The "Genius,"* and $5000 was just too large an outlay for the young firm to spend at this point in its existence for the opportunity to republish the three-year-old novel.

Placated by Liveright's explanation and by a $1000 advance, Dreiser submitted his next work, *Twelve Men*. The following year, this volume of journalistic portraits, edited by Liveright to remove "inept expressions and slovenliness," along with *Hey, Rub-A-Dub-Dub*, a collection of philosophic plays and essays the novelist had written for liberal and Leftist periodicals (though few had been accepted) , was issued by Boni & Liveright.[44] Neither of these works made publisher or author much money. What the public was waiting for, Liveright reminded the writer, was a new novel. It was eight years before Liveright got this book, his original objective in signing Dreiser, but soon monthly checks of $333 were being sent out regularly: twelve equal installments of a $4000 advance Liveright gave Dreiser in an attempt to encourage him to finish this book.[45] In return, the publisher received second-rate works, petulant letters, and demands that Liveright share in, and pay for, the abortive or unprofitable enthusiasms of his literary lion.

Next to the "rediscovery" of Theodore Dreiser, Boni & Liveright's most important early publications were translations of works by a Russian, Leon Trotsky, a Frenchman, Henri Barbusse, and an Hungarian, Andreas Latzko.[46] Boni had found a copy of Trotsky's work, *The Bolsheviki and World Peace*, in the Greenwich Village apartment of his uncle, Thomas Seltzer. Seltzer, who was well known for his translations of French, German, Polish, and Russian works, agreed to translate Trotsky's book in addition to two novels, Barbusse's *The Inferno* and Latzko's *Men in War*, all of which were published in the spring of 1918.[47] Topical and controversial, each met an unusual reception in a war-minded America. *The Bolsheviki and World Peace*, written in Switzerland before the overthrow of the Czar, sold over twenty thousand copies to Americans sympathetic to or curious about the Revolution, until the Red Scare arrested the book's sale.[48] *The Inferno* did not succeed at all, despite the fact that Barbusse had been awarded the *Prix Goncourt* the year before. *Men in War*, which had appeared in Holland, Denmark, Sweden, France, and Switzerland, went through two small editions of two thousand copies each, before it was suppressed by the United States government in June, shortly after its publication, as "injurious to the morale of our armies, or detrimental to the proper conduct of the war."[49] These European novels were much alike in content; in both, the authors had recorded their war experiences. They were further marked by anti-militarism, intense pacifism, and overt

Bolshevism. Their hostile reception in a chauvinistic, war-crazed America now seems understandable. Americans did not want the war debunked or their salvation of Europe obscured by propaganda; rather, they preferred to read the "authentic" heroics of a native son in Arthur Guy Empey's best-selling *Over the Top* or the equally successful *Dere Mable*, by Edward Streeter, inane, comic letters purporting to depict army life as seen through the eyes of an American doughboy writing to his sweetheart.[50]

Liveright's protests about the government banning of *Men in War* were, predictably, unsuccessful. In fact military intelligence officers kept the firm's office under surveillance for a time to be certain the ban was obeyed. On August 14, 1918, he wrote to Latzko that the volume was no longer on sale here.

> You will easily understand why the Government authorities of our country feel that as long as the war lasts the circulation of such a book as *Men in War* is not advisable. As appears from the reviews of your work which I am sending you, most of our critics have construed the significance of your book correctly, and took it to be an attack on Prussian militarism, not an attack on the defensive war which we, the Allies, are fighting. Nevertheless, it could hardly have been expected that if there was any doubt as to the effect *Men in War* might have upon the fighting morale of our soldiers, the Government would not [sic.] step in to prevent its circulation. My own personal opinion is that the book could not possibly prove harmful in any way, that on the contrary it is plainly on our side and would therefore be helpful to our cause. But the times are out of joint and we are all nervous.

When the ban was lifted in February 1919, the reissue of this prototype of some war-debunking novels that were to follow in the Twenties met an even more ignominious fate; it was ignored. After Latzko complained to Liveright that he was receiving no royalties and that the advance the publisher had offered him for his next work was too small, Liveright responded:

> I have made . . . a very fair offer considering the great loss we had on *Men in War* and the fact that the book trade and the book buying public in this country will look with suspicion on a new book by you. Pacifist literature is extremely unpopular in this coun-

try just now. You must not overlook in your consideration of our publication of *Men in War,* the fact that on this book we advanced . . . something over $1100 which applied against royalties . . . has not been earned up to this date.[51]

Latzko's next work, *The Judgment of Peace,* translated for Liveright by Ludwig Lewisohn and equally pacifistic, was published in 1919 and also did very poorly.[52] The initial edition of only twenty-two hundred copies was never sold out. While the books of Barbusse and Latzko went through countless printings on an unsettled Continent, Liveright's editions of their works were rebuffed in America, where readers gobbled up copies of *The Four Horsemen of the Apocalypse,* a story of romance and war, written by a non-revolutionary foreigner, Vicente Blasco-Ibáñez.[53] Nevertheless, Boni and Liveright continued to issue pacifistic and socialistic literature. With books on politics, economics, ferment, and insurrection here and abroad making up a large portion of their lists, they came to be regarded by other publishers as radicals or fools—and commonly both.[54]

Forgotten now, as they were ignored in postwar America, the titles of these volumes contain an impressive record of important controversies of the time; but they were, at best, dubious sales prospects for a company still struggling to be well established financially. In 1918 they included Karl Ludwig Krause's *What is the German Nation Dying For?*; James MacKaye's *Americanized Socialism;* Nora Connolly's *The Irish Revolution of 1916;* Paul Kellogg's and Arthur Gleason's *British Labor and the War;* and in 1919, Walter Guest Kellogg's *The Conscientious Objector*; Lionel D. Edie's *Current Social and Industrial Forces*; Samuel Roth's *Europe: A Book For America*; and H. M. Hyndman's *The Awakening of Asia.*[55]

Sensitive to the intellectual currents of the day, but in growing awareness of an unfriendly audience and a bearish market, Liveright, Boni, and Seltzer watched most of their first ventures in promoting imported works fail.[56] This triumvirate, consisting of Liveright as president, Boni as treasurer, and Seltzer as vice president and editor of the Modern Library, was temperamentally suited for partnership only by virtue of its common sympathy for radicalism. The firm was constantly plagued by editorial disputes and financial disagreements. Liveright was eager to expand and to publish Greenwich Village unknowns as well as big names; his partners favored the socio-political works and the novels of Continental writers. As a result, the two-thirds majority vote which decided all such controversies produced logrolling and resulted in bitter feelings. Finally, Liveright and Boni reached an impasse concerning the direction the firm would take. Since neither was willing to sell out to the other, they decided to flip a coin. Liveright won the toss, and in July 1918 he became the majority owner of the firm.[57] The following year Albert Boni departed for Europe, and, attracted by the glamor of the Russian revolution, went to the U.S.S.R. There, in 1920, he was imprisoned on spying charges; upon his release, he returned to the United States and eventually re-entered the publishing business with his brother Charles.[58] Beginning in 1923, they issued works by Upton Sinclair, Carl Van Doren, Marcel Proust, and D. H. Lawrence, as well as their most successful volume, *The Bridge of San Luis Rey*, by the then unknown Thornton Wilder. About four months after Boni's departure, Seltzer left the company too, and soon established himself as Thomas Seltzer, Inc. After publishing volumes by Ford Madox Ford, Proust, Lawrence, and Arthur Schnitzler, he merged his firm with that of the Bonis in 1926.

The withdrawal of Boni and Seltzer from the firm left Liveright much reduced in funds but free to follow his own enthusiasms. He recouped some of his outlay by selling one vice presidency to Julian Messner, who was then the firm's sales manager, and by selling another vice presidency to Leon Fleischman, who took on the added responsibilities of secretary and treasurer for the house.[59] Solvent again and in control, Liveright at last turned to the native-born radicals—political and literary—of Greenwich Village.

The Radical Writers

The writers had been ready to be heard from for some time, for since the early years of the twentieth century New York's Greenwich Village had offered them an atmosphere, an uninhibited milieu, for generating, investigating, and frequently discarding ideas. It was there, shortly before America's entry into World War I, that intellectuals gathered in small groups and cliques, mutually indifferent to, or secretly suspicious of, each other, since there was no common center for the Village as a whole.[1] Beyond their own tongues and a handful of little magazines, there were few means for the expression of their opinions. Whether the genesis of Liveright's firm can be attributed exclusively to the existence of the Village cannot be exactly determined, but it does seem that the presence of these people and their common need to talk and to write set in motion a series of events which ultimately resulted in fulfillment for many of them and important literature for the world.

Liveright's penchant for gambling on unknown writers was soon evident to young American authors. His determination to sell their books through aggressive publicity was also dramatized to them early in his career, and one by one, members of the Liberal Club, the Washington Square Players, and the Provincetown group, as well as former browsers in the Bonis' book store, found their way to Liveright's office at 105 West Fortieth Street. Some were the legacies of Albert Boni; others were sought out by Liveright himself. Several were published by the firm regularly through the Twenties; the works of others were issued sporadically by the house during the same time. These Villagers included Mary Heaton Vorse, Hutchins Hapgood, Harry Kemp, Max Eastman, Maxwell Bodenheim, Michael Gold, Alfred Kreymborg, Marsden Hartley, Upton Sinclair, Art Young, Djuna Barnes, Kenneth Macgowan, and Lawrence Langner. Since many of these writers were also contributors to *The Masses*, their works often mingled social criticism and art: a combination always regarded with favor by their publisher.[2] The first of these sometime-radicals, sometime-artists, to be published by Liveright with considerable success was a graduate of Harvard, a frequenter of the Bonis' bookshop, and a flaming revolutionary—John Reed.[3]

During his short career as a journalist and amateur labor organizer, Reed took part in or reported proletarian unrest in the United States, Mexico, and Russia. At first his on-the-spot coverage found favor with readers in New York, but soon his emphasis on radical propaganda brought him into disrepute. In trouble with both national and local officials in 1918, Reed stood trial in New York with the other editors of *The Masses* at almost the same time he was being threatened with jail in Philadelphia.[4] His eager sympathy with Russian Bolsheviks and American workers alike soon found him under surveillance by United States agents who warned him not to criticize the government. While he was under indictment in Philadelphia on the charge of inciting a riot, he began to write a book on the Russian Revolution as he had observed it the year before, his only means of support a generous advance from Liveright. This work, based on his notebooks and documented by Russian newspapers, was issued in January 1919 as *Ten Days that Shook the World*, a powerful title suggested by Arthur Garfield Hays. Despite a suspicious citizenry, the book stimulated great interest among reviewers—both favorable and critical; for example, the *Chicago Tribune* critic took the opportunity to pray for the sudden death of Trotsky and Lenin in the course of his review, while the *Boston Transcript* reviewer wondered aloud why Liveright had stooped so low as to publish the book.[5] Nevertheless, Reed's volume sold over nine thousand copies during its first months on the market. The most impressed reader was Lenin, for as Reed recorded in one of his letters to Louise Bryant, "All my love, and greetings to all. Tell Horace the big chief thinks my book the best."[6] For Liveright in 1918, *Ten Days that Shook the World* represented his first major success as the publisher of young Americans.

Three other Greenwich Village intellectuals, securely dug in below Fourteenth Street, found a great deal to criticize in America.

But their efforts, published the same year as Reed's, were considerably less successful.[7] The first of these was Harold Stearns' collection of essays, *Liberalism in the United States.* Now overshadowed by his symposium, *Civilization in the United States,* this early indictment of America's moral and social failures anticipated its creator's—and countless other young intellectuals'—subsequent escape to Europe and temporary exile. Another approach to social criticism was exemplified by David Karsner's *Debs: His Authorized Life and Letters.* The publication of this eulogy found its subject serving a ten-year prison term for violating the Espionage Act; in 1918 Debs had made a speech condemning government prosecutions for sedition. From jail he campaigned for the Presidency, and, in 1920, received nearly a million votes. But only a few of his supporters bought this book. The third member of this trio of rebels had come into contact with Liveright while he was an associate editor of the short-lived *Seven Arts.*[8] Their long friendship was to result in Liveright's publication of eight volumes by Waldo Frank which appeared in the next ten years.[9] Liveright lost money on all but two of them, though the novelist-critic more than repaid the favor by directing many other young writers to his publisher—most notably, Lewis Mumford, Evelyn Scott, Hart Crane, Gorham Munson, and perhaps Jean Toomer. The manuscript Frank presented to Liveright in 1919 was a collection of essays reflecting his concerns while running *Seven Arts.* When the magazine foundered, Frank withdrew from the periodical field, registered as a conscientious objector, and began writing books. The first result of this was *Our America,* Frank's now famous indictment of the "Puritan-pioneers," who, he asserted, had been responsible for a utilitarian, spiritually empty twentieth-century America.[10] Four thousand copies of the book were sold, but Liveright's profit totaled only about $600.[11]

The manner of Liveright's introduction to Eugene O'Neill, who became the publisher's most successful Villager, has never been established. It could have occurred through a number of different people: Richard Madden, the playwright's agent; Frank Shay, who had issued two of O'Neill's one-act plays, *Bound East for Cardiff* and *Before Breakfast,* in his series of Provincetown play pamphlets; or fellow Provincetowners like Otto Liveright, the publisher's brother; Mary Heaton Vorse, an early Liveright author; and Waldo Frank. In any case, Liveright issued a volume of O'Neill's one-act plays four months after the MacDougal Street production of *The Moon of the Caribbees*.[12] It is doubtful that any other publisher would have taken a risk on the dramatist in 1919, let alone have given him a $125 advance, but Liveright accepted his plays and gave him the money on the chance that the firm might break even and that the cash would be all he would lose.[13]. O'Neill's collection of one-acters, *The Moon of the Caribbees* and *Six Other Plays of the Sea* (*Bound East for Cardiff*, *The Long Voyage Home*, *In the Zone*, *Rope*, *Ile*, and *Where the Cross is Made*), appeared in April 1919. This volume paid for itself in fourteen months, for in June 1920 O'Neill was awarded the Pulitzer Prize. He won the honor with *Beyond the Horizon*, his first play to receive an official Broadway production. When it began on February 3, 1920, the published version was already at the printers; it was issued three months before the dramatist's public and critical acclaim reached any great proportions.[14]

Liveright cannot be credited with discovering O'Neill, who had been the subject of scattered newspaper attention and whose three one-act plays, *Voyage*, *Ile*, and *The Moon of the Caribbees*, had appeared in *The Smart Set* in 1918.[15] But the publisher's sponsorship of a playwright unknown to Broadway and without even an uptown producer for his work was most unusual. Established houses, if they published plays at all, issued them only after they had achieved notable success uptown. This was Liveright's rule too.[16] He broke it only in the case of O'Neill, and a long association, soon to be financially rewarding for both, began. Liveright's sponsorship of O'Neill, then, was an early example of his critical acumen and his willingness to gamble on unknowns.

Writers of all kinds flocked to this young, unconventional, daring publisher. Daily, the mail truck unloaded bundles of manuscripts at his door, over a hundred a day at the height of his career; all were read and reported on by readers, though often less meticulously than works that came to the office through the personal recommendation of one of the Liveright stable of authors. Fearless, eager to print anything the public would buy, and somehow able to get the money he needed, Liveright pushed his way ahead. He loved notoriety. He was noisy and aggressive. In the early Twenties when Harry Hansen, then literary editor of the *Chicago News*, met him for the first time at the small B & L offices, he was impressed by the brashness of the publisher. "Why can't you do something for Mary Austin's *Outland?*" Liveright asked. "It's a great book. What are you doing for Dreiser? I've got Dreiser and O'Neill, the two greatest American authors, and what have you editors done for me? Nothing!"[17] While other publishers apologized for the volumes they issued and courted the favor of literary editors, Liveright did not. He was confident that he published great books and demanded that the book world and the public acknowledge them. Glamor-struck by big names in literature, he followed the age-old, though unadmitted, publishing practice of trying to lure notable writers from other houses with promises of larger advances, greater advertising, and better sales; almost always, they came, attracted by his enthusiasm, his daring, and his money. Moreover, they knew him to be honest with their fellow writers, and they respected the uniquely brilliant editorial staff he soon surrounded himself with and—what is even more unusual—listened to. They were aware that at Boni & Liveright the inhibitions, if any, of the president and his readers would never be imposed on a writer, for about the place was an air of freedom, an atmosphere conducive to the free functioning of author and editor.

Above all there was Liveright himself. Once an author joined the house he discovered what it was that Liveright offered that was more important than advertising and royalties: attention, the undivided attention the publisher paid to each writer, whether he was a first-time author or was already well known.

Besides learning quickly about book promotion, Liveright handled the editorial side of the business as well as his executive duties until 1921, when he hired T. R. Smith, then editor of the *Century Magazine*. Smith took over the position as Liveright's editor-in-chief after twenty years of experience in publishing.[18] In 1911 he had helped organize Moffat, Yard & Company, which he managed for the next three years. Later, at the *Century*, he had done a number of editing jobs for Boni & Liveright; his function as their unofficial literary advisor made his selection as editor-in-chief a natural one. The arrival of the forty-year-old Smith at Liveright's not only provided the firm with an erudite and discriminating reader, but widened its already valuable contacts with writers in the Village, editors of little magazines, and budding theatrical groups to include such well-known critics and editors as H. L. Mencken, George Jean Nathan, Burton Rascoe, and Ernest Boyd, all of whom were good friends of Smith. It was Smith too who recommended that James G. Huneker and George Moore join the Boni & Liveright list of authors, before he himself became officially connected with the firm.

Within the time of Boni's departure and Smith's arrival, the Volstead Act became law, the League of Nations was rejected, Socialists made one of their last grasps for power, and amateur psychoanalysis came into vogue. These events effected major changes in America, the Village, and publishing. At Boni & Liveright, the emphasis on unsaleable topical nonfiction dealing with revolution and socialism quickly shifted to equally daring, but flashier books dealing with sex. Liveright's publication of Moore, Huneker, and Sigmund Freud in 1920 exemplified this changeover. The publisher, first considered disreputable by his competitors because he was a Jew and because he promoted radical literature, politics, and economics, became even more notorious for his publication of polite pornography and serious works that were outspoken in their treatment of sex.[19] And in Edward Bernays, a young public relations counsel and the brother-in-law of one of the publisher's vice presidents, Leon Fleischman, Liveright found a man with the energy and imagination to do his kind of selling.

The publisher hired Bernays in 1919 and soon discovered something of the financial rewards that came with unconventional, inventive book promotion. When Bernays joined the house, routine publishing practice consisted of distributing a firm's catalogue as well as mailing out authors' biographies, photographs, and book descriptions to literary editors and booksellers.[20] Newspaper and magazine advertisements were mostly limited to brief, formal announcements. Bernays and Liveright, however, created a show-business approach to book publishing and promotion.

First, Bernays devised a series of circulars which were sent to three hundred major bookstores in the United States each week. Then Boni & Liveright offered newspaper editors across the country free books and about one hundred newsworthy articles on the firm's books and authors.[21] Soon feature stories based on these releases began appearing everywhere, and, thanks to increased exposure to the public, Liveright's books began to sell better than ever. Other publishers quickly copied the methods the house had initiated, but during his brief association with Liveright Bernays kept ahead of them. Working with a few books selected by Liveright for special promotion, Bernays wrote 1000-1500 word feature articles about them. Within weeks articles were running in newspapers around the United States focused on one of the volumes, *Our America*, and entitled "Psychoanalyzing Chicago," "Psychoanalyzing New York," and "Psychoanalyzing New England." Two other promotional campaigns had mixed success.

To popularize Hutchins Hapgood's anonymously issued *The Story of a Lover* Bernays decided to get definitions of love from American movie queens and to use these comments in advertising the novel.[22] His success was immediate and the sales of *The Story of a Lover* climbed rapidly thanks to the newspaper ads touting it under the romantic effusions of Mary Pickford, the Gish sisters, or their press agents. Bernays' next effort, to repeat his triumph with Christopher Morley's *In the Sweet Dry and Dry*, was not nearly as successful. Morley's work was a satire on the attempts of a moderate drinker to survive during Prohibition. In order to publicize it, Bernays persuaded the owner of the Majestic Hotel in New York to convert his empty bar into a booklovers' tavern. The opening of the drinkless bar was to coincide with the appearance of Morley's book. Various B & L authors were invited to the ceremonies and instead of bottles, their books were displayed behind the bar. Bernays' press release stressed Morley's work, but the reporters who covered the story at the Majestic failed to mention it. They were much more impressed with the novel idea of a book pub and the presence of the president of the New York County Chapter of the WCTU behind the bar of a metropolitan hotel. Hit or miss, Liveright was enthusiastic about Bernays' new ideas, excited about each new list, and he seemed to identify himself with the new volumes he selected for publication. His interests were wide, and he believed that every work deserved some sort of dynamic treatment—that it ought to be promoted as if it were a new play or a sporting event.

While Liveright's new publications were a powerful factor in attracting young writers, the Modern Library remained, perhaps, his most prestigious offering in the eyes of young intellectuals; from its inception, this series had become a mainstay of their libraries.

Priced at 95 cents a volume, the one-hundred-and-four-volume Modern Library offered a distinguished list of native and foreign authors and critics. The Modern Library of 1921 reflects the legacies of Boni and Seltzer as well as the new influence of Smith.[23] Reprint volumes by British writers such as Moore, Beerbohm, Dunsany, Pater, Swinburne, Gissing, and Blake were edited by Floyd Dell, Francis Hackett (then on the staff of *The New Republic*), Padraic Colum, Arthur Symons, Ernest Rhys, Paul Elmer More, William Butler Yeats, and Edgar Saltus, respectively. The Continental authors Gorky, Ibsen, Nietzsche, DeMaupassant, Turgenev, and France were similarly represented by volumes assembled by G. K. Chesterton, H. L. Mencken, Willard Huntington Wright, Michael Monahan (formerly editor of *The Phoenix*), John Reed, and James Branch Cabell. Shortly after Boni's departure, Liveright added to the Modern Library the works of some American writers. They included *A Modern Book of Criticism*, edited by Ludwig Lewisohn; *The Great Modern American Short Stories*, edited by William Dean Howells; Henry James's *Daisy Miller* and *An International Episode*; Frank Norris' *McTeague*; and Stephen Crane's *Men, Women, and Boats*. These were soon joined by Gertrude Atherton's *Rezanov*, introduced by William Marion Reedy; Walt Whitman's *Poems*, selected by Carl Sandburg; W. H. Hudson's *Green Mansions*, with a preface by John Galsworthy; and John Macy's *The Spirit of American Literature*. In the next five years, pioneers of the twentieth-century renaissance—Ezra Pound, T. S. Eliot, E. E. Cummings, Sherwood Anderson, Ernest Hemingway, Robinson Jeffers, and William Faulkner—joined O'Neill and Dreiser on the Boni & Liveright roster; they appeared in catalogues alongside such best-sellers as Rose Macaulay's *Potterism*, Samuel Hopkins Adams' *Flaming Youth*,

Hendrik Willem Van Loon's *The Story of Mankind*, Ben Hecht's *Gargoyles*, Gertrude Atherton's *Black Oxen*, Harry Kemp's *Tramping on Life*, Emil Ludwig's *Napoleon*, Maxwell Bodenheim's *Replenishing Jessica*, and Anita Loos's *Gentlemen Prefer Blondes*.

This perfect union of quality books and best-sellers began in 1920 with the appearance of Freud's *General Introduction to Psychoanalysis*, and Rose Macaulay's *Potterism*. The publication of Freud's work was due in part to the efforts of his nephew, Edward Bernays.[24] Prior to the Liveright publication of Freud, there were scores of books on the market that dealt with psychoanalysis in layman's terms, but there was no single authoritative volume by Freud himself. To remedy this situation and, hopefully, to secure for his uncle a stable income in American dollars, Bernays persuaded Freud to accept Liveright's offer to publish his introductory lectures on psychoanalysis, and in July 1920 the *General Introduction* appeared. Within a year, five thousand copies at $4.00 apiece had been sold, and Freud was "rejoicing," having earned $3000 in royalties. Moreover, the yearly royalties from *A General Introduction to Psychoanalysis* never fell below $500 during the Twenties, and there were often substantial additional royalties from the other volumes by Freud that Liveright subsequently issued: *Beyond the Pleasure Principle, Group Psychology and the Analysis of the Ego*, and *The Future of an Illusion*.

Liveright's discovery of Rose Macaulay came as a result of Harry Hansen's early enthusiasm for her work.[25] Liveright took over *Potterism* after it had already been set up by another New York publisher, and with extensive promotion, this satire on the English upper class in the postwar period stayed on the best-seller lists for many weeks. Leftist literature was less conspicuously represented and not nearly so successful. Class conscious prose like Doris Stevens' *Jailed for Freedom*, George Lansbury's *What I Saw in Russia*, and H. M. Hyndman's *The Evolution of Revolution*, along with works by Upton Sinclair, Mary Heaton Vorse, and Romain Rolland often did not pay. The War was over; revolution was no longer in style. So, in an attempt to capture one facet of the public taste, Liveright began to mine the lode of limited editions.

His early strikes and the greatest moneymakers were the works of George Moore and James G. Huneker and the *Intimate Journals of Paul Gauguin*. Smith brought the Irishman into the house when Moore's regular publisher, Brentano's refused to issue *A Story Teller's Holiday* without cutting it.[26] Acting as Moore's agent in America, Smith sold the book to Liveright. On his later volumes, *Heloise and Abelard* and *Memoirs of My Dead Life,* which were Boni & Liveright subscription offerings of 1920, Moore received advances of five hundred pounds each and was guaranteed, a 15 per cent royalty (as opposed to the more usual 10), for every copy of the two thousand signed volumes that were sold. All three sets were exhausted shortly after their appearance. No less successful was Huneker's novel, *Painted Veils,* which arrived at the firm in 1920, also on the recommendation of Smith.

In 1919, Huneker, a biographer, short-story writer, and critic of music and art, had written a lengthy essay on the opera season for Smith to publish in the *Century*.[27] In June of that year he asked Smith to read and pass on to Liveright his new novel *Istar: Daughter of Sin,* which had recently been returned by his regular publisher, Scribner's, with the offer to publish it in an expurgated version. When the editor and the publisher showed interest in his work, Huneker decided to polish his transcript for publication in a limited edition.[28] With an advance of $1,000 and the promise of more at publication, Huneker later vacillated between fear of John Sumner and a desire to see himself in print once more; but the subscription edition of *Painted Veils* sold out immediately upon publication without incident. Boni & Liveright grossed $13,000, for there were evidently thirteen hundred people anxious to read the work at $10 a copy.[29] In both 1928 and 1929 Liveright reissued the novel with considerable success, but *Painted Veils* never achieved its real triumph until 1953, when, as a paperback, it sold over two hundred thousand copies.[30]

Publication of works by Moore and Huneker reflects more of Liveright than just his eye for a dollar and his daring in the face of censorship; it also shows his willingness to recognize quality writers, even those of minor significance. His list in 1921 contained many important books from which he could expect little, if any, profit.[31] There were two sets of letters by famous figures: the hitherto unpublished correspondence between Nietzsche and Wagner, which was issued with a preface by H. L. Mencken, as well as a volume of George Sand and Gustave Flaubert letters with a preface by Stuart P. Sherman. The sale of these two collections was limited to a very small audience as were the *Poems: 1918-1921* of Ezra Pound.

When Liveright published Pound's own work, he often lost money, but his respect for Pound's judgment always remained high. In 1919 Liveright accepted the poet's volume of classic studies, *Instigations*, after it had been turned down by Knopf.[32] Later that year, Pound interested the publisher in printing James Joyce's *Ulysses* in unexpurgated form. Negotiations involving Joyce and Huebsch, his original American sponsor, as well as Pound and Liveright went on intermittently until early in 1921. At that time issues of *The Little Review* containing episodes from *Ulysses* were barred by the United States Post Office and successfully prosecuted by the New York Society for the Suppression of Vice. These actions led both Huebsch and Liveright to decline Joyce's novel. The forces of censorship were simply too strong in the early Twenties for either publisher to take the risk on a work that had already been banned.[33] But Liveright did issue three of Pound's other recommendations— John Cournos, Hilda Doolittle, and T. S. Eliot—without hesitation. Moreover, the publisher also accepted the volume Pound offered him in 1921, one which included "Hugh Selwyn Mauberley" in addition to Cantos IV through VII.[34] It marked the first appearance of both works in America in book form. Like his earlier work, the *Poems* sold poorly.[35] In contrast to his verse, Pound's translations were often much more successful; the proceeds from his version of Remy de Gourmont's *The Natural Philosophy of Love,* brought out the same year, more than compensated the publisher for his loss on the poetry. As a result, Liveright and Pound signed a contract on January 4, 1922 to run for two years and to provide the poet with an income of at least $500 annually for translating from French into English whatever works his publisher requested. Pound made sure he protected his reputation through the stipulation that Liveright agreed not to place Pound's name on the translation of any work that he issued which Pound considered a disgrace to humanity.[36]

In 1921 Liveright issued three collections of verse: *Padraic*

Colum's Anthology of Irish Poetry, *The Richard Le Gallienne Anthology of Poetry*, and T. R. Smith's choice of "rare and curious amatory verse," called *Poetica Erotica*.[37] Marsden Hartley's *Adventures in the Arts* was a volume of criticism in the Huneker manner; the author was a painter, a member of the Liberal Club, and a protege of Waldo Frank. Complementing the plays of O'Neill was *The Theatre of Tomorrow*, an early attempt to describe and evaluate the new drama and stagecraft, as seen by Kenneth Macgowan, the drama editor of *Vogue*, the *New York Globe*, and one of the important members of the newly organized Theatre Guild. The final volumes under the classification of "general literature" were *The Dance* by Ivan Narodny, *The Literature of Ecstasy* by Albert Mordell, *Culture and Ethnology* by Robert H. Lowie, and the last, for a while at least, of a number of works on Russia, *In the Days of the Revolution* by Albert Rhys Williams.

The other books Liveright offered in 1921 varied enormously in prestige. A collection of O'Neill's new plays—*The Emperor Jones*, *Straw*, and *Diff'rent*—sold quite well on the basis of the playwright's growing reputation on Broadway; its successor, *Gold*, did not. Although it had been written in 1909, Ferenc Molnar's *Liliom* was first produced on Broadway in 1921. This drama, which established Molnar's reputation here, appeared along with O'Neill's works. Rose Macaulay's *Dangerous Ages* followed successfully on the heels of her first best-seller, while Claire Sheridan's diary, *From Mayfair to Moscow*, a chatty volume devoted to gossip about the international set and descriptions of famous Bolsheviks, appealed to readers interested in the notable but not in propaganda. There were first novels by two Americans, Eunice Tietjens' *Jake* and Evelyn Scott's *The Narrow House*, in addition to *Quiet Interior* by E. B. C. Jones, a new British writer. Konrad Bercovici, some of whose earlier efforts had appeared in *The Masses*, was represented by *Ghitza and Other Romances*. Since the title story had been selected by Edward O'Brien as the best short story published during 1920, the gypsy storyteller's career seemed to be in the ascendant. And finally, Liveright added the first fruit of the new literary epoch to the Modern Library. This was Sherwood Anderson's *Winesburg, Ohio* with an introduction by Harold Stearns.

Even with this diversified list of works, Liveright would have foundered had it not been for his remarkable gift for finding writers and encouraging them with both personal enthusiasm and money. The first of his early gambles to pay off in a big way was the spectacular success of Hendrik Willem Van Loon's *The Story of Mankind*.[38] Van Loon, who had come to the United States from Holland in 1903, had established himself as something of an authority on the history of his native country through the publication of three works, none of which was particularly successful. During World War I, he alternated between lecturing at Cornell and acting as a correspondent for the Associated Press. After the Armistice, he was dismissed from Cornell, because his views on the war did not coincide with those of the patriots of Ithaca. Failing to make his way by writing advertising copy, Van Loon began to revise the first volume of a proposed twelve-volume history of the world for children, which he had begun at Cornell.

At the first sixteen publishing houses in New York, Philadelphia, and Boston where he applied, the manuscript was rejected; at the seventeenth, the Century Company, T. R. Smith recommended his work but was overruled by the sales department, which explained that such a series was too expensive to produce and all but unmarketable, since Van Loon had no following as an historian or as a writer for children. Nevertheless, Smith was enthusiastic enough to send Van Loon to Liveright, who promptly staked the writer for four months while he finished the first book, *Ancient Man*. In 1920, the first volume in Van Loon's "primer history of the world" appeared. It was acclaimed by Heywood Broun, who called it "the most fascinating book for children . . . we have seen in years." The *Times* critic said, "This is the way to tell history to children—and to the rest of us," while the *Globe* critic called *Ancient Man* "one of the most original books ever published. When Mr. Van Loon's work is completed," he predicted, "we will have an outline even more fascinating than Wells's."[39] Evidently Americans didn't agree; while they bought thousands of copies of H. G. Wells's *Outline of History*, *Ancient Man* remained on bookstore shelves.[40]

At this time, Smith changed jobs. As soon as he became editor at Boni & Liveright, he and the publisher persuaded Van Loon to give up his idea for a twelve-volume series and condense the rest of his history into one volume for publication the next year.[41] They also urged him to revise it so that it would appeal to adults as well as to children. Since a current survey had revealed that the I. Q. of the average doughboy in World War I was that of a sixteen-year-old, this upgrading posed no problem for the author. After Van Loon had completed his revisions, this early example of creative publishing, made possible by Smith's editorial intelligence and Liveright's faith in his hunches, appeared late in 1921. It was called *The Story of Mankind*. At five dollars a copy, the first fifty thousand volumes moved quickly. It was the second best-selling work of nonfiction in 1922 and remained among the top ten during the next year as well. In fact, during the Twenties this retelling of the development of civilization, written in simple language and illustrated by Van Loon's own drawings, went through thirty American editions and was translated into a dozen foreign languages. More than anything, its sale was a tribute to Liveright and his advertising department, for they catapulted this "disreputable" scholar into international fame.[42] The revenue Boni & Liveright received from *The Story of Mankind* paid most of its overhead for that year and part of the next; with his share of the sales Van Loon bought an elegant Dutch colonial in Westport, Connecticut.[43]

In 1922 Liveright found no other best-seller of the magnitude of Van Loon's; moreover, it took four books—two novels and two autobiographies—to equal the profit from *The Story of Mankind*.[44] The first of the novels was an imitation and vulgarization of Fitzgerald's *This Side of Paradise*, which was currently in vogue. *Flaming Youth*, as it was titled, was hack work designed to shock the timid, and it racked up huge sales. Supposedly written by a newcomer and young rebel, Warner Fabian, the novel was actually the creation of Samuel Hopkins Adams, a middle-aged journalist, who found his new anonymity so profitable that he later produced a number of similarly lucrative books ostensibly representing the revolt of modern youth in America. Like other popular novels of the day, Adams' book featured open discussion of sex and sexual morality, as well as marital infidelity, and was characterized by a postured cynicism. Its companion on the 1922 Liveright list was Ben Hecht's *Gargoyles*, which was similar in content though not so successful in sales. With this work, Hecht, formerly a member of the Chicago School and a recent arrival in New York, became popular with the hardcover trade as well as the readers of *The Little Review.*

Both novels were slick and sexy, a surefire combination, but the two autobiographies were a different matter. The more successful was Ludwig Lewisohn's *Up Stream,* in which the critic recalled his early youth in the South. Lewisohn was far from unknown to American readers; his poetry had appeared in the Greenwich Village *Moods,* his criticism in *The Smart Set,* and his short stories in *The Delineator.* In addition, he had done a number of books on Continental literature and the theatre. His autobiography, written when he was sixty while an associate editor of *The Nation,* seemed an unlikely best-seller; once more, however, heavy advertising put it across. An even more dubious prospect for the winner's circle was the story of the bohemian poet, Harry Kemp. Kemp had come to Liveright in 1920 with a distinctly unpromising offer. His wife, Dreamy, had developed tuberculosis, and Kemp, impoverished, needed $100 a month to send her to a Lake Saranac sanitarium for treatment. He asked the publisher to give him some money on account, and in return he promised Boni & Liveright a book of poetry. Without questioning him further, Liveright gave him a $1200 advance, but earmarked the money for a novel. In this way, Liveright circumvented any problem with his treasurer, who would have taken a dim view of an advance of this size on a book of poems. Unless it was Brahmin-bred, poetry was a notoriously poor seller, even in the Twenties, and Kemp was, of course, nothing but a Village bohemian.

A year passed, and Kemp returned to Liveright in despair. His wife, he said, hadn't died yet. The sympathetic publisher renewed the contract and gave Kemp another $1200. After Dreamy finally departed this world in 1922, Kemp appeared one day with the bulky manuscript of his "novel." It was neither fiction nor poetry, but his autobiography. Published immediately, *Tramping on Life* met with enough success to promise Liveright a generous reward for his gamble. But he overshot the advertising budget, and his paper profit of $10,000 was cut in half.[45]

Although 1922 was the year when Liveright introduced many

new or at least recently established authors to the public—for instance, Noel Coward by way of his *Terribly Intimate Portraits*—it was the writers of substantial reputation whose continuing successes paid for losses on the newcomers.[46] Liveright brought out Molnar's latest Broadway hit, *The Swan*, along with an earlier play, *Fashions*. While Molnar was receiving the French Cross of the Legion of Honor on the Continent, O'Neill won his second Pulitzer Prize in America for *Anna Christie*. This popular success and his outstanding experimental drama of the same year, *The Hairy Ape*, were both issued by Liveright to a receptive audience. Furthermore, Freud's *Beyond the Pleasure Principle* and Rose Macaulay's *Mystery at Geneva*, though less successful than their predecessors, made money for the firm.

Along with *Flaming Youth*, Liveright also published in 1922 the first book by E. E. Cummings, *The Enormous Room*, the record of Cummings' impressions during his confinement in a French prison in World War I. The author's father, Dr. Cummings, took the manuscript to Boni & Liveright because the house published exciting books and was reputed to be sympathetic to unknowns.[47] Cummings himself had given his father instructions that the work was to be issued untouched. He then departed for Europe and did not return to the United States to see *The Enormous Room* through the press, preferring to rely on his father and Liveright's staff to read the proofs of his novel. This turned out to be an unfortunate decision, for when the book appeared—probably in May 1922—many passages had been omitted, and there were mistakes in spelling and punctuation as well as misprints and mistranslations. Cummings, naturally, was furious; Liveright was perplexed. The publisher said he knew of only a few omissions which he had approved before the book went to the printer—simply "a few phrases or words which we felt it was necessary to delete in order to make the publication of the book possible in this country." Moreover, just before the book was sent out to reviewers, Liveright received a report that Sumner planned to raid the firm and prosecute the publisher because the novel contained the word "shit." As a result, Liveright directed one of the secretaries to go through the entire edition inking out the offending word. With the exception of this kind of "editing," the publisher claimed ignorance of any larger omissions and was apologetic about the careless mistakes. Dr. Cummings eventually accepted the responsibility for all the errors, though he insisted he would have caught them had the firm not pressured him to return the proofs immediately; moreover, he felt that bringing the textual omissions to Liveright's attention would only delay the book's appearance still further. Clearly, the responsibility for issuing what was a very inaccurate and sloppy text rests with all three of those most closely involved in its production: Dr. Cummings, Liveright and his staff, and certainly Cummings himself, who was having too good a time in Europe to read the galley proofs.

In any event, Cummings' memoir, one of the first and probably the finest of American war-debunking writings, had what publishers like to call a respectable sale. Its total sales of two thousand copies at $2.00 each would normally have allowed the publisher to break even, if he had been careful not to spend more than 8 to 10 per cent of the book's gross retail income on advertising and promotion. Cummings was doubtless disappointed when his total royalties did little more than cover Liveright's advance; however, the publisher, who lost money on the transaction, was pleased by the very favorable press *The Enormous Room* received and looked upon his discovery as a good future investment.

After word reached New York in 1927 that Lawrence of Arabia had praised *The Enormous Room* and recommended its publication to an English firm, Liveright issued a second edition and then a third. Both were bolstered by large-scale advertising campaigns. But each time the results were disappointing. Isidor Schneider, who handled the promotion, later recalled some of the details of the republication of *The Enormous Room*.

> I was working at Liveright's when they decided to put out a new edition of *The Enormous Room*. Here was an instance where a publisher had faith in a good book and was willing to bet good money on it. The occasion for the new edition was the praise given it by Lawrence of Arabia. This praise was printed either as a preface or a jacket blurb, I don't remember which, but even the praise of the British Sheik didn't turn the trick and *The Enormous Room* settled back into its brilliant obscurity. I say brilliant obscurity purposely because the book, while it went into retirement, so to speak,

was lit on its way by critical pyrotechnics and by a publisher's advertising campaign that turned on the headlights.

I don't mean to suggest that *The Enormous Room* was then or at any time after its publication without readers. The critics' send-offs, and the reminders of it in general literary articles and surveys, and the efforts of its several publishers have pushed it, I should judge, into the hands of five thousand book buyers. Relatively, however, this is obscurity, and I have often tried to think out the reason for it.

The Enormous Room wasn't published in a bad year, and if it had been, it was reissued enough times to have known a good year.[48]

The history of Lewis Mumford's first book to receive extensive promotion, *The Story of Utopias,* is much the same.[49] Mumford, a frequent contributor to *The Dial* and *The New Republic,* used his first published volume as a vehicle for an evaluation of American culture in the machine age. For Liveright, he too was an investment with a future. In the years that followed, Mumford and Cummings had eight books published by their early sponsor. However, none came anywhere near the success of the works of their fellow novice, Maxwell Bodenheim. His book of verse, *Introducing Irony,* was the first of many Bodenheims published by Liveright. Although his poetry never sold well, Bodenheim's fiction, tawdry and oversexed (at least by the standards of the Twenties), soon established him as one of the most consistently successful authors of the day. His first prose work, *Replenishing Jessica,* appearing on the 1925 Liveright list, plunged its publisher into a much-publicized and comic battle with the censors and went on to sell thirty thousand copies.[50]

Less popular with the public, but of much greater literary significance, was T. S. Eliot's *The Waste Land,* which Liveright issued in 1922. The manuscript was directed to the publisher by Ezra Pound with definite instructions as to its handling—it was to be left untouched.[51] The obscurity of Eliot's masterpiece doubtless puzzled Liveright, but he issued it exactly as he had received it, giving orders that the work have careful treatment. In October 1922 part of *The Waste Land* had appeared for the first time in *The Criterion,* the London literary periodical that Eliot himself edited; then the whole poem was printed in *The Dial* in New York the following month; and finally the work appeared under the Boni & Liveright imprint in book form at the end of the year. Liveright's publication was the first to include Eliot's notes, which added an interest and value of their own to what was his second major poem and his most influential one.[52] By the time of its hardcover appearance *The Waste Land* was becoming the center of its own critical battle, and when Eliot won *The Dial* award for it later that winter, it was subjected to numerous attacks and rebuttals by such critics as Louis Untermeyer, Burton Rascoe, Edmund Wilson, and Christopher Morley.[53] Despite this critical attention, the public bought only about twenty-six hundred copies of the poem during the next eight years.[54] Once more, this was a respectable sale, but it certainly turned no significant profit for Liveright. Priced at $1.50, the book finally brought in a little over $100 in excess of its costs. The publisher's revenue could have been substantially increased had he not been so eager to promote the poet; he had gone all out and spent 25 cents per copy for advertising instead of holding with a more realistic budget of 12 to 15 cents a book. This was foolhardy extravagance in the case of a relatively unknown poet like Eliot. For an established author like Dreiser, on the other hand, large outlays for advances or promotion represented sounder investments.

Theodore Dreiser

In the early Twenties Theodore Dreiser was living in Los Angeles, across the continent from the Village apartment where Liveright had found him in 1917. Before he left New York Dreiser had involved Liveright in a series of the writer's literary interests: a book-magazine devoted to realistic and radical writing, called the *American Quarterly*, which Liveright was to publish and Dreiser edit, but which never materialized.[1] Then, there was a new writer, Charles Fort, a pseudo-scientist whom Dreiser had tried to get published for several years. When pressed by Dreiser, who threatened to quit Boni & Liveright if the firm refused Fort's work, called *The Book of the Damned*, Liveright capitulated and the book appeared and disappeared in 1920.[2] Liveright finally balked, however, at a five-volume work by John Maxwell that Dreiser urged him to take. Maxwell was a newspaper man who was convinced that Shakespeare was a fraud. In his exhaustive study he set out to prove that the plays of Shakespeare had actually been written by Robert Cecil, first Earl of Salisbury; but Liveright would have none of the Shakespeare hoax or Mr. Maxwell.[3]

The spring of 1920 found the Liveright-Dreiser association no better than ever. The checks went out each month to the author. Liveright had heavily exploited *Hey, Rub-A-Dub-Dub*—although it received the "rottenest sort of reviews"—and the publisher was trying to place *The Bulwark* serially with *The Cosmopolitan Magazine* prior to its hardcover publication.[4] Moreover, Liveright reaffirmed his intention of taking over all of Dreiser's works and issuing them in a uniform edition—a gesture accorded only very popular writers, and one, of course, that had tremendous appeal to Dreiser. For his part, Dreiser was still unhappy about the promotion of his works and was unable to finish *The Bulwark* on schedule.[5] Apprised by the author that his novel would be delayed, Liveright responded:

I am not excited about the fate of *The Bulwark*; I am simply disappointed that our biggest Fall book and the biggest book we were to have published should be more or less definitely postponed.

I sincerely hope that *The Bulwark* will be finished by August 1st. This should make possible publication in November.

I do wish that you could get it out of your mind that we have been asleep at the switch on *Free, Twelve Men,* and *Hey, Rub-A-Dub-Dub*. I reiterate that we've done pretty well, considering the fact that the reviewers have been anything but kind and that you are known as a novelist and every time anything by you is published, except a novel, people ask for a novel by you. I'll guarantee that if *The Bulwark* measures up in the critics' and the public's opinion with *Sister Carrie* and *Jennie Gerhardt,* we'll make a killing on the book.[6]

Later, after Dreiser had offered to substitute one volume of his autobiography for the unfinished novel, Liveright replied:

I'll be very glad to read *Newspaper Days*; but frankly, what I want is *The Bulwark*. I wrote you some time ago, asking you if you couldn't fix a time when the script would be finished. . . . *The Bulwark,* as you know, was to have been our big Fall number. Everyone is waiting for a Dreiser novel. When I tell some of the most important people in the trade that I have already received the first third of the book, they laugh and say "Oh, that was written several years ago; we thought Dreiser was West finishing the book." Other people whisper in my ear that they hear through some subterranean channels that you haven't been doing anything on *The Bulwark*. Now is the time for a big Dreiser novel. Please don't let it wait too long. And please write by return mail and give me some definite date.[7]

Evidently the writer had chosen to accept the money but keep Liveright in the dark about his actual progress. Despite advance publication releases to generate an enthusiastic market, the work Liveright counted on to be their "biggest book to date" failed to materialize.[8] In July the publisher indirectly discovered one cause of its delay. With candor and quite natural annoyance he set the facts before Dreiser:

After all, a small publishing concern must have one head to make decisions and to outline policies. Now that I am alone and have plenty of cash to make things hum I want to have a pretty clear idea of what I can expect from you. There is a check due you on our contract,—the one you so kindly said we could hold up. This will be sent to you as soon as you let us know whether to send it to Los Angeles or whether you expect to come East.

About the novel, I was disappointed when Lengel [William Lengel—one of Dreiser's agents] casually remarked to me that you had written him that you did not know when *The Bulwark* would be finished, and, as a matter of fact, you were working on another novel. I wrote you some days ago telling you that I have heard from another source that *The Bulwark* is far in the future, but this does not tally with one of your more recent letters in which you say you hope to have *The Bulwark* completed this summer. Won't you be perfectly frank with me? After all, $4,000 is a large sum to any publishing house, Macmillan not excepted, and you know perfectly well that nothing like this sum will be earned by the rest of your books in this office for a very long time to come. You also know that you are known as a novelist and that your novels sell and sell well and that $4,000 was advanced to you against your next novel. The public is greatly anticipating this book, and even Francis Hackett, when he "roasts" your other books, speaks of you as "our leading novelist," and adverse as the criticisms of *Hey, Rub-A-Dub-Dub* were, by and large, 50% of them spoke of waiting with great interest your forthcoming novel.

I write you at this great length because I consider this matter one of the most important things for Boni & Liveright to get straightened out on.⁹

Liveright knew nothing of Dreiser's efforts to place his next book, the autobiographical *A Book About Myself*, with another publisher on the promise of giving his new benefactor his current novel when it was completed.¹⁰ Meanwhile, in another letter Liveright outlined his future publishing ideas in great detail. In doing so he gave an objective, capsule appraisal of both the current book field and its audience:

As I take it from your letter, there will be a novel for Spring. In this connection, you might be interested to learn about my new publishing policy. . . . To my mind there is no fun in publishing a lot of books for the mere satisfaction of getting up big lists each Spring and Fall, trying to shoot for best sellers, publishing journalistic stuff for the consumption of a small group of liberals, radicals, etc. I've been spending hours examining the lists of all the publishers, and with the exception of Macmillan, there isn't one of us who doesn't get out a lot of trash and flub-dub. I thought we were above this but the anxiety for growing big and making money put lots of things on our list that shouldn't be there. When a fine publisher like Knopf finds he has to issue second-rate detective stories, wild west tales, etc. in order to make ends meet, it shows in what a rotten condition the publishing business is. I think I have hit a solution. When we started it was to do the *Modern Library* and a few really fine books each year. Then we got carried away by more or less false ambition and decided to be publishers, propagandists, friends of the needy, etc. Now I'm going back to the first principles, weed out our entire list and from now on publish only fine worthwhile books, books which in our mind will have a life of at least five years. It is impossible for contemporaries to judge what will live for several generations, but we're going to try to do this. If only two books come our way in a year, that's all we'll do. If 200 come in we have a sound financial basis on which to do them. We know perfectly well that 20 books in a year will be the limit unless some new genius has cropped up. Sticking to this policy as we absolutely shall, not being breathlessly rushed to make up big lists to suit either our salesmen or the book trade (God knows the public doesn't want them) we'll make our imprint stand for even more than it does now. And of course it will give us the time, capital, and energy to do a great deal more for the few books we do publish. Our spring list will not be as fine as I might wish because there are a few hangovers for which I have contracted. But even now I'm trying to make arrangements and settlements on some of these contracts taking losses whenever necessary. What say you?[11]

But Liveright's plans were, apparently, of little interest to Dreiser, who had confided to Mencken his decision to look elsewhere for a sponsor.

Quietly and under cover I am negotiating a return to Harper & Brothers. All my books published by Liveright are published on a *5-year lease,* so I need only assign the leases to Harper's or any other firm. I have the feeling that Liveright cannot sell books for me.

Harper's & the Century have always done well with mine. *A Traveler at Forty* has sold 10,000 and a new 5,000 edition at $3.50 in cheaper paper has been issued.[12]

Actually, only 4662 copies of *A Traveler at Forty* were sold between its publication by the Century Company in 1913 and September 30, 1920, but Dreiser seems to have significantly increased the sales.[13]

Besides dickering with Harper's, Dreiser soon opened up negotiations with the Century Company and Scribner's too.[14] Yet to Liveright he wrote:

> All I can say is that sometime ago, finding that I was not doing as well with the *The Bulwark* as I had hoped I began another, working on *The Bulwark* at spare moments but giving the main line of my attention to this new one. Having made various promises with every intention of keeping them but having failed so to do, I now prefer to say nothing until I have the completed thing before me. It is very likely that it will be done by April, possibly before, but I would not swear to it. That it will be a good novel at least in the judgment of some whose opinion I respect goes without saying or it will not be presented to anyone for publication.
>
> In the meantime you go on shrewdly, as you think, endeavoring to rouse my seemingly indifferent soul by reference to the appearance of novel-writing geniuses on every hand. Floyd Dell has written a novel which strips me of all my alleged laurels. Sherwood Anderson the same. Sinclair Lewis the same. Ben Hecht the same. I am supposed, I imagine, at this news to grasp my pen or typewriter, and with nervous envy and trembling or sweating with fear, grind out chapters after chapter[s] in the hope of resuscitating my fading laurels. I wish your prescription might work. . . . The truth is, as you ought to know by now, that my love is for the work itself and after that I would like to see it sold so that I might get a little something out of it. Beyond that little interests me, not even the arrival of a thousand geniuses. They do not help me to write my books and they do not stop me. As I say I do the very best I can.
>
> By the way, Floyd Dell has written a very fine book and I have so written him. It is exceedingly good. Four book stores here carry window displays, a fact which sorrows me a little from a practical point of view, for when *Hey, Rub-A-Dub-Dub* came out I could not find a copy here. Knopf at least has the knack of getting his product displayed.[15]

Liveright, however, astutely read between the lines of Dreiser's complaining or evasive letters; it was clear that all Dreiser wanted was an opportunity to quit him:

> I can only say that since we have had the privilege of publishing your books, we have had nothing that in any way approached the chances of success that a novel gives the publisher. When you tell me about window displays of Floyd Dell's book, you seem to overlook the many window displays that we got on some of your books at the time we sent out the very good looking poster of Theodore Dreiser; you also seem to overlook the fact that we gave the dealers all over the country a chance to buy all your books through us, even though, in many instances, we got a smaller discount than we were obliged to give the trade. However, I am not going to enter into a controversy with you whether or not Knopf or someone else would have done a great deal better for your books than we have. You have rubbed this in on me right along and nothing that I can say would change your ideas. Another thing you seem to overlook is that I wrote you twice, and not once, asking you to send in *A Novel About Myself* telling you that it would have my immediate consideration.
>
> So far as *The Bulwark* and the other novel are concerned, you seem to entirely overlook the fact that when we made the arrangements to advance you $4,000 in monthly installments, you said that *The Bulwark* would be ready for publication, and this without any equivocation on your part, not later than this present fall season.[16]

Upon Dreiser's reply, Liveright wired the author requesting him to send in the manuscript of *A Novel About Myself* (retitled *A Book About Myself* when it was issued) for spring publication.[17] Then Dreiser responded at length:

> Your first letters on the subject of *A Novel About Myself* were so positive in their assumption that it would be a mistake to publish anything but an out and out novel of *The Bulwark* brand that I was convinced that not only did you not want it but that, assuming it were more or less forced on you, that your publishing attitude toward it would be one of indifference. So I gave up hope of really seriously interesting you in it and for that reason, when it was done turned to others with [it]. Yet the real reason why I hurried to finish it last spring when I saw that *The Bulwark* was not coming out as

well as I had expected was to turn in this manuscript as a pledge, and as something out of which you could easily take your money. Your idea seems to have been that for some insane reason I was deliberately shirking on *The Bulwark,* a notion which to me seems so ridiculous that I cannot imagine anyone who really knows me assuming any such thing. Nothing in the world would give me more pleasure than to finish *The Bulwark* as I have schemed it out and turn it in and so be done with it. It will be a fine bit of literary property when it is finished and I will only be too glad to turn it in and make good and so restore good feeling all around.

On the other hand working on as I have, first on *The Bulwark,* later on *A Novel About Myself* and more recently on this third novel which I hope to have done by spring, I have reached the place where I must secure some more money from some source. Now, as things stand I can take $2,000 in advance from Harper's on *A Novel About Myself,* or I can hold it for a little time and try to market a series of chapters out of it as magazine papers. This same I set Lengel to do sometime ago, but as I now learn it has been only within the last ten days or two weeks that he has seriously set himself to this matter. If that is done, and he now wires that he has a tentative offer from the *Metropolitan,* I will not need any immediate aid, but if it is not I will. But seeing that the small amount of cash I owe you seems to trouble you so much I scarcely see how we are to come together on this work unless you with Lengel's aid can see your way to either marketing the material indicated by me to Lengel, and which he has evidently separated from the main body of the work in some form, and turning this cash over to me, or making me an additional advance against this and the other books now in your possession. Personally I can see no reason why you should not do this.

I have no objection to you as a publisher. Where you are really interested you seem to be able to do a great deal. The only thing for an author to do though is to get your real interest or move. For more reasons than one I always feel that I am entitled to considerable interest and aid, because I have had it proved to me in more ways than one that my public connection with a house is of great value to it.

As for this next novel on which I am working but concerning which I do not care to make any predictions, nor will I enter upon any contract for it now, it will be every bit as good as *The Bulwark* if not better,—in every sense as dramatic.[18]

In a letter written the same day as Dreiser's to Liveright, December 21, 1920, the publisher frankly and sorrowfully anticipated the writer's admission of sending *A Novel About Myself* to another firm, which was naturally just as eager as Liveright to get a novel from Dreiser. Through his former associates at the *Century* magazine, T. R. Smith had probably discovered that Dreiser had been negotiating with the Century Company and Harper's.

> Your last few letters show me that you have no feeling of regard or loyalty for me, personally, so our affairs must be regarded in the strict light of business proceedings. . . . I feel that we have done very well by you considering the materials you have provided us with. I have no apologies to offer or any cheap rosy promises to give you. You have never been looked on by me or anyone connected with this firm as an accident or a probable failure. We have considered you just as you wished to be considered, as a literary property and the most distinguished American author. I have looked into the matter of collecting your works and bringing out a set not once but ten times. I am of the same opinion today that I have come to after each one of these investigations, and that is that a set of your works would have twice as good an opportunity of being successful after your next successful novel as they could now. For the last two years you know as well as I that manufacturing costs have been staggering and that the set could not be priced at a figure that would promise success.
>
> I have published everything you brought to me without qualification; even *The Hand of the Potter*. . . . You know perfectly well the tremendously hard work I did on *Twelve Men* and you, yourself, acknowledged that my work on it was of great value. You could have at least written to me first and told me how dissatisfied you were before making me, more or less, Grub Street talk.

A wire from Liveright offering Dreiser a $1,000 advance for *A Novel About Myself* followed this letter.[19] Early in January, after Liveright had heard nothing from the author, he wrote again.

> I have already wired you making you a definite cash offer for *A Novel About Myself*. It may not be as good as the Harper offer, but after all you know that an advance is really more or less in the nature of an evidence of good faith. . . . I feel rather confident that I will have a wire from you today or tomorrow accepting my offer,

and I do hope that from now on you won't feel it necessary to go to any other publisher with any proposition. If you would only put yourself in the frame of mind of believing that we do as much for you as any other publisher could, we would both be happier. It is ridiculous for you to make anyone your agent for serialization or anything like that. I'm glad to do it for nothing, and I'm as good an editor as the people whose assistance you ask. If *A Novel About Myself* is going to be published by us this Spring, I sincerely hope that you're going to allow me to "edit" it and not anyone else. This would be done in close consultation with you by letter and wire. You know that I did the best job on *Twelve Men* that any of your friends ever did on any of your books. It would be fine to have *A Novel About Myself* for this Spring, and the other novel that you mention for the fall. On the novel to take the place of *The Bulwark* you're quite right. We must pay you just what it is worth regardless of the *Bulwark* contract. It's too bad that you have not finished *The Bulwark* but I have high hopes for it eventually.

I maintain with unswerving confidence that the collected works should not be attempted until business conditions are better, and until the publication of the next "real" novel. Before the novel is issued, however, steps should already have been taken to secure rights, plates, etc. from other publishers.[20]

But Dreiser, while willing for Liveright to read his manuscript, was not ready to agree to any proposition the publisher offered. He was anxious that Liveright secure his books from Lane, especially *The "Genius"*—which Dreiser was convinced would have a successful sale—and that Liveright continue acquiring his earlier works so that a collected edition of Dreiser would soon be a reality. Moreover, while he tested Liveright's courage and commitment to him, Dreiser, with Mencken's encouragement, continued to barter with other firms.[21] Liveright, more or less unaware of what was going on, wrote:

This leaves the matter of *A Novel About Myself* pretty much up in the air. Mencken sent the manuscript to me and I've read about half of it and want to tell you that I think it's wonderful stuff. I feel that I could edit it to great advantage. . . . I haven't been in any rush to write you about *A Novel About Myself* because you have been determined not to have it published in book form until you could get something out of it from serialization. On January 7th you wired me that you preferred to sell articles before issuing it. Now if there are to be any chapters taken from *A Novel About Myself* and published in the magazines, this would, undoubtedly, defer publication until the Spring of 1922. This would be a fine time for it to come out if in the fall of this year you publish a regular Dreiser novel. Will you let me know who is handling the serialization-end of *A Novel About Myself* and what progress is being made? It is a wonderfully fine book and I'll be proud to publish it when you say "Go ahead."22

While Liveright waited for directions to proceed, Dreiser continued to negotiate with Harper's. However, on March 11, 1921, the author wrote his publisher and enclosed a letter from Harper's which said, in effect, that the moment was not right for them to issue Dreiser's autobiographical works or to make him a long-term publication commitment. Rather, the powers at Harper's believed that Dreiser should first publish a successful novel to hold and extend his audience before his nonfiction was issued.23 In his own letter to Liveright, Dreiser wrote:

When I sent the ms. to Briggs [William H. Briggs, an editor at Harper's] it was with the idea of interesting [them] in the series of articles . . . which could be used in the magazine. Despite anything I could do—I wrote at least four letters—they proceeded to consider the manuscript not only for possible magazine articles, but as a book to be published by Harper's, with what result the enclosed letter shows. Since the proposition they put to me rather complicated matters I recalled the manuscript in order to think out for myself just what would be best. As you will learn from this letter I am still thinking. What I finally decide will depend very considerably I think upon what you have to say after thinking over what I have to say. Here is the situation as briefly as I can recite it.

Several years ago, before I ever wrote *A Novel About Myself*, I started what I proposed to call *A History of Myself*. I think I spoke of it to you once but without any desire to do anything about it at that time. It was and is to be a work in four or five volumes. Volume I.—no final name, as yet, I completed in about six months and laid aside because, at that time I was undecided what to do about it. I covered my life from infancy to Newspaper Days, which was the title I originally gave to *A Novel About Myself*. Because of certain personal and family reasons I laid it aside waiting such time as conditions might warrant its use. Since then several of the people whom parts of it might offend have died. Besides that reflection has made me see how parts of it could be temporarily eliminated. Even so I would not have thought of doing anything about it now if it had not been for this letter of Harper's and certain letters from Mencken who from the first view of *A Novel About Myself* has insisted that I ought to write a volume concerning my earlier years and one about my literary experiences. And this without knowing that I had written volume one.

All this by way of answering your questions concerning the fall publication of *A Novel About Myself*. As I see now I will need a little more time than I thought to finish the book on which I am working. That will probably throw its use over until fall. Then in so far as *A Novel About Myself* is concerned, I am inclined to think that Harper's and Mencken are right and that I ought to launch the series as this Harper letter suggests. What I need to know now is your attitude toward this series. You may not see it as, evidently, Harper's see it. Assuming that volume one is as good as volume two and that after finishing this novel I could finish volumes three and four would you be interested to publish [*sic*] the series, one volume a year for four or five years? And do you feel that you would have the same faith in the idea which Harper's apparently have. From this and several other letters written me by Briggs, I gather that they are genuinely excited or enthused by the critical and financial prospects of such a series. It is entirely possible that you would not see it in quite the same light or that you would not be willing to undertake so long drawn out a series. Personally I would rather take the series to the one who would feel the keenest about it. Plainly if Harper's could have it they would do their best to make it a success and they do pretty well with a lot of their things. At the same time I am sure that if you had a real proposition and were really enthused by it, you would do as well as anyone.

However, such is the story and now you may think it over. I would have written you before but I had not quite made up my mind as to whether it would be advisable to attempt that series now. Since I have finally concluded that it would be I am putting the facts before you. Your silence in regard to the second volume has made me wonder whether you see it kindly as do some others.[24]

Liveright was ready to oblige, even if it meant accepting four volumes of autobiography to get a novel from Dreiser; moreover, he reopened negotiations with the Lane Company to secure Dreiser's books—an action Harper's, apparently, was uninterested in pursuing, though it was one of Dreiser's major concerns. On April 12, 1921, Liveright wrote Dreiser:

> I have been trying to find out . . . what the lowest figure would be that would induce Lane to turn over all your books that they control. Up to date I have been unable to get any information that amounts to anything. In this connection, I would greatly object to having *The "Genius"* expurgated in any way at all. From what I understand of the case, we would at least stand an even chance of not being interfered with except in a few isolated places if we republish the book as it was originally brought out. In an expurgated edition I don't think it would sell very well, and it would not be a particularly creditable piece of publishing.
>
> Naturally, I can't make you any definite proposition until I see how much money the whole thing is going to involve. I must be sure, above all things, that whatever obligations we enter into with you can be rigorously lived up to, and I also have in mind the publication of a complete set of your books, taking over your books from all other publishers if they agree to this.
>
> Assuming that fair arrangements cannot be made just at this time with Lane, what do you want me to do for you (a) on the new novel to be published this coming fall, (b) on the publication of your autobiography commencing with volume one in the Spring of 1922 and volume two which I suppose is *Newspaper Days* in the fall of 1922?

Liveright's activities seemed to convince Dreiser, temporarily at least, that Boni & Liveright was his proper home. His reply to Liveright was most cordial.

> About the manuscript of the novel. When it is done, and if it pleases you, I would like an advance in some form, according to my needs and plans at the time, but no more than I could get anywhere against that particular book. . . . As for the works in general I certainly want a guarantee that they will be assembled if I am to turn over this novel, *A Novel of Myself* and such additional works as I turn out. . . . I want to ask you about certain other books that

I have and which I feel are worth publishing, especially in a set. One of these is the second book of short stories, previously mentioned. Another is a book to be called *Pictures of American Life*, and contains pen portraits of places and institutions with their accompanying moods, urban and rural. Then there is a book of poems. Assuming that the material is accepted as intrinsically meritorious would you be satisfied to include them in any eventual set?

As to the terms on all of the books, I would like twenty per cent. For that I will give a long time contract, of course. I want a definite understanding as to what in the way of advertising is to be done. Briggs writes me, and you can verify this by asking him, that the sales of *Jennie Gerhardt* and *The Financier* have doubled—I think he said more than doubled, in the last two years. That is why I am anxious to get the Lane books away because they do not sell any of my books now. They have literally dropped out on the theory that I can go to hell, I assume. But *A Hoosier Holiday* will sell, if advertised. And so will *The Titan* and *The "Genius."* People are always trying to get those two books from me direct. I rather agree with you that once *The History of Myself* is started, in a publishing sense, the volumes ought to follow each other at intervals of six months and I have such a lead that I could easily do volume three and no doubt four, in time. Then I would like to stop and finish *The Bulwark*.

Let me have an outline of your own thoughts and what you think is best. I most sincerely hope you take over the Lane volumes.[25]

That Liveright was willing to do almost anything Dreiser demanded in order to secure a novel from the author is substantiated by the fact that every one of Dreiser's demands was met long before the completion of the new novel was near. While Dreiser delayed committing himself on *A Novel About Myself*, the fall season of 1921 came and went. His correspondence with Liveright included letters from the publisher describing the publishing situation and still another plea from his sponsor for enlightenment about their future plans. First, Liveright wrote Dreiser on August 10, 1921:

You ask what the trade outlook is for fall. There is a peculiarly mixed up situation in the book trade. General business is bad. The merchandise managers of such concerns as The American

News Company, McClurg's, etc, have given orders to buy from hand to mouth except on what they call "sure fiction." It happens that this fall brings with it the biggest collection of this "sure fiction" that has been offered in one season for some years past. There are new novels by Hall Caine, Kathleen Norris, Harold Bell Wright, Gene Stratton Porter, Joseph C. Lincoln, Ethel Deal, John Galsworthy, H. G. Wells, Winston Churchill, E. Phillips Oppenheim, merely to mention the ones that come to my mind. They are all what the trade looks upon as a cinch. The first printing of Gene Stratton Porter's new novel was 250,000, of Hall Caine's 100,000, etc. With this embarrassment of riches on easy money merchandise, the bookseller is going to take very few chances.

But, again, I *implore* you to let me know when the novel will come on.

Second, the publisher wrote on October 8, 1921:

There seems to be mix-up in our ideas about where we stand on *A Novel About Myself* and where we stand in other matters too. . . . As far back as March 31st you sent me a wire saying: "Devoting entire time to novel not *The Bulwark* which should be done about August 1st. When completed will be glad to deliver it and *History* providing arrangement is entered into soon." As you know you always attached some sort of string to any arrangements with me saying that we first had to take over the Lane volumes, and, as you know, up to date Lane has been absolutely unwilling to make any decent offer.

As I understand my position with you now, if we give you an advance of $1000, against royalties on *A Book About Myself*, we can publish it either in the spring or fall of 1922. . . . But how about the typical Dreiser novel that you wrote on March 3rd [sic] would be done before August 1st? Then again how about *The Bulwark*? I've already written you that I would be perfectly willing to make you a liberal advance on the other novel not considering it as a substitute on your *Bulwark* contract. And are you going to send me the manuscripts of the other books in the *History* series? . . . Everyone in the trade is asking us when another Dreiser novel is coming out and we have talked in rather vague way about one and also about *A Novel About Myself*. I'd like to start some publicity as soon as I can. Won't you please answer me as definitely and as fully as you can about what you think your plans and our plans for publishing your books should be.

Still, Dreiser continued to hold out. He made inquiries, proposals, and counterproposals to several houses without Liveright's knowledge. While Dreiser consulted a lawyer, Arthur C. Hume, in the hope of somehow securing personal control of the plates and copyrights to all his books, another alternative emerged: the American branch of the John Lane Company failed, and its contracts were taken over by Dodd, Mead & Company.[26] Hence Liveright was held up in his attempt to secure Dreiser's works, but the writer discovered another firm to bargain with. In debt to Lane for $1597.92 and Liveright for $1338.13, Dreiser immediately proposed to Dodd, Mead that they give him a $3000 advance on his next novel.[27] With this money he proposed to wipe out his debts to both Lane and Liveright and become a Dodd, Mead author. But Dodd, Mead was a conservative house; it met Dreiser's proposal with caution. Moreover, the author had developed a reputation as being bad-tempered and difficult to deal with. Dreiser began to have second thoughts. He wrote to Hume:

> They [Dodd, Mead] want *The Bulwark*. Why? Because Lane claims he advanced me some money against it? I can scarcely see another reason. They approach me with a tricky offer to knock off one thousand of the alleged Lane claim if I will reduce my royalties and by the process they will make more than they will lose. Outside of that they will advance $1,000 when I can go to Harper or Liveright and get $3,000. And this offer of theirs is really tentative. They will look at *The Bulwark*. If it isn't too radical for them and I will make such changes as their conservatism would dictate then the aforesaid offer holds good.
>
> If they stall around with a few select ifs, ands, etc. you may know that they are not for me. I want none of them. I will get the book published and the publisher who gets it will be delighted to get it. And he will come to the front and do some talking about it. Will it be an old line publisher. I doubt it. I doubt it very much.[28]

Mencken received an even greater indication of Dreiser's contempt for the old line.

> The Dodd people are not publishers of liberal books. They approach me about [as] a Baptist snouts a pervert. I am to alter my books. I am to let them pick and choose. They will see whether I

can do anything worthy of them. They do not want *The "Genius"* unless it is properly pruned around the vitals.[29]

In contrast, Liveright apparently wanted to issue *The "Genius"* in unexpurgated form. It was simply a question of securing the rights to it.

> I have seen Sumner who told me that *The "Genius"* had never been actually suppressed. He went to the Lane Company and they voluntarily stopped selling it because Sumner warned them about it. This being the case have you a suit against Sumner? Of course, I suppose you'll take this matter up with your attorneys. Sumner reiterated that in its present form *The "Genius"* would be open to action on the part of his Society. He promised to go over the whole case as soon as he could and send me a list of the changes that would have to be made. From the way he talked I should say that the book would be pretty badly emasculated when he gets through with it. I'll let you have the stuff from Sumner just as soon as I get it.
>
> I would like to begin publicity work as soon as possible on your fall novel if you feel pretty sure that it will be ready. Won't you let me hear from you about it?[30]

It became increasingly clear to Dreiser that of the three publishers—Harper's, Dodd, Mead, and Liveright—he had been dickering with most seriously in 1921 and 1922, Liveright was the least conservative, the most anxious to reissue *The "Genius"* in unexpurgated form, and the best able to exploit that work in the fullest possible way. Though denied a novel year after year since their initial association in 1917, Liveright accepted Dreiser's abuse and accusations in the belief that Dreiser was a great American novelist and would, eventually, justify his faith by producing a best-seller. Finally, Liveright proved his readiness to confront Sumner for the sake of free expression, and this must have impressed Dreiser. The writer accepted the $1000 advance and, after nearly two years of bartering, sent *A Novel About Myself* to Boni & Liveright. After working on the manuscript for weeks, Liveright wrote to Dreiser just prior to its publication.

> You'll see that I've done a whole lot of editing, mostly cutting because you left very little else to clean up despite what the damn-

fool critics say who love to reiterate that your writing is so sloppy at times.

I feel almost confident that you'll approve of most of my cuts. . . . I should say that I have cut the book about 200 pages although I haven't estimated it carefully at all.[31]

After Liveright edited Dreiser's autobiography, he devised a proposition to set before his suspicious, cantankerous author. First, the publisher relinquished any rights to *The Bulwark*, a book that had been hanging fire for five years. With reluctance Liveright wrote, "I'm returning the contract releasing you on *The Bulwark*, but I hope that this doesn't mean that I'm not to have any chance of publishing it. You'll find that I'll do better for you than anyone else if I get a chance at your real work which I think is the writing of novels."[32] Next, in a contract that Dreiser signed on January 18, 1923, Liveright promised the novelist a drawing account of $4,000 annually for the next four years. In addition to buying the rights, plates, sheets, and bound volumes of all Dreiser's earlier works from Harper's, and Dodd, Mead (Lane) at a total cost of $9631.38 Liveright agreed to pay Dodd, Mead & Company slightly more than $1300 to cover Dreiser's personal indebtedness to them. *The "Genius"* was to be reissued immediately, and the author was to receive a straight 50 cent royalty on each $3.00 volume sold as opposed to the more usual 10 or 15 per cent of the retail price. For all his other works reprinted or issued by Boni & Liveright, Dreiser was guaranteed a royalty of 20 per cent. A collected edition of these writings was to begin appearing in January 1927 and, after a sale of one thousand sets, Dreiser was to receive a minimum royalty of $10,000. In return, Dreiser promised the house all his works for the next four years at the rate of two volumes annually. Among the projects specifically mentioned in the agreement were at least two full-length novels, a limited edition of poetry, an autobiography, and a collection of short stories. Dreiser's works were to be issued in the following order:

The "Genius"—Spring, 1923
A new novel or *Twelve Women*—Fall, 1923
The Color of a Great City or a novel—Spring, 1924
Youth (volume one of the autobiographical series) —Fall, 1924

A volume of short stories or a novel—Spring, 1925
A volume of short stories or a novel—Fall, 1925
The third volume of his autobiography—Spring, 1926

Dreiser's persistent crankiness and his inability to finish a new novel soon seemed to indicate that Liveright had gambled over $25,000 and achieved very little. The publisher spent an additional $2000 to advertise the elusive *A Book About Myself,* and yet this volume had an initial sale of fewer than 3000 copies.[33] Dreiser's reaction to the public's apathy was to accuse Liveright of falsifying his sales records and failing to promote his work.[34] Liveright responded on March 27, 1923:

> I cross my heart and swear to our Lord that your note of yesterday absolutely mystifies me.
>
> You say that before I forward you a statement for the last six months that you wish I would think over something which you said to me one day not long ago, etc., etc. You say further on in the letter that you would like to stick and work with me, etc. but upon the condition only "that I absolutely get a square deal."
>
> Your letter leaves no interpretation open other than that you question whether you have always gotten a square deal from me. Thank God our books are open to all our authors or to anyone else who has any direct or indirect right to be interested in them. Our authors can know day by day what orders are received for their books. We will be glad to get them at any time affidavits from our printers and this holds good from the first day when the place opened shop. The only thing in this business that I have the slightest regret about is that when I first came in and knew nothing about publishing ethics, Albert Boni put several titles in the Modern Library which legally were non-copyright, but all of which we should have paid for. And as soon as I learned of these things, I paid back every cent that was ethically due, although it hurt pretty badly when I did it.
>
> Let me reiterate what I have frequently said to you: That I am heart and soul for your work, that we now have a very big investment in it, and that from now on you will see a very much greater concerted campaign for the sale of all your work. Up until recently, as you know, we have had no feeling of security which justified us in spending a lot of money on your work as a whole. In this con-

nection, by the way, won't you please within the next few weeks let me have some idea of the sales for the last two years of your books which we have taken over from the other publishers? I certainly do not want to fall behind their figures and I think it will be a good thing for my sales department if I could give them figures upon which they must improve.

In spite of your letter, which it is possible I have misinterpreted, my admiration and affection for you remains the same.

And later, on August 2, 1923:

Messner told me that you didn't think we were doing anything for your books. Don't think for one moment that with the very big investment we now have in them I'm damn fool enough or inactive enough not to have laid my plans long ago. . . . I am now laying out at home a $2000 campaign on Dreiser, as an institution, so to speak, most of it to run in the *New York Times Book Review Section*, and I will be ready to show you this plan in the rough Monday or Tuesday, or whenever you drop into New York. . . . When you ask the obvious question: "Why haven't these plans been put over?" the answer will be just as obvious, because up until now we haven't published a Dreiser novel, and I say over and over again that no one could sell any more of your books than we have sold. I hope to show you real results on The *"Genius"* although it's only a *republication* and we may have some real trouble from Sumner who is more active than ever. We have been told from what looks like unimpeachable authority that he is going to try to get a grand jury indictment on the book in spite of the unofficial imprimateur which we got from the District-Attorney's office.

When I see you here in New York I'll make you a solemn promise never again to give you any figures of sales from order records. From now on whenever you ask about the sales of your books, I shall gently lead you down by the hand to Mr. Pell's [Arthur Pell, Liveright's treasurer] office and we will have the ledgers opened and find what the sales were, not the orders as reported by some clerk who has either forgotten cancellations, entered orders two or three times, etc. But I haven't forgotten either that I have always told you that I'd stand behind any figures I gave you, and although I only did give you a penciled memorandum which I got hurriedly one day, I am going to make you believe more and more that Liveright's word is as good as his bond. How do I know that you didn't spend this extra royalty on 2 or 3 new gowns—I should say suits? But when, as and if, you demand your pound of flesh—you old fundamentalist—it's going to be accompanied with a sworn statement of printings from the printers, and you, yourself, will be able to see the books on hand here and at the warehouse. Then the sales and review copies must be the difference.

The promotional campaign Liveright promised was begun with large ads announcing that all of Dreiser's works were now Boni & Liveright publications. Besides individual descriptions of these volumes and a picture of the author was the following text:

> We announce with pleasure and pardonable pride that we have acquired the publication rights for all of Theodore Dreiser's work.
>
> As a realist he is looked upon by an ever increasing audience as not only one of the first, but as perhaps the greatest exponent of the naturalistic school in American fiction.
>
> Many younger writers are his disciples. Realism today has become almost a cult, but the discerning reader turns ever to the master mind.
>
> Historically Dreiser has his companions, for he belongs with the movement toward naturalism and realism which came to America when Stephen Crane, Frank Norris and others were dissenting in their various dialects from the reticencies and the romance then current.
>
> Mr. Dreiser is an eminent spirit brooding over a world which, in spite of many condemnations, he deeply and soberly loves.[35]

Liveright had once said to Dreiser, "Stick to me, kid, and you'll wear diamonds," and his faith in Dreiser as a novelist soon rewarded them both, when, in the fall of 1923, new editions of *The "Genius"* reached the same bookstores from which they had been recalled by an intimidated John Lane Company seven years before.[36] Believing that the changes Sumner had suggested would emasculate the work, Liveright had encouraged Dreiser to revise if he wished, but not to expurgate.[37] The publisher soon proved how well he knew the reading public. His belief that a novel by Theodore Dreiser would sell, even if it was one of his poorest and a reprint at that, was confirmed, for the work sold 12,301 copies by the end of the year.[38] Moreover, Liveright's surprising success with *The*

"*Genius*" seemed to mellow Dreiser somewhat. Together they had defeated Sumner—at least temporarily—for the Vice Society took no action. For a while letters from Dreiser complaining about the way his books were being handled arrived at the house less frequently— but they still appeared. There was one to Messner, chiding the sales manager about the lagging sales of *A Book About Myself*. Messner's reply, that they were promoting him as well as they could, that they were in business to make money, and that a new novel would increase the popularity of all his books, sounded enough like Liveright so that Dreiser did not complain to Messner again.[39] But Dreiser remained as suspicious as ever. He confided to Mencken that he thought Liveright was cheating him, despite the fact that *The "Genius"* was having the largest initial sale of any of Dreiser's books up to that point.[40]

John Sumner's Vice Society

The New York Society for the Suppression of Vice was chartered in 1873 by the New York State Legislature in order to secure enforcement of laws prohibiting the "sale, distribution, and production of any obscene, lewd, lascivious, filthy, indecent, or disgusting book, magazine, and motion picture."[1] Ostensibly an instrument of society in general, and presumably following standards determined by law and court decisions, this organization soon came to control—or at least exert a powerful influence over—the sources of its own power in Albany and New York City. With misguided zeal it kept a watchful eye on all current books and periodicals; it made impossible the sale in unexpurgated versions of such classics as the *Odes* of Horace, *The Wandering Jew*, and *The Three Musketeers*. Protests might be signed by respectable intellectuals and leaflets gotten up by the Authors' League, but the Society thrived. Few publishers were willing to risk the pressure of public opinion or a term in jail by opposing these defenders of decency headed by John S. Sumner. The emergence of Sumner was recorded by Floyd Dell:

> In [1915] the infamous Anthony Comstock died and went to hell, and an obscure person named John S. Sumner took his place as the hired agent of a private organization which, in cahoots with a corrupt police force, exercised an unofficial Censorship over American thought, and art, and literature; and a cowardly and hypocritical American public allowed this tyranny to go on.[2]

Even today it would be difficult to show that Dell maligned Comstock, Sumner, or their vigilantes in the least. With Sumner in New York and the Watch and Ward Society in Boston, the East's most prominent centers of culture and cosmopolitanism seemed doomed to a bland diet of carefully screened reading. The ardent chauvinistic credos of the mighty censors, "to uphold our standards of decency more than ever before in the face of this foreign and imitation foreign invasion, rather than to make those things which are vicious and indecent so familiar as to become common and representative of American life and manners," put liberals on the spot.[3] The new publishers were no more in favor of dirty books per se (although their sales income was welcome), than they were against the Flag, but rather than risk being called purveyors of obscenity, they, at first, quickly withdrew works that had been threatened by the censorship society.

Soon the younger, more adventurous publishers found two ways to circumvent Sumner and prosecution.[4] The first was to "limit" the sale of questionable books to a white-collar group consisting (supposedly) of doctors, lawyers, ministers, and teachers. The assumption seemed to be that if you offered indecent books to professional people, they would know what to do with them! This ruse was mainly successful, but it occasionally backfired by limiting the sale of a real rouser, which might have been a best-seller on the open market. Semiannually, Liveright's catalogues announced certain "scientific" books for the edification of "physicians, the legal profession, and other educators, legitimately interested in the subjects they discuss."[5] In the Fall 1921 catalogue the publisher presented *The Natural Philosophy of Love* by Remy de Gourmont, as translated by Ezra Pound, and *Sex Happiness* by André Tridon. De Gourmont's work was guaranteed to "prove an illuminating document to every person who should properly read the book," while Tridon's volume was restricted to those who were married or contemplating matrimony. *Sex Happiness* was the more topical and daring, for it promised to supply the reader with the "basic physical and psychological reason for the restless and dissatisfied modern wife," and with "sanity" and "delicacy" reveal the "methods which most normal men and women follow." The purity and doubletalk of this capsule catalogue description probably bewildered the censors. Moreover, the price of science was high—$5.00 a copy.

Works which were obviously belles-lettres were issued under a different aegis, since they didn't qualify as scientific treatises.[6] Lacking the "educational" selling point, ingenious publishers borrowed a practice from their old-line rivals: the publication of limited editions. Soon Brahmins in boxed volumes and leather-bound sets were replaced by their less sacrosanct counterparts. Offered at the highest price the market would bear, limited editions more than compensated their publishers for the chances they took and sometimes paid a firm's overhead for the year.

For almost a decade, until houses began to saturate the market with them, these special editions—gotten up on large thick paper, heavily bound, and often autographed—were eagerly sought by American book collectors and autograph afficionados.[7] The more gold on the cover, the more unusual the design (and many volumes were, indeed, handsome examples of the book-making craft), the more eager the public was for this boxed wonder. Usually printed in editions of one thousand, fifteen hundred, or two thousand copies, and advertised with flourishes suggesting the famous author had personally signed each copy after he had leafed through it and blessed its pages, these hoaxes were in reality the creations of enterprising publishers and anonymous binders. The latter were responsible for tipping into each volume a sheet with the author's signature, one from a stack of blank pages he had signed prior to the book's final manufacture.

Like other publishers, Liveright offered his limited editions on a subscription basis; his early selections sold out shortly after publication.[8] They included four volumes by George Moore, Huneker's *Painted Veils,* Paul Gauguin's *Intimate Journals,* Pierre Louys' *Aphrodite,* and T. R. Smith's collection of bawdy verse, *Poetica Erotica.* Liveright's grandest scheme, the publication of the complete works of George Moore, began in 1922. Its immediate success surely bears out the ingenuity of its daredevil sponsor in dealing with a portion of the American public. The twenty-two-volume set of Moore was called the Carra edition, and the writer's signature appeared in the paper itself, replacing the common watermark. The complete Carra retailed for $180. When Liveright gave Moore an advance of $30,000 before the appearance of a single volume, he risked bankruptcy. However, the publisher proved his knowledge of the market when the entire edition of one thousand sets was subscribed to.

Although Sumner and his Society allowed Liveright's limited

editions and "scientific" works to pass into the hands of avid, prosperous collectors, the crusader and his supporters constantly threatened the sale of books offered the general trade. Liveright's first local run-in, on March 22, 1920, was not with Sumner but with a bluenose detective. At that time one hundred and thirty-seven copies of *The Story of a Lover* were seized at the Boni & Liveright office.[9] This novel, published anonymously, was written by Hutchins Hapgood, a cofounder of the Provincetown Players.[10] It had already moved into a third edition—with eleven thousand copies sold—before Detective John C. Pooler of the New York City Vice Squad picked up a copy, perused it, and decided that it "was not a desirable volume for public circulation."[11] Appealing to a sympathetic city magistrate, William G. McAdoo, who didn't bother to read the whole volume, Pooler was granted a warrant, and Liveright was issued a summons to answer charges of publishing and distributing an indecent and obscene book in violation of Section 1141 of the Penal Law. Pooler, accompanied by two other detectives, proceeded directly to the firm, where they seized all copies of *The Story of a Lover* and took them back to police headquarters. There the volumes remained until after the trial. Liveright appeared before the court on March 29, and asked that a committee representative of public interests be appointed to examine the book for alleged violations rather than continuing the hearing on the basis of a reading by a single policeman. This was refused. The next month, however, before Magistrate Frothingham in the Jefferson Market Police Court, the publisher was cleared and the case dismissed. Frothingham held that there was insufficient reason shown by the prosecution that the book was likely to corrupt and deprave the morals of its readers.[12] Liveright's trouble with the policeman over the Hapgood book was a comparatively minor one, when compared with his official introduction to Sumner two years later, but both Detective Pooler and the Secretary of the Society for the Suppression of Vice used the same means to bring Liveright to court.

According to the statute under which Detective Pooler had acted in 1920 and Sumner would use later on in the decade, the mechanics of getting a book withdrawn from circulation appeared to be fairly simple.[13] Once any citizen saw or professed to see indecency and obscenity in a book, he could apply to a city magistrate within his jurisdiction and have the sale of the work stopped. According to the law the magistrate was ordered—once he had received a complaint and if he too decided that the book was actionable—to issue a warrant directing the police to confiscate all copies of the book in question and deliver them to the District Attorney's office, where they were to remain until the seller had been tried and the status of the book had been determined.

If a citizen was reluctant to initiate an action against a publisher himself, he had only to apply, anonymously if he chose, to the Society for the Suppression of Vice about the work he objected to. Once a complaint was received by the Society, an officer of the organization read the book, and if he too found it distasteful, the Society applied to a city magistrate for a warrant to search and seize as well as for a summons to bring the publisher into court. If the court decided against the publisher, he was allowed to appeal to the Court of Special Sessions. Here three judges decided the fate of the work, and if they held it was objectionable, they had the authority to suppress it for good. Obviously, the operation of the plan could and did in fact involve publishers in costly, protracted legal fights.

During the summer of 1922 Sumner and his group suddenly became very active. First, they seized several hundred copies of three works at the firm of Thomas Seltzer, Inc., and charged the publisher with issuing and selling obscene literature.[14] The books in question were *A Young Girl's Diary*, by an anonymous Austrian girl with a preface by Freud; *Casanova's Homecoming*, by Arthur Schnitzler; and *Women in Love*, by D. H. Lawrence. The next on Sumner's list was Liveright and a book that had been around for a long, long time (but generally in Latin), *The Satyricon* of Petronius Arbiter. T. R. Smith, with one eye on the classics and the other on contemporary taste, had seen to an idiomatic English translation of this work as well as its production in a two-volume, $30 limited edition.[15] But it took Sumner only a glance at its pages alluding to heterosexual orgies as well as friendly relationships between men and boys to take Liveright to court. As in Sumner's prosecution of Seltzer, the real target was the publisher not the book.[16] While both cases were pending, the *New York Times* editorialized that it would be "a serious loss to human knowledge to suppress Petronius, whatever may be thought of Schnitzler and D. H. Lawrence."[17] The extant fragments of *The Satyricon* revealed the talent of a brilliant mind and above all presented a unique picture of social conditions within certain classes of Roman society during the First Century A.D. Moreover, the *Times* continued:

> It used to be assumed by courts which construed the law that persons who could read the classical languages were already corrupt beyond hope of redemption; hence the obscene classics were usually allowed to circulate without interference. Mr. Sumner has now attacked that interpretation of the law. And he is quite right, if one assumes—as he must—that in a work containing obscene passages nothing else is real, and that matter which might pervert some readers must be withheld from all readers.

Neither the Seltzer nor the Liveright case was decided until September, but during August 1922 Sumner, aroused by the "extreme" manner of authors of the younger school, invited representatives of publishers', authors', and booksellers' organizations to meet with him in the hope of establishing a program of voluntary censorship for books.[18] This was to be under the direction of an arbiter or dictator, much as the Hays Office functioned for the motion-picture industry and the Baseball Commissioner for the Major Leagues. While the National Association of Booksellers and writers in general immediately rejected Sumner's plan, the publishers were divided. Some, like Brentano's and Holt, were inclined to approve it, but others sided with G. P. Putnam, who met the proposal with one word: preposterous.[19] In the public discussion that was current, Liveright gained most of the publicity. First, he said, he was preparing to bring suit against Sumner for libel, because of public statements the publisher alleged Sumner made about both the Boni & Liveright *Satyricon* as a "free and slangy translation of an alleged classic" as well as Liveright's practice of issuing limited editions to anyone who would buy them rather than the special clientele of "mature and incorruptible persons" the publisher claimed he had built up for these special works. Liveright said these statements reflected unfavorably upon his reputation and integrity as a publisher as well as upon the dignity and character of the people who bought his books. Moreover, Liveright said that he had earlier proposed to Sumner a plan of having fifteen public-spirited men and women consider questionable manuscripts.

> At that time Mr. Sumner and I communicated with each other, but it was never my intention then, nor is it now, that any sort of body should be constituted that would act as censors before the publication of a book. I said two years ago, and say now, that instead of the tremendous expense of money, time and energy, and the notoriety that attends all cases of censorship, as we have seen them to date, these cases might better be brought before the committee which I suggested. I realize, of course, that the decision of even such a committee as I suggested two years ago might be extremely unfair to the fine work of a fine writer. But rather than submit to the stupid persecutions and indignities of today's procedures, the vote of such a committee would, I think, be accepted by most publishers.
> But to organize a censorship committee presided over by some Pooh Bah of literature who could decide upon the advisability of publishing a manuscript would, to my mind, sound the death knell of literature. I, for one, would not submit one manuscript to such a committee, and from conversations that I have recently had, know of no intelligent publisher who would.[20]

Soon the idea of a publisher's offensive against Sumner even became popular, and it was rumored that several firms planned to follow Liveright's example by suing the crusader, should their books be seized and eventually cleared.[21] In fact, once the charges against Seltzer's three books were dismissed on September 12, he instituted a suit against Sumner for $10,000.[22]

Two weeks later Magistrate Charles Oberwager dismissed the complaint against *The Satyricon* as well.[23] In his rather lengthy decision, Oberwager held that the book was both a recognized classic and an important historical document—too important to be judged by isolated sentences or separate paragraphs taken out of context.

> The legislature did not intend to confer upon any individual or society in general powers of censorship over literary works, for if such were the case the power could easily be abused and the destruction of freedom of speech as well as freedom of the press would be resultant effects of such a state.

It is generally believed by scholars that the book in question was written by the Roman in the time of Nero. The English translation, which the New York publishing house printed in a limited edition of 1,200 copies, was offered to their subscribers at $30 a set for two volumes.

With this prosecution the Society for the Suppression of Vice seeks to impose a duty upon the Court to exercise a censorship over literature with a view of suppressing a work of literary merit that has lived for nineteen hundred years.

If *The Satyricon* is to fall, the contemporaries of Petronius such as Ovid, Juvenal, Horace, Martial, and Tacitus must come under the ban.[24]

The following day the *Times* rejoiced at Sumner's defeat in an editorial, Liveright said he was suing Sumner for $25,000, and Seltzer raised the amount of his suit against the Society to $30,000.[25] But Sumner announced he had no intention of dropping his action against the publisher of *The Satyricon*. "There is nothing too indecent to be safely published," he said, if Oberwager's decision on *The Satyricon* was allowed to stand as a precedent.

If this decision holds, anything that has ever been written by anybody may be safely printed and circulated without limit. This may be a limited edition in the number of copies issued, but the readers are not limited, as is claimed, to highly moral, intellectual and sophisticated readers. It is strictly limited to those who have the money to pay for it.

My investigator, who was sent to the offices of the publisher, sent in a card which read "Carl Becker, dealer in rubber goods and sundries" and asked for a copy of the book. There was nothing else to identify him. That was accepted as sufficient proof of his high moral and intellectual calibre and the only question asked was whether he had the [money].[26]

In October, Sumner sent *The Satyricon* to the District Attorney, Joab A. Banton, who eventually announced he would start a new action against Liveright for issuing the work.[27] Although it was most unusual to reopen this kind of case, Banton announced he was convinced the book was indecent and was submitting it to the Chief Magistrate William McAdoo, who could overrule Oberwager's decision.[28] Sumner concurred: *The Satyricon* made *The Decameron* look like a Sunday School book, he said. Besides, in their circular touting the work, Boni & Liveright emphasized the frankness and boldness of the translation. Although the house announced that the limited edition was directed to a select group of mature and incorruptible persons, the circular went on to offer 40 per cent discounts to booksellers who purchased the work in lots of fifty two-volume sets.

Chief Magistrate McAdoo refused to reopen the case, however, and, while denouncing *The Satyricon*, publicly criticized the Society for the Suppression of Vice for encouraging public interest in the book by continuing to prosecute it.[29] District Attorney Banton then turned to the Grand Jury to decide whether or not Liveright might be indicted for issuing a dirty book. Not to be outdone, Liveright maintained that he was guiltless, and in a magnificent gesture announced that he was presenting to each of the twenty-three members of the Grand Jury his own $30 set of *The Satyricon* to read at his leisure.[30] But by the time the case came before this body, Liveright found it impossible to obtain twenty-three sets, so it was decided that the Assistant District Attorney would read both volumes to the Jury. Since the Grand Jury sat only two hours each day, it soon became clear that they had well over a week's listening before them. They voted to adjourn without hearing Petronius and deciding the fate of *The Satyricon*.[31] Although District Attorney Banton threatened to place the book before the next Grand Jury, he apparently decided against this move. In the meantime, the sales of *The Satyricon* rolled merrily along.[32]

Sumner, by now frustrated in his aims and, of course, publicly embarrassed, next broadly hinted to the press that only state censorship in the form of a new stricter law could be the answer to the failure of the courts and the apathy of some segments of the public in dealing with obscenity.[33] The prestige of the Vice Society remained high, for an impressive number of well-known people inside and outside the literary community shared Sumner's views and supported his efforts, publicly or covertly, to suppress books.[34] Outspoken adherents of Sumner from the literary world included writers like Mary Roberts Rinehart and Booth Tarkington, critics like Brander Matthews and Stuart Pratt Sherman, and publishers like

George H. Doran—all of whom expressed at one time or another their distaste for the new, iconoclastic, postwar literature. Soon, thanks to the rather badly timed activity of a circulating library, John Ford, a justice of the New York Supreme Court, became Sumner's most powerful and articulate ally in the struggle to impose stricter censorship.

A copy of *Women in Love* sent to Justice Ford's sixteen-year-old daughter by a circulating library in 1922 led to the Judge's alliance with Sumner and the Society for the Suppression of Vice.[35] So scandalized and angered was Ford by what he read of Lawrence's novel, that he immediately called the press and issued a statement. He was, he said, going to find the means to prosecute all those responsible for the publication and circulation of *Women in Love*; he was prepared to have a bill introduced into the legislature to strengthen the current law against obscene literature. "What can ail our Magistrates?" he said. "This book is a terrible thing. It is loathsome. The fact that a Magistrate may have approved of it doesn't alter the fact. A Grand Jury can still act. . . . I'll find some way of acting, or I'll go to the Legislature with a law that will stop this sort of thing." When told that the Sumner organization had unsuccessfully prosecuted the Lawrence novel and that Sumner himself had pronounced the novel a Sunday School book compared to some of the other volumes also upheld by the magistrates' courts, Ford said, "I don't know what we are coming to if that is so . . . I have never seen anything worse than this."

By February 6, 1923, an alliance had been formed between Ford and Sumner, and within a week the two had decided upon their strategy.[36] The present law was to be amended so as to make it possible to prosecute booksellers and publishers more effectively should they sell or issue objectionable works. Sumner explained the plan more fully.

> It may be possible to prosecute with more success by a new method. Hitherto, the publisher has been prosecuted for publishing a certain book. The courts have held that the entire book must be taken into consideration in such a case. This complicates the problem. Hereafter the prosecution may be based solely on immoral and objectionable passages, the foregoing and subsequent pages being

left out of the consideration. This will narrow down the issue and simplify things greatly.

As a practical matter, these books must be judged by their worst passages, because they are circulated on the strength of the worst passages.[37]

Once the general nature of the plan was established, Ford began to build an organization and, of course, to rouse public support. What was to become the Clean Books League was unofficially launched at a two-and-a-half-hour meeting in the Astor Hotel on February 24.[38] The city magistrates, the court of appeals, greedy publishers, and "blasé literati" (literary columnists) were proclaimed the apologists and promoters of vice, those who "pollute the minds of our children, undermine the teachings of Church and parent, and desecrate the family shrine of purity and innocence." On the side of virtue were civic and religious organizations represented at the Astor meeting along with the Girl and Boy Scouts. *Women in Love*, *A Young Girl's Diary*, *Casanova's Homecoming*, James Branch Cabell's *Jurgen*, and, naturally, *The Satyricon* were among "the volumes produced at the meeting and assailed."

Following the Astor organizational meeting, the editors of the *Times* pointed out that the new crusade, backed as it was by strong clerical support, offered a serious threat to the press.[39] Far from being ridiculous, one editor said, the Ford-Sumner proposal, if it were passed, would render half the literary masterpieces of the world obscene, since one indecent passage equalled an indecent work in the eyes of Ford, Sumner, and their followers.

On March 8, 1923, Ford officially announced the formation of the Clean Books League, a coalition of civic, religious, and welfare interests headed by Justice Ford himself.[40] The objective of the League, he proclaimed, was to make the law describing objectionable literature "horse-high, pig-tight, and bull-strong." The following amendments to the penal law were proposed: (1) that words like indecent, lewd, and obscene "shall be taken and construed in their common and generally accepted meaning;" (2) that "opinion or expert testimony shall not be received for any purpose whatever upon any hearing, examination or trial"—"That the evidence of artists, professional writers and all others having a personal or pecuniary interest in [a work] was incompetent;" (3) that it shall not "be a necessary constituent element of the crime charged that the matter on which the prosecution is based has a tendency to excite lustful or lecherous desire;" and (4) that the prosecution of a work may be based "upon the whole, or exclusively upon a part or parts, of any publication," and that if the action is based on a part, "only such part or parts shall be admissible in evidence or considered for any purpose"—in effect, a single phrase or sentence would suffice to condemn a book.[41]

While the League's first provision was editorialized by the *Times* as "grotesque but unimportant," the second was characterized as more dangerous—as one which prevented anyone who knew anything about a book or a situation from testifying. The League's third amendment was interpreted by the *Times* to mean that it made "no difference that the alleged indecency implanted no impure thoughts in anybody's heart, so long as the prosecutor [said] it was indecent." The fourth was the most dangerous of all. It alone seemed to put more books at the mercy of Sumner and the Society for the Suppression of Vice than Anthony Comstock, Sumner's predecessor, had ever dreamed of. It would, according to the *Times*, destroy modern literature on false grounds.[42]

> [The proponents of these amendments and their supporters] are intensely shocked by what they find in modern novels, as well they may be, but their suffering seems to be due to having found in print revelations which they have not been accustomed to finding there. Apparently, they have not asked themselves whether the revelations printed are true or not, nor has it occurred to them that if the revelations are true, the thing to do is not to stop the printing, but to stop the commission of the crimes described.
>
> In book after book they read about boys and girls, young men and young women, who are destitute alike of brains, of morals and manners. If these strange creatures do form a large, or even measurable, fraction of the generation soon to occupy the world's stage, that is indeed a most terrible phenomenon—a sufficient reason for loud outcries and for strenuous efforts to remedy a situation leading straight to social deliquescence and national destruction.
>
> But it is not the books that make the situation; it is the situation that makes the books—it is, that is, if these writers are veracious,

and the question of their veracity is vastly more important than the question whether or not they violate in their writings the conventional proprieties and reticencies.

Regarding the second of the questions just propounded, there is no excuse for assuming, or even for suspecting that the more able writers of this day are less keen observers than were their predecessors, or that they are less eager to tell with exactness what they see. Many of them just now are devoting whole chapters to the "flapper" and her masculine playmates. GERTRUDE ATHERTON, in "Black Oxen," has done it as well as anybody, perhaps, but she has rivals in the performance of this task. ARTHUR TRAIN in "His Children's Children," WARNER FABIAN in his "Flaming Youth," and there are dozens more, all agreeing in the presentation, as a visible and audible part of "society," of young girls who ought to be in Bedford Reformatory and of young men who not many years ago would have been soundly thrashed by the first father or brother who learned of their behavior in the presence of daughters or sisters.

If these pictures of "high life" are accurate, the novelists in painting them in full detail, are performing a duty, not committing the crimes charged against them. Presumably, they exaggerate a little and concentrate more, but that is the privilege of every artist.

The moral of these books is not that vice is attractive, but that parents, and especially mothers, have changed for the worse far more than has the younger generation—which probably has not changed at all—which probably is doing just what the younger generations always have done, and that is to use all the liberty, and even all the license, that the negligence of their time accord.[43]

It serves no purpose to point out that under this law SHAKESPEARE's plays and the Bible are obscene works, unfit to circulate in New York. Like some other laws, this one, if enacted, will apply to many, but under it only a few will be prosecuted. . . . For arrest and prosecution are in the hands of the Society for the Suppression of Vice. The Secretary of that society will not prosecute the Bible. He may even spare SHAKESPEARE and FIELDING; anybody else who made a complaint against the sellers of SHAKESPEARE and the Bible would be laughed out of court by the police.

But profane writers, unless they had attained the repute of SHAKESPEARE, would be wholly at MR. SUMNER's mercy. He could suppress such classics as he dislikes; he could and certainly would suppress such modern works as he dislikes. For under this law almost every book is guilty, and all evidence for the defense is excluded. If this bill is passed, MR. SUMNER will be an absolute and irresponsible censor of all modern literature. We hardly want that.[44]

The Clean Books League moved quickly. On March 22, its bill sponsored by Representative George N. Jesse, a Republican, and by Senator Salvatore A. Cotillo, a Democrat and chairman of the Judiciary Committee, was introduced into the State Legislature.[45] It quickly passed the Assembly by a sizeable majority and smoothly passed its first and second readings in the Senate.[46] Representatives of the League left New York for Albany under the leadership of Ford to testify before a routine Judiciary Committee hearing. Among the delegation were representatives from the Salvation Army, the Federated Catholic Societies, the New York Federation of Churches, the Society for the Suppression of Vice, the Y. M. C. A., the Holy Name Society, the Minerva Club, the League of Catholic Women, and metropolitan religious leaders representing the Roman Catholic Archdiocese and the Protestant Episcopal Church.[47] The *Times* reported that not a single person appeared at the hearing to oppose the League. The amendments seemed certain to pass. But then, on the eighteenth of April, a last-minute hearing was arranged at the request of a small, determined band of insurgents.[48] Challenging the Clean Books Bill were, initially, a novelist, two journalists, a lawyer, a teacher, and one publisher—Horace Liveright.

Having made the most of the notoriety connected with his early, largely insignificant difficulties with the censors, Liveright had earned the jealousy of his competitors as well as the wrath of Sumner. More brazen than the rest, Liveright seemed to them to be prospering on a diet of polite pornography, limited editions, and publicity. His radical books of the pre-Twenties had not sold particularly well, and this failure, naturally, had aroused no envy in other publishers, who simply waited for his bankruptcy. But Liveright's seeming Midas touch in the early Twenties and his success with the sensational, not to mention the theft of an author or two, was one of the factors leading to the silent and somewhat unlikely union of some old-line houses with the Society for the Suppression of Vice and the Clean Books League.[49] It was even rumored that two publishers had aided in the preparation of the Clean Books Bill, while others were purported to have advised the League.

Sumner himself announced he had gained the support of many "respectable" publishers, although he never named them.[50] Generally, the alliance was an informal one, since the publishers, wishing to retain their anonymity, remained in the background and showed their support for Sumner and Ford mainly by doing nothing. Where, asked the *Times* in an editorial on April 23, was the opposition in Albany?[51] Where were the organizations of publishers and authors? Why were three or four writers and a single publisher the only ones present to be heard? As for Liveright himself, he had scarcely planned to be a spokesman for so apparently small a following.

The spring of 1923 had found Liveright busy in New York running his business; in particular, he was involved in answering those critics of Van Loon's newly issued *The Story of the Bible* who protested the historian's omission of the Resurrection.[52] But he also found time to make a statement about a subject on which he was soon to become more of an expert. The following excerpts from his article, "The Absurdity of Censorship," which appeared in *The Independent* in 1923 made his position clear:

> The absurdity of censorship lies mainly in its application. *Only* the highest quality of intellect and understanding is capable of acting as a censor, and it is obvious that no man or woman of fine intelligence will act in any way as a censor of the arts; therefore such activity is left in the power of those individuals who have little, if any, sense of value in literature, drama, and art generally. Certainly if there has ever been any doubt of the truth of this contention it has been recently dispelled by the printed statements of certain men who are trying to organize a board of censorship over literature and the drama. Some of their opinions on books would put a schoolboy to shame. "The difficulty with any censorship," states an editorial in the New York *Sun*, "is that it can accomplish nothing which cannot be just as well accomplished without its help." This is a truth which can be understood by anybody. No man or committee of men is qualified either by nature or education to decide whether a book is indecent or not. A social judgment is necessary and this can only be had from a wide-spread public opinion.
>
> Unlike many of the men whose absurd opinions are now

breaking out publicly, every publisher knows the exact difference between frankness and obscenity, and he functions according to his understanding of this. The editorial minds in any publishing house are severe and competent censors, but they judge only by intelligent standards. In a book they demand, as H. L. Mencken puts it, "that it be dignified in conception, artistically honest, faithful to life, and fine in workmanship." There is nothing pornographic in any work of literature, or even such books as can hardly be classified as literature. Pornographic books have been issued, but they are manufactured by obscure printers, in Europe and America, and are sold by peddlers; they are not issued by publishers or reliable printers.

Certain facts of life exist, and their relation to other facts and to human behavior can only be expressed through the medium of words.

Certain fiction, which seems to be the principal object of attack today, expresses itself according to the contemporary interpretation of science, abnormal psychology, psychoanalysis, and other methods of study of human behavior. Art and mind are always in process of change; a new age has a new literary and philosophic expression. But this affects only the intelligent-minded; never the ignorant. Good art lives and bad art dies, that is all we know; and intelligent Americans are as capable of appreciating this fact as any other people. There is only one test and that is the test of intelligence, though a work may not be good art and yet have a useful or entertaining place in the world. "Obscenity—the word already vague enough after such repeated use—would come to mean little or nothing. If the people who most fear it have their way, it is a word that will quickly be so diluted and enlarged as to drown all literature." (*The New Republic*, March 7)

Frankness in literature relating to sexual matters never corrupted or depraved any one, adult or child. It is difficult for some people to realize this, but any judge of a criminal court should know what every student of life and society knows, viz.: that the so-called depraved or vicious classes or types have no contact whatever with literature beyond the daily newspaper. This is so well known that it has become a platitude. We may become depraved by, or vicious by, economic or physical conditions, but certainly not by literature.

A censorship over literature and the other arts is stupid, ignorant, and impudent, and is against the fundamental social principles of all intelligent Americans. There is no place for such crudity in our present civilization, and even the most conservative press and individual opinion have expressed themselves against it most emphatically. Who is really in favor of it?[53]

In Albany during April the Senate Judiciary Committee studied Chief Justice Ford's bill with favor. Its passage seemed certain. But no other New York publisher stirred to protest; even the Authors' League remained aloof. Failing to enlist support from the National Association of Book Publishers—its president, John W. Hiltman of Appleton's flatly rejected a request to become involved in the fight—Liveright led the opposition to the capital alone.[54] Armed with pamphlets (hastily conceived and thrown together by T. R. Smith), containing relevant quotations and court opinions ranging from Thoreau to Jefferson and Brandeis, Liveright and his supporters—Gertrude Atherton, Max Fleischer of the *New York American*, Thomas E. McEntegart of the Hearst Corporation, a psychology instructor from Union Theological Seminary, and Francis D. Gallatin, a lawyer and former Park Commissioner of New York City—entrained for Albany eager to defend the liberty of the press.[55]

This caravan was met at the station by a fellow liberal, but no literateur, James J. Walker, then minority leader of the State Senate. Immediately drawing the publisher to one side, Walker is purported to have asked Liveright, "For God's sake, Horace, what's this? What did you bring these nuts for?" Liveright explained that he had brought them to testify against the Clean Books Bill.[56]

On April 18, Liveright and the others met Sumner and Ford as well as their much larger following before the New York State Senate Judiciary Committee which had been hastily convened at Walker's request.[57] The opposition group condemned the Jesse-Cotillo sponsored Clean Books Bill which threatened to "establish a censorship over printed matter so severe in its character that if it should be rigidly enforced . . . the Bible, Shakespeare, the Encyclopedia Britannica, practically every dictionary, the classics with few exceptions and even some works of the early church fathers of the Catholic Church would come under the ban." Pleading for at least a year's delay, Liveright condemned the advocates of the bill as anti-American and anti-religious. Gertrude Atherton announced that she had read *The Decameron* at sixteen and had not understood it. Moreover, she said, if she had been sophisticated enough to do so, "What harm does the book do that hasn't already been done?" When Sumner said he was surprised to hear her say that no bad book could injure a teenage girl, Mrs. Atherton retorted, "Most of those books are so dull and deadly that they carry their own antidote."

Furious, Justice Ford rose, pointed his finger at the novelist and Liveright who was sitting beside her, and said:

> These publishers, editors and authors profess to be greatly concerned about protecting the Bible and Shakespeare. They don't care about the Bible. All they are interested in is the profits from their own filthy books. Here is a New York City newspaper attacking me in one column and carrying in an adjoining column an advertisement for one of these filthy books. The man who wrote that attack on me [Heywood Broun, one of Liveright's authors], is hired to get that sort of thing in the paper. I hold the editors responsible.[58]

The *New York Times* reported that Justice Ford was waving a copy of the *New York World* in the air as Gertrude Atherton rose "calmly" and addressed the Committee. "This is perfectly absurd and it is entirely unfair," was all she said. "It is the editors and their filthy profits that's responsible," cried Ford, and "the air was filled for a moment with protest."[59] In the final gesture on this day of confrontation, Sumner placed in the hands of the assembled committeemen sealed envelopes which contained offensive passages from current novels: concrete evidence guaranteed to establish the need for a stricter law.[60]

After this stormy session, Liveright returned to the Ten Eyck Hotel where Walker had stationed him.[61] Evenings there, in another room that the senator had taken for the duration of the proceedings, Liveright and some of the most powerful leaders from both parties gathered to play poker. Liveright's luck was always to be with writers, never with cards. Regular calls went out from the publisher in Albany to his treasurer on West Forty-eighth Street in Manhattan for additional gambling money, and a steady stream of office boys arrived in the capital with cash for their boss.

After Liveright and Mrs. Atherton had spoken against censorship, and while Liveright remained in Albany dealing the cards and losing game after game, publishers and writers in New York apparently realized the threat posed by Ford, Sumner, and their followers. An alliance to block passage of the Clean Books Bill was formed by the magazine and newspaper publishers along with the printers' associations. On April 20, 1923, this body issued a statement asserting that the Jesse-Cotillo Bill struck "at the fundamental constitutional amendments prohibiting the abridgment of the freedom of the press."[62] Unfortunately, the union of these powerful organizations seemed inclined to do little more than make public pronouncements and file a brief in Albany. Their counterpart in the book publishing world, the National Association of Book Publishers, did even less. Its executive committee, composed of the presidents of or representatives from Doran, Longmans Green, Grosset and Dunlap, Appleton's, and Stokes rejected the recommendation of the association's censorship committee that the body oppose the Jesse-Cotillo Bill. Instead, the association leaders deplored "the growing tendency on the part of some publishers unduly to exploit books of a salacious character for purely pecuniary gain."[63] Following this official pronouncement, George Palmer Putnam and Alfred Harcourt resigned from the censorship committee in protest, and Putnam even announced his support of Liveright.[64]

While periodic protests emanated from the divided publishing industry in New York City, the majority and minority leaders of the senate arranged for the introduction of and voting on the Clean Books Bill. Arriving for the May 3 session, Liveright heard only a handful of legislators speak in favor of the censorship measure.[65] Senator Walker led the opposition:

> In a speech which at times had his listeners on the verge of tears and at others laughing he called advocates of the censorship insincere. "There is not one among us," he said, "who cannot tell the story of my dad's sweetheart who afterward became dad's wife, and who lived in days when there were as many salacious books as there are today and who for all that grew into a life of saintliness and went down to her last resting place just as clean and pure in mind and heart as the day she was born. That is all there is to this talk about books of the kind against which this bill is directed ruining

our young girls. They haven't got to read them and they won't read them if proper influences dominate their homes."

"No woman was ever ruined by a book," he continued. "It is one of those strong men who are worrying about salacious books in the hands of little girls who are ruining them. This debate makes me think of the Volstead Act and in connection with that of how many vote one way and drink another. Some of the best tellers of shabby stories in this Senate have been worrying their hearts out during the debate today about somebody reading something which may not have been good for him or her."[66]

Following Walker's speech, the Clean Books Bill was defeated by a two to one vote that did not follow party lines. In an editorial entitled "A Danger Deferred" the *New York Times* called the senator's speech the best he ever made, one which promised "a return of common sense to our legislative bodies, from which pessimists thought it had been exiled forever." Walker had reminded people "that purity did not become wholly extinct in the several thousand years during which the human race has got along without a Clean Books Bill."[67]

Back in New York City, Ford, now joined by a new ally, a representative of the D. A. R., announced that his struggle was far from finished.[68] He planned a new assault on the Legislature in 1924, and promised that a decisive victory would be won. Ford did indeed introduce similar legislation the next year, and annually during the remainder of the Twenties, but the serious threat of state-wide censorship had passed.[69]

With a modesty uncharacteristic of a congressman, Senator Walker later asserted, however, that Liveright was "solely responsible for defending the freedom of the press."[70] Walker made this statement at a testimonial dinner that was held in Liveright's honor at the Hotel Brevoort on June 14, 1923. The dinner committee was headed by T. R. Smith and included Heywood Broun, John Emerson, Fannie Hurst, Walter Guest Kellogg, Lawrence Langner, Elizabeth Marbury, Eugene O'Neill, Burton Rascoe, Charles Hanson Towne, and Edgar Selwyn. In addition, H. L. Mencken, Zoe Akins, Ernest Boyd, and Carl Van Vechten were among the writers, artists, and public figures present. The honor was officially paid Liveright "in recognition of his unselfish and untiring efforts in fighting and eventually defeating the recent Book and Press Censorship Bill before the New York Senate." But for the publisher's prompt work, the dinner announcement read, "this iniquitous bill would have passed the Senate as it did the Assembly."[71] In his own speech Liveright thanked those present for their support and announced that he had formally resigned from the National Association of Book Publishers. He had done so, he said, because of the group's failure to act in the recent struggle.[72]

Liveright's testimonial dinner, in effect, honored him for a real accomplishment, but one he had achieved by methods he had not planned to use. The publisher himself viewed the activities of the spring of 1923 with a mixture of amusement and relief, as shown in a letter to Francis Hackett.

> For the last five weeks I've done practically nothing except lead the fight against the so-called Clean Books Bill up in Albany where it passed the Assembly and almost got through the Senate when I jumped into the fray and finally licked the powers of darkness. The National Book Publishers' Association tacitly supported the bill and the only publishers who helped at all were Seltzer (who had three books on the list which Justice Ford issued); Huebsch (who had one) and Macrae of Dutton who had been attacked by Sumner in the public prints. Fortunately, none of my books was mentioned in any of the recent rumpus so I could lead the opposition with fairly clean hands. Most of the newspapers have been very generous in giving me credit for defeating the bill, and I understand there is to be given a dinner in my honor. I know, too, that a lot of authors are disgusted with the way their publishers acted, although the Authors' League, itself, did nothing except send a couple of telegrams. Of course, the bill is going to be brought up again in January, but I understand the Legislature now as I never did before, and while I don't feel comfortable, I feel hopeful that no utterly ridiculous bill will pass next year. The whole fight took 3 weeks of my undivided time. I could write you an interesting 64-page booklet about it, but I'll wait until I see you and you can look forward to a rather amusing evening on Albany, gin mills, stud poker games, the sanctity of the home and its relation to mixing cocktails.[73]

The B & L Offices

The offices of Horace Liveright were perhaps so unusual because their owner considered his business life to be his main interest; he thought of his office as a second home, and his employees followed suit.[1] While his old-line competitors thrived on the dignity and dust of spacious, book-lined reception rooms managed by efficient, bespectacled secretaries, and chastely decorated offices inhabited by scholarly editors at orderly desks, Liveright's experimental business practices and his nonconformity were apparent throughout the premises and especially in the extraordinary staff of young people who assisted him. In May 1923 the firm moved into larger quarters in an old four-story brownstone at 61 West Forty-eighth Street. The brownstone housed not only a flourishing publishing firm, but an opulently furnished informal club and, briefly, a homemade still. The ground floor, a low-ceilinged basement, served as both stock room and shipping department. The Modern Library was stored there in soft lambskin covers, which periodically became stiff and hard. Since flexible leather bindings had become part of the Modern Library trademark, Julian Messner insisted they be kept and suggested that shipping-room clerks soften the covers with castor oil. The castor oil promptly turned rancid, but the *modus operandi* was established. Employees now recall their horror at being sent to the basement on business, where the smell was enough to overpower them.

The floor above housed the business offices, with the accounting department managed by the head bookkeeper and treasurer, Arthur Pell. The only businessman in the place, Pell, who had been hired as a bookkeeper in 1921 and had gradually taken charge of the company records, kept a watchful eye on the clerical force and the company expenses. The treasurer was exceedingly cautious in financial matters, and he and Liveright were constantly at odds over the publisher's extravagances. For many years Pell secretly kept his report of the current bank balance $5,000 below its actual figure; otherwise the cash would have taken wing to feed some struggling author, to pep up the lagging sales of a book, or to pay off the bootlegger. In the end, Pell's stricter methods triumphed, for he gradually assumed control of the business after lending Liveright money on his stock.

The reception room, at the rear of the second floor, was done in a heavily ornamental style then called Italian Renaissance. According to Liveright, it was "the prettiest reception room or play room—call it what you like—of any office in New York City."[2] Besides an enormous fireplace and three Italian double doors, the stucco walls displayed the works of whatever artist—Alexander King at one time—Liveright or his staff currently esteemed. In one corner stood a bust of Dreiser by Onorio Ruotolo, the publisher's tribute to an author whose works he was convinced would endure.[3]

A day at B & L might bring fifty or more people up the late nineteenth-century staircase to this reception room. Famous and unknown authors, bootleggers, chorus girls looking for parts in a Liveright musical, and the inevitable hangers-on simply looking for cash came and went. Once, in the mid-Twenties, a small, gray-haired man remained seated there almost the entire day waiting to see the publisher. Neither the receptionist nor Liveright's secretary had recognized his name or understood much of what he said because of his thick accent. Finally, after passing in and out of the publisher's private office several times, T. R. Smith was unable to control his curiosity any longer. The editor approached the patient, unassuming stranger and discovered the Swedish geographer and explorer, Sven Hedin. Hedin had brought his autobiography, *My Life as an Explorer*, directly to Liveright, the only publisher he wished to issue it. Hedin's work appeared in 1925, but some others who came and waited, patiently or not, were less successful. Despite the legend that grew up about the firm—that anyone could walk into the house and receive $500 on a new book without being pinned down about its contents—there were some who failed to get an advance or a contract. These included several self-proclaimed Jesus Christs, as well as a woman who claimed she had written a treatise on love cults which she proposed to follow with her definitive work on reading the phallus.[4]

When Liveright branched out into show business in 1924, the wall which joined the publishing brownstone and his production offices next door was removed and an elaborate false bookcase was installed. Manuel Komroff, who designed this sliding façade, created the original titles that adorned it.[5] They included a narrow volume entitled *The Complete Works of Sir Walter Scott*, a bulky edition called *The Love Life of Ludwig Lewisohn*, and other amusing, sometimes off-color titles. In a second burst of interior decorating, Liveright turned the extension roof, which opened out beyond the double doors, into a lavish, awning-covered porch. Adorned with an oversized pergola, and equipped with furniture upholstered in shades of coral, mauve, and jade, the new roof garden, while useful for entertaining visitors, became famous as the setting of Liveright's celebrated parties.

Initially, there were two kinds of parties given at Boni & Liveright, although the distinction between them soon disappeared.[6] The A parties were more respectable affairs, like those given by other publishers for their authors or to celebrate the publication of a new book. The B parties were impromptu, come-by-for-a-drink gatherings and were less restrained, less bookish, and more bacchanalian with heavy drinking, and guests who became unmanageable or passed out or both, while others became publicly amorous. The B parties sometimes moved to the apartments of either Liveright or Smith. In any event, by the standards of New York in the Twenties, Liveright parties were scarcely remarkable affairs in terms of the amount of liquor consumed or the behavior of the guests. What did distinguish them for all time were the setting—the reception room of a publishing house—and the prominence of the guests and the gate-crashers.

In their way, Liveright's parties replaced the informal get-togethers at the now defunct Village Liberal Club. The reception room and the porch at B & L replaced the club and the Bonis' bookstore, while bootleg whiskey and a well-catered table were the answer to Paula Holladay's wine and cuisine; Bolsheviks were, to a great extent, supplanted by Follies girls, newspapermen, and Liveright authors. Otto Kahn of Wall Street, Jesse Lasky of Hollywood, and Jimmy Walker, the mayor of New York, mingled with Herbert Bayard Swope, editor of the *New York World*, Paul Robeson, Ruth Chatterton, Anna May Wong, Kay Francis, and John Barrymore. On hand as well might be writers like Thomas Wolfe, the Millay sisters, Carl Van Vechten, Madeline and Ernest Boyd, Elinor Wylie, and Sinclair Lewis, in addition to whatever Liveright authors were in town. In less than a decade, the bonds of fellowship had stretched a bit, but the uninhibited atmosphere remained the same.

Often the parties moved into Liveright's own spacious office in the front half of the second floor. From the narrow carved Italian table-desk to a huge Chinese jar for wastepaper, almost nothing about it resembled regulation old-line quarters. It had a fireplace, soft lounging chairs, a grand piano, the inevitable bar, and a series of extravagant, flamingo-colored panels—brilliantly painted with frogs, underwater plants, and seaweed—which concealed the entrance to an adjoining bath and zinc-lined shower. In fact the only reminders that he was a publishing executive were the photographs of O'Neill, George Moore, Rose Macaulay, Lord Dunsany, Gertrude Atherton, and Theodore Dreiser which covered the walls. In addition to serving the publisher as a studio apartment, the office was the scene of the weekly Monday morning editorial meetings at which Liveright, Messner, Smith, Komroff, the current vice president, and a reader or two gathered. They began late in the morning and rarely came to an official ending; rather, the participants simply drifted off to luncheon engagements. Discussion of actual business was interspersed with phone calls, gossip, and clowning. Despite the unconventional atmosphere, a great deal of serious work was accomplished. They discussed advertising and promotional plans, debated proposals for new books, considered manufacturing specifications and prices, and, most importantly, decided whether to accept or reject new manuscripts.[7]

Liveright held sway. He was king and this his kingdom, as some associates aptly said. It was the right background or stage setting, perhaps, for a man who seemed to play different roles. Some saw him as a flamboyant exhibitionist; some knew him as a ruthless buccaneer who was brusque, curt, and insultingly crude; some found him irresistibly charming, gregarious and fun-loving, a man with sex appeal for many women. He was tall, lean, and well-tailored with a shock of long (for the times) black hair, piercing eyes, and a John Barrymore or Mephistophelean profile, depending on one's point of view. Whatever his true nature, Liveright let his authors and his staff be themselves, and this was perhaps his most remarkable quality. The lengthiest statement the publisher ever made, which may be taken for his credo-in-brief, was issued from this office soon after he had settled in it. Asked what he thought of being called a radical publisher, Liveright replied:

> If you mean by "radical," getting at the roots of things, I cheerfully plead guilty. We think that Theodore Dreiser gets at the roots of things, and have been his publishers practically since we opened shop. And when other publishers thought Eugene O'Neill's one-act plays so radically different from what plays should be that they had no chance either on the stage or in book form, we made arrangements to publish them.
>
> And when we published Jack Reed's "Ten Days That Shook the World," and Andreas Latzko's "Men in War," and Freud's "A General Introduction to Psychoanalysis," and Waldo Frank's "Rehab," and Nora Connolly's "The Irish Rebellion of 1916," Albert Rhys Williams' "Through the Russian Revolution," and "The Authorized Life and Letters of Eugene Debs" (most of them appearing during the war hysteria), we did so because we felt they got at the bottom of things.
>
> But so-called conservatives can also get at the roots of things, and we feel that John D. Rockefeller Jr.'s "The Personal Relation in Industry," "Flames of Faith," a novel by Samuel Harden Church, and Jeremiah Jenks's "We and Our Government" are just as radical in the correct sense of the word as are our many books by George Moore, Ludwig Lewisohn, Horace Kallen, or Edgar Lee Masters.

In reply to a question about his motives, Liveright responded:

> Motivating impulses? First, to maintain an open forum and to publish books so long as I believe they are good, no matter what side of any question they take; no matter how frank they may be in their expression of the life of yesterday, to-day, or to-morrow; to fight the good fight for the freedom of the press, no matter whether it leads

me to Albany or Washington. Above all, to make our home on Forty-eighth Street a place where young and unknown authors may bring their books or their ideas.[8]

This, then, was Liveright in his greatest role, that of progressive publisher.

Above Liveright's office and the reception room, the editorial, sales, advertising, and manufacturing offices were crammed into the third and fourth floors. Inside one small, enormously chaotic room just above Liveright sat his editor-in-chief, T. R. Smith. Tommy Smith was a dapper, bald, cherubic little man, who affected a pince-nez on a cord and seemed all fatherly benevolence. His door was invariably open, a condition which often caused some confusion among the manuscripts piled high on his desk, and his ear was always available. So, for that matter, was the offer of a drink, and his stingers were reportedly lethal. Perhaps the most erudite editor of the Twenties, Smith daily exercised "his critical acumen and his encyclopedic knowledge of what had been published by Macmillan in 1888 and who wrote how many pages for whom in the spring of 1919."[9] This authority on the erotic and the pornographic and, happily, one who knew the difference between them, seemed to be able to smell out best-sellers and masterpieces alike. Once he advised Liveright to pay $1,000 for the English-language rights to an unread biography of Napoleon which had been written by a little-known German named Emil Ludwig. Smith was confident that they would at least break even on the work, since no book on Napoleon had ever sold fewer than two thousand copies on either side of the Atlantic. Besides, he counseled, the title would enhance their list. It did, indeed; Ludwig's *Napoleon* sold over two hundred thousand copies.[10]

As editor-in-chief, Smith worked with a brilliant young staff of readers which included Beatrice Kaufman, Louis Kronenberger, Edith Stern, and later Saxe Commins, together with special editors and translators like Lewis Galantière and Eden and Cedar Paul. Beatrice Bakrow, Mrs. George S. Kaufman, was a member of the Algonquin Round Table and reflected the taste of sophisticated New Yorkers in her critiques. She preceded Edith Stern who had arrived at the house fresh from college and a few months experience at

Knopf's.[11] Mrs. Sterns's departure from Knopf's came after a series of minor jobs which ranged from shelving and dusting books to the prospect of becoming a cookbook editor. Making $15.00 a week and facing a series of recipes, the first of which began "Take 600 crayfish," the nonculinary Mrs. Stern made a beeline for West Forty-eighth Street and less alien ground. At twenty-one, Louis Kronenberger had just graduated from college too, and after eking out a living tutoring and reviewing books, he joined the firm in 1926.[12] Years later he recalled the initial appeal this unorthodox establishment had for himself and others: "Boni & Liveright . . . stood for America in the process of exposing and defining and aspersing itself; stood for the *Zeitgeist*, itself all too fluid and mercurial; stood for something brooding and lonely in American life as well as unruly and defiant."[13] Since their approaches to literature were often diametrically opposed, the reports of two or three of these readers, plus the reactions of Smith and Liveright, produced quite balanced evaluations of a new manuscript.

Julian Messner and the sales department were down the hall from Smith and his readers. As sales manager for the firm throughout the Twenties, Messner trained Edward Weeks, later editor of the *Atlantic Monthly*, along with such neophyte entrepreneurs as Richard Simon and Bennett Cerf. Simon was with the firm from 1921 to 1923, when he left to found his own house with Max Schuster. Cerf joined Boni & Liveright in 1923, soon bought a vice presidency, and left in 1925 to begin Random House.[14]

Next to that of Pell, Smith, and Messner, Manuel Komroff's association with Liveright lasted longest.[15] Prior to joining the publisher, Komroff had been, successively, art critic for the *New York Call*, editor of the *Russian Daily News* in Petrograd, reporter for the *China Press* in Shanghai, editorialist for the *New York Daily Garment News*, and, finally, movie critic for *Film Daily* in Manhattan. In 1920, exhausted from seeing twenty movies a week, he took over the production department and the Modern Library at Liveright's. In the next eight years he saw several hundred current and reprint volumes through the presses. His job included such varied tasks as letting the contracts for printing, binding, and jackets; designing title pages, book covers, and dusters; getting up dummy copies of approximately the first sixteen pages of text and a table of contents for use as salesmen's samples; selecting paper, type, and bindings; estimating the number of pages; calculating line lengths, margin areas, and the total printed material; and all the proofreading. At the same time he suggested new titles for the Modern Library, which he saw through the same manufacturing steps.

Since the multiple facets of book-making took place in six or seven different cities in New York, Massachusetts, and New Jersey, Komroff lost two or three books during his first year on the job. To prevent other books from going astray, he put up a large blackboard across one wall of his office. After ruling it, he entered the situation and condition of each book under his supervision. It was safer if Dreiser didn't know how many copies of Anderson the house was issuing, and vice versa, so Komroff used code numbers to befuddle curious authors. When asked what the code stood for, and he often was, Komroff replied with complete seriousness that it was Hebrew.

In addition to managing production, Komroff devised an efficient interoffice memo system. The head of each section of the business—Smith, editorial; Messner, sales; Komroff, production; Pell, accounting; and Liveright—had a different colored notepaper. Hourly, an office boy went up and down the four levels collecting and delivering this rainbow of correspondence. In connection with the basic aspects of his job, Komroff spent about one third of a million dollars annually. Liveright never questioned a nickel of it. "Just bring me a good book, Manuel, like *The Three Musketeers*," the publisher told him.

Despite his overtime job running Boni & Liveright production, Komroff found time to do some writing himself. Although his early works had only a limited audience, they did appear in *The Dial*, *Reedy's Mirror*, and *Broom*. In 1925 he completed a work on Marco Polo, which he finally convinced a reluctant Liveright to accept. In an attempt to work up some enthusiasm on the publisher's part, Komroff explained that the book told about Marco Polo's travels and his adventures with the Kubla Khan. Still unconvinced of its selling powers, Liveright replied, "It should have been a biography of Otto Kahn." However, he issued *The Travels of Marco Polo* in

1926, and the work was so successful that the publisher apologized to Komroff.

On the top floor of Liveright's brownstone, the advertising staff labored, first under little magazine poet and Bolshevik enthusiast, Isidor Schneider, who left B & L for Paris and his own writing, and later under the talented eye of Aaron Sussman.[16] In their top-floor nest, "all the accepted ideas about publishing had been thrown out the window and every book was a new challenge to the ingenuity of the oddly assorted staff. Everything, in their opinion, was worth trying at least once. And the results were spectacular in the extreme."[17] At one time or another, Schneider and Sussman had as assistants Manuel Siwek, who began his tenure in publishing under Pell and climaxed his career by becoming head of Grosset and Dunlap, and Leane Zugsmith, who along with her job at Liveright's began to write novels that brought her greater fame. Maurice Hanline, then the author of one privately printed poem, was another of Schneider's assistants, at least for a time. Then he became Liveright's man Friday and minister without portfolio.[18] He was even installed briefly in London as the firm's representative abroad, and finally he went on to Hollywood where he wrote scenarios. A decade before she became famous as a playwright, Lillian Hellman worked briefly as a copywriter in the advertising department and then graduated to reading manuscripts. One of the most pleasant, nonliterary memories of her life, she later recalled, was sprinting up and down the long staircases at Boni & Liveright to avoid being pinched.[19] Liveright himself, as well as any other member of the firm who was interested, contributed his ideas to Schneider and Sussman. They devised schemes to improve upon Bernays' earlier promotions.[20] For example, the staff came up with the idea of offering a free copy of one of their publications, *The Mental Side of Golf*, to any golfer who scored a hole in one. When four hundred requests, accompanied by scorecards signed by pros (a condition of the offer), were delivered in a matter of weeks, they learned what liars golfers are. Another idea backfired when they advertised Moore's latest works as deathless prose in the tradition of Anatole France. It was a testy Irishman who cabled them that a superior writer should never be compared to an inferior one.

Two successful stunts involved more controversial matters.[21] Prior to his publication of a book on nudism, Liveright invited all the literary editors in New York to join him in a visit to a nudist camp upstate. The columnists had a field day with the safari, and the book orders came in. About the same time, on the day marking Liveright's publication of Judge Benjamin Lindsey's book, *Companionate Marriage*, the publisher called a press conference. To newsmen he announced in apparent seriousness that he stood by the Judge's sympathetic discussion of premarital sexual relations. His purpose, moreover, in publishing this work was not to make money, but to cut down the divorce rate.

Boni & Liveright were also noted for their unusual newspaper and magazine advertisements—heavy black borders framed photographs, bits of gossip about authors, and book descriptions printed in very bold type. At the top and the bottom and often along the sides of each advertisement was the B & L symbol, a cowled monk seated at a writing table, the most misleading trademark that ever existed in the book trade, "for never in publishing, and seldom anywhere else, has there been an atmosphere so unmonastic, so unstudious, so unsolitary as at Liveright's."[22] The amount spent in promotion by this middle-sized firm was, comparatively speaking, enormous. But Liveright believed that books should be advertised like cars and just as extravagantly. He constantly increased the promotional budget on new books, especially if their authors had received generous advances. His advertising expenditures, the despair of treasurer Pell, bear out the faith he had in this policy. During the Twenties Liveright spent over a million dollars promoting his publications in various magazines and newspapers.

The final office on the third floor belonged to the current vice president. When the need for new capital arose, as it often did, Liveright sold a share in his business to some young man interested in beginning a career in publishing. After the departure of Leon Fleischman in 1920, two young executives had their headquarters here. The first, Bennett Cerf, brought to Boni & Liveright a degree from the Columbia School of Journalism and three years' experience on Wall Street.[23] A complete novice in the publishing world, he was hired by Liveright to replace the firm's top salesman, Richard

Simon. Cerf's first day on the job consisted of lunch with Simon, Liveright, and Theodore Dreiser at the Algonquin, and then Cerf accompanied Dreiser—an awesome figure to the young man—to a ball game. Cerf was soon eager enough to invest $25,000 in the firm, receive a vice presidency, and then make Liveright an additional loan of $25,000 as well. He learned the business quickly, and the Modern Library sharpened his growing desire for a firm of his own. He had studied volumes from this series in college, and he soon noticed that Liveright neglected it because it was not as exciting to work with as new books and authors. In 1925 Cerf talked Liveright into selling him the Modern Library for $200,000—$150,000 in cash plus the $50,000 Cerf had already invested in the house. Liveright regularly needed money for his ventures in publishing, the theatre, and the stock market, but in 1925 he was particularly anxious to pay off a long-standing debt to his father-in-law, who had a considerable interest in the firm.

Liveright's associates were furious when they learned he planned to sell the Modern Library. But, in the midst of their attempts to dissuade the publisher from doing so, another literary man purportedly arrived at the office with a gun and threatened to kill Liveright because he was having an affair with the man's wife. Messner, the chief opponent of the sale, was dispatched to calm the gunman, that is, to ply him with as much liquor as possible, and, in the confusion, the deal went through.

At B & L the staff had called Cerf Jesus Junior, since he was perpetually shocked at what went on. There were, apparently, occasions when he had real reason to be. Whatever his extra-literary education, Cerf departed with the Modern Library, probably the most distinguished backlist in publishing history, and established his own firm with Donald Klopfer three blocks away. Initially, their firm was called The Modern Library Incorporated, but in 1927, as they began to issue new titles, they changed the name to Random House.

Evidently Liveright spent the profits from the sale of the Modern Library very quickly, for during the same year, 1925, Donald Friede bought a half interest in the firm for $110,000 and at twenty-four became the youngest vice president in publishing.[24]

Friede had actually been hired a year before by Manuel Komroff to assist him in the manufacturing department. There had to be something good, Komroff later recalled, in a young man who had been dismissed from three Ivy League schools and had failed at Knopf's in accounting and selling. The role Friede envisioned for himself was, in some respects, similar to that Liveright had taken: the discoverer and promoter of new talent in the arts. The size of Friede's investment in B & L clearly allowed him to follow his enthusiasms in literature. At the time Liveright sold him a half interest in the house, it was arranged that Liveright would remain head of the company and control the publishing policies, although each partner owned exactly the same number of shares of stock. If either wished the firm to issue a book that the editorial committee had rejected, he could achieve publication by personally guaranteeing the house against any losses which might be incurred by the work's failure.

Friede, who apparently uncovered a new genius semi-weekly, regularly exercised his right to force publication. His choices were catholic in scope and uniformly unsuccessful: *Thérèse* by François Mauriac; *Tropic Death* by Eric Walrond, a volume of short stories important in the fiction of the Negro Awakening; and *The Fifth Child*, a novel by Klaus Mann, the son of Thomas Mann. To help the sale of this one Friede arranged an American tour for the young German, only to be amazed by the discovery, when Mann arrived in New York to begin his scheduled engagements, that the young novelist spoke no English. There were also a book on Caruso's voice methods, written by one of Friede's cousins, a book on glands by a perfect stranger, and an English novel that appealed to Friede only because its main character was named Donald.[25]

Besides losing money in several plays, a couple of them Liveright's, Friede's career as an impresario of the other arts came to an abrupt climax on April 10, 1927, when he produced George Antheil's *Ballet Méchanique* at Carnegie Hall.[26] Tickets to this single, much publicized performance were scaled from $110 to 75¢. The *pièce de résistance* of the evening, the *Ballet Méchanique* itself, required ten pianos and ten pianists, six xylophones, two bass drums, a mechanical piano for Antheil, along with mechanical sound devices such as electric bells, a wind machine, and, at the climax of the presentation, a fire siren. Besides the deafening sound effects, the wind machine was mistakenly directed at the orchestra seats instead of above them and the fire siren—once it was finally started, long after its cue—refused to stop and continued to blare after the performance was over and the audience, or what was left of it, had departed. A few days later Antheil and Friede escaped to Europe following the critical lambasting of their avant-garde fiasco.

On the whole Liveright hired employees of consistently high quality. They gravitated to his house for a number of reasons. They knew the publisher to be truly generous to his employees, just as he was to his authors. The staff not only received annual bonuses and never had to ask for raises, but might also share in any financial windfall an unexpected best-seller brought in. Liveright called his house the only real socialistic firm in New York, in the sense that he wanted his employees to share in its prosperity.[27] Once when the surprise sale of some subsidiary rights to *Napoleon* amounted to $20,000, Liveright divided the money among his associates. People came to him because they knew they could advance at Boni & Liveright, in a time when opportunities at old-line houses were limited by latent, if not open anti-Semitism. Finally, they were drawn by Liveright's vividness, impulsiveness, and high living. His combination of openmindedness and flamboyance was reflected in the list he published whether it was the Modern Library reprints, representing "the sophisticated, the subversive, and the avant-garde," or each list of new books, reflecting the ferment in American letters.[28]

What made their associations with Liveright and each other so remarkable and fruitful was that once they were hired, they were allowed to run themselves. In contrast to what seemed to them the bleak orderliness of rival houses, there was no sense of institutional piety or of rules at Boni & Liveright. Employees came and went as they pleased, free of clocks and the fear of being fired. By and large, they were allowed to follow their own enthusiasms; an employee could move from accounting or sales into editing or advertising. Sometimes one combined his interests and followed his favorite new work through all its steps of production and publication. Liveright's credo that literature be new and free encouraged his staff to fulfill its own interests in literature and publishing. The office became part of their daily lives, a quasi-social club to which each had a key and at which each found fellowship and a chance to work at what he enjoyed. Practically everyone in the house was a part-time publisher. Stenographers and shipping clerks, along with salesmen, who got first crack at mysteries, read manuscripts and offered their ideas for advertising and promotion. There was, in fact, almost daily excitement at Boni & Liveright as books were discovered or famous authors stopped in at the office to meet the newest staff members and renew acquaintances with the old. There were, naturally, periods when efficiency and order were imposed, and the house began to look as polite and organized as Knopf or Harcourt, Brace. These interludes were infrequent. Mostly, it was an untidy, easygoing, and altogether agreeable place.

Over twenty years later, Edith Stern captured something of both the feeling and significance of Liveright and his house most successfully, if rather romantically. Part of her brief essay illuminates the man and the era as can only the reminiscence of one who was present:

> Whether Horace Liveright was a great publisher because he set off the Renaissance of the twenties or, sensitive to its currents, acted as its chief conductor, it is still too early to say, and that is as unimportant as deciding between the hen and the egg. That, par excellence, he embodied it, is enough. He had flair—hunches—instincts —call them what you will, for they transcended judgment—which he applied both to choosing employees, and titles for his lists. Sometimes his flashes seemed almost visible, like lightning. The lightning, of course, did not always strike. . . . But more often than not, against apparent reason, he was right. He had no truck with nonentities, whether personalities or books. The titles he published were literature, of current significance, or flamboyant. The employees he chose had vivid personalities, keen minds. Both they and his authors stayed with him, because for all his trying unpredictability and exhibitionism he had the heroic quality, rare in both publishers and employers, of encouraging you to be yourself. The longtime result was the galaxy of office alumni; the contemporary, a remarkable list.
>
> Some place, in some firm, there may be a similar group of young people unobviously being fertilized for as spectacular a flowering a decade and a half from now. But in this socially-conscious and

hard-pressed world, I cannot imagine where. The Boni and Live-right office was the Jazz Age in microcosm, with all its extremes of hysteria and of cynicism, of Carpe Diem, of decadent thriftlessness, and of creative vitality. To recapture its atmosphere one would not, like Proust, dip a madeleine into a cup of tea, but a canapé into bathtub gin.

Yet though the madness, the extravagances, the orgies, the empty bottles that occasionally littered the stairs in the morning and the parties that cut into office hours are the truth, they are by no means the whole truth. So much did they fascinate contemporaries for whom Horace loved to put on a show, so much have they been publicized in print, on the screen, and by word of mouth, since his death, by both the tenderly nostalgic and the jealous, that they have tended to obscure the profound emotional and intellectual ferment whose end products were literature—and people.[29]

New Writers and New Ventures

The 1923 relocation of the publishing house in larger quarters was prompted by Liveright's desire to publish a greater number of books.[1] His success with the works of Van Loon, Adams, Lewisohn, Rose Macaulay, and others, in addition to the appearance of new capital through the sale of a vice presidency to Bennett Cerf, guaranteed the publisher the cash he needed to expand. Moreover, his backlist, made up principally of the Modern Library, offered as secure an annual income as any middle-sized American publishing firm has probably ever enjoyed. Even Liveright's lifelong penchant for playing the stock market and his overgenerosity to broken-down hacks and unknown writers seemed less dangerous at this time of comparative prosperity. The publisher had demonstrated his flair for selling books of all kinds; his success with the "Warner Fabians" allowed him to gamble on the T. S. Eliots. His genuine dedication to freedom of expression, complemented, it appeared, by his love of publicity, had earned him the kind of attention no other publisher received. Consequently, Liveright soon effected an increase in production from about forty new and reprint volumes, Boni & Liveright's annual average output from 1917 through 1922, to almost eighty books yearly. This reflected no desire on his part to create a large house, even in terms of book production in the Twenties. Furthermore, by the standards of today, when Doubleday issues over seven hundred volumes annually, Liveright's expansion seems minuscule. But in 1923, it was a major step forward for the publisher, and in time, many untried authors, as yet unknown to Liveright and the public, would benefit from his move.

The first fruits of Liveright's expansion produced no great profit for the firm, nor did they include any new major American literary figures.[2] The most significant new fiction Boni & Liveright published in 1923 and 1924, with varying degrees of success, included two novels by Waldo Frank, *Holiday* and *Chalk Face*, which didn't sell, and two novels by Ben Hecht, *The Florentine Dagger* and *Humpty Dumpty*, which did.[3] Two Englishwomen joined the firm briefly, when Elizabeth Bowen's short stories, *Encounters*, and Dorothy Sayers' early mystery, *Whose Body?*, were issued. Since neither volume had a significant sale in the United States, both authors were dropped.[4] Two established American writers, Edna St. Vincent Millay and Edgar Lee Masters, were approached by Liveright and offered lucrative contracts for novels.[5] Miss Millay promised him *Hardigut*, but she later abandoned her work because of ill health.[6] While the poetess preferred to remain with Harper's, Masters left Macmillan and signed up with B & L to write two novels. The books he submitted to Liveright, *The Nuptial Flight* and *Mirage*, were consecutively issued to an unresponsive public. Francis Hackett, supported by Liveright, retired from his editorship of *The New Republic* to write a novel, *That Nice Young Couple*. Taking a loss on this volume, the publisher continued to support Hackett for the next six years, while the writer researched his next project, a biography of Henry the Eighth, a subject suggested by Liveright and another instance of his creative publishing.[7]

Probably the most interesting commercial failure of these two years was *Cane*, by Jean Toomer. After it appeared in 1923, this miscellany of stories, sketches, poems, and a one-act play sold only about five hundred copies.[8] Toomer himself belonged for a while at least to the Crane-Frank-Munson-Kenneth Burke coterie and had seen the publication of his stories and poems in several little magazines.[9] But the work that perhaps inaugurated the Negro Renaissance soon disappeared from public view, and, eventually, so did its creator. Copies of *Cane* became collectors' items in the fifties and sixties, until 1969 when it was reissued first, by the University Place Bookshop, New York City, and then by Harper and Row and took its place among American Negro letters as a classic.[10]

Despite a sizeable loss from the publication of all these books, a few novels did make money for Liveright: Ludwig Lewisohn's *Don Juan*, Rose Macaulay's *Told By an Idiot*, Samuel Hopkins Adams' *Siege*, "Warner Fabian's" *Sailor's Wives*, and Dreiser's *The "Genius."* However, Gertrude Atherton was the chief writer whose book saved the firm from financial crisis in the midst of Liveright's expansion.[11]

When Liveright persuaded Mrs. Atherton to leave the Frederick A. Stokes Company and join his house in 1922, he gained a writer who was already very well known.[12] Like her contemporary, Edith Wharton, Gertrude Atherton had a tremendous potential audience. In the Twenties, when sensational books attacking the older generation were greeted enthusiastically by reviewers, she retained their respect as one of the few older novelists who, like Howells, focused a critical eye on society. Moreover, like her new publisher, Mrs. Atherton knew the value of publicity to book selling. Some of her extra-literary prominence had come about through the newspaper coverage of her shocking habits. Photographs of her smoking at the South Shore Country Club in Chicago brought cries of "scandalous!" and when she showed no remorse but vigorously defended her actions, more attention from the press followed.[13]

When, at sixty-six, Mrs. Atherton joined Boni & Liveright, she had written nearly thirty books. Any new work of hers was assured a cordial reception from the reviewers. Its profit, however, might be modest, because many of her readers had grown tired of her favorite format of historical novels set in early California or on the Continent. On the other hand, a new novel set in present-day America, passably written but still spicy, would reestablish the author on the best-seller lists.

The manuscript Mrs. Atherton submitted to Liveright as her first Boni & Liveright publication was entitled *Black Oxen*. Laid in contemporary New York society and centered on the love affair between her man-about-town hero and a mysterious countess whose charms were the result of physical rejuvenation by the Steinach treatment, the novel caught the popular fancy immediately. This time there was no need for the writer to promote its sales in her own adventurous way; Liveright's advertising staff gave her book the kind of costly, extensive publicity she had never before enjoyed. In 1923 Mrs. Atherton watched *Black Oxen's* unflagging progress upward on the popularity charts. She and Liveright had made a mutually profitable agreement, for in 1924 the best-seller compilation in *The Bookman* revealed that the two leading works the previous year had been Emily Post's *Complete Etiquette* in nonfiction and Gertrude Atherton's *Black Oxen* in fiction.[14]

While Mrs. Atherton led the list of Boni & Liveright novelists,

Liveright's mainstay in the drama, O'Neill, continued to head the firm's output of playwrights and poets.[15] O'Neill's *Fountain, Welded,* and *All God's Chillun Got Wings* were issued then as was an expensive two-volume limited edition of the dramatist's earlier works. Other plays the house published included Molnar's *Her Husbands and Lovers,* Lawrence Langner's *Moses,* and the George S. Kaufman/Marc Connelly comedy, *Beggar on Horseback.* Two limited and two trade editions of poetry were all the important verse Liveright published at this time. For the collector there were Masters' *New Spoon River* and François Villon's complete, unexpurgated poems; for the cognoscenti there were Bodenheim's *Against This Age* and Sacheverell Sitwell's *One Hundred and One Harlequins.*

During 1923 and 1924 Liveright's offerings in the novel, drama, and poetry were the least impressive he had ever issued. A review of his publications outside these categories reveals, however, a fascinating group of books, wide in their appeal and varied in their significance. As representative types of writing, they may be found on the lists of most trade publishers today, but it is unlikely that a single small firm ever issued, almost simultaneously, so many diversified titles.

In the Boni & Liveright catalogue side by side with Dreiser's *The Color of a Great City,* sketches of New York filled with deterministic Spencerian overtones, was a popular edition of Charles M. Doughty's *Arabia Deserta,* which had first appeared in 1888.[16] Issuing Doughty's famous adventures in Arabia was the inspiration of T. R. Smith.[17] After Jonathan Cape had brought out a small limited edition of this travel book in 1921, Liveright's chief editor began to urge him to offer a less expensive reprint. Smith admitted to Liveright that the house stood to lose $5,000 on an edition of two thousand copies if the work failed to sell, but, he maintained, it was a prestigious book to add to their list. The publisher agreed to take the chance, and the popular two-volume edition of *Arabia Deserta* with an introduction by T. E. Lawrence was issued in 1923 priced at a steep $17.50 per set. Two thousand readers soon bought it out.

In addition to portraits of twentieth-century Broadway and nineteenth-century Arabia, Boni & Liveright offered other miscellaneous works including Van Loon's *Story of the Bible,* which was written in the manner of his earlier best-seller but was considerably less successful; *These United States,* a collection of essays by well-known writers like Mencken, Lewisohn, and Edmund Wilson; and, for good measure, there was *The Common Sense of Music,* the first volume by the late editor of *The Music Journal,* Sigmund Spaeth.[18] Spaeth's work was an early example of the appreciation books that have been so successfully marketed from that time since. Books that Boni & Liveright issued in limited editions or those "restricted" in sales were in some cases noteworthy and sometimes had sensational appeal. Literary volumes included Moore's autobiographical *Conversations in Ebury Street*; *The Intimate Letters of James G. Huneker,* consisting of letters that Scribner's (Huneker's regular publisher) had believed too indelicate to issue; and two biographies —*Beatrice Cenci* by Corrado Ricci, whose respectability was assured through his position as Minister of Fine Arts in the Italian Cabinet, and *The Private Life of Louis XV* by Mouffle d'Angerville, who offered no similar qualifications. Liveright's list of scientific books was headed by Freud's *Beyond the Pleasure Principle,* as well as *Group Psychology and the Analysis of the Ego.* Others were Dr. Paul Kammerer's *Rejuvenation* and *The Inheritance of Acquired Characteristics,* and Dr. Wilhelm Stekel's *The Peculiarities of Behavior.*

Volumes of literary history and miscellaneous criticism included *The Story of the World's Literature* by John Macy, *Main Currents of Nineteenth Century Literature* by George Brandes, *Salvos* by Waldo Frank, *Sticks and Stones* by Lewis Mumford, and *Waldo Frank: A Study* by Gorham Munson.[19] In this abundance of nonfiction, the firm's offering of biographies, autobiographies, and reminiscences was probably the most widely appealing group of all. There were Samuel Ornitz's anonymously published *Haunch, Paunch, and Jowl,* Maxim Gorky's *My Intellectual Life,* Marcel Schwob's *Imaginary Lives,* Elizabeth Marbury's *My Crystal Ball,* Mme. Pierre Berton's *The Real Sarah Bernhardt,* John D. Rockefeller's *The Personal Relation in Industry,* Samuel Harden Church's *Flames of Faith,* John T. McGraw's *My Seventy Years in Baseball,* and, for contrast, the naturally anonymous *Real Story of a Bootlegger.*[20]

By the mid-Twenties Liveright had become the most exciting

publisher in the United States. He had accomplished the meteoric rise in less than ten years. Yet with success—his publication of seven Nobel Prize winners within a six-year span would be success enough for any firm—came, or was to come, disaster.[21] In two years alone, 1925 and 1926, the house grossed over two million dollars, but its net profit remained tiny, as low as $8,609.12 in 1925.[22] Liveright's own business mismanagement as well as his early ventures into play production and his disastrous gambles on the stock market accounted for large shares of his losses; furthermore, a different kind of financial drain, the expense of his own personal problems, was responsible for a sizeable portion too.

The turning point in Liveright's picaresque career probably came in 1925, the year he issued his most important list. By the fall of 1925 he had published or accepted for publication the early works of Nobel Prize winners-to-be Hemingway, Faulkner, Roger Martin du Gard, François Mauriac, and also the work of Hart Crane, Robinson Jeffers, Hilda Doolittle, V. F. Calverton, Djuna Barnes, Liam O'Flaherty, and Dorothy Parker.[23] For most of these young writers, it was the first major publication of their work in the United States. Among Boni & Liveright's best-sellers were Anita Loos's *Gentlemen Prefer Blondes;* Sherwood Anderson's *Dark Laughter*; Theodore Dreiser's *An American Tragedy*; O'Neill's *Desire Under the Elms*; Bodenheim's *Replenishing Jessica*; Frances Newman's *The Hard-Boiled Virgin*; and Gertrude Atherton's *The Crystal Cup*. There were new books of verse by Kreymborg, Cummings, and Pound—*Scarlet and Mellow, Is Five*, and *Personae*, respectively—*The Dybbuk* by S. Ansky, as well as new plays by Molnar, the Kaufman/Connelly team, and Stark Young; new fiction by Bercovici, Adams, Conrad Aiken, Heywood Broun, Rose Macaulay, Sarah Gertrude Millin, Paul Morand, Naomi Royde-Smith, and Frank Sullivan, all either popular or potentially successful authors. Liveright's new nonfiction included Van Loon's *Intolerance*; Lewisohn's *Israel*; Moore's *Avowals*; Frank's *Virgin Spain*; Mumford's *The Golden Day*; Kreymborg's *Troubadour*; Eastman's *Since Lenin Died*; Sven Hedin's *My Life as an Explorer*; Otto Kahn's *Of Many Things*; Judge Benjamin Lindsey's *The Revolt of Modern Youth*; Dr. Morris Fishbein's *The Medical Follies*; and Bertrand

Russell's *Education and the Good Life*. Moreover, there were luxurious limited editions of *Droll Stories* and *The Decameron*, Waldo Frank's translation of Jules Romains' novel *Lucienne,* the first volumes of the Scott Moncrieff translation of Stendhal, and finally, in the Modern Library, over one hundred titles in literature, economics, psychology, and history.

At this time the fortunes of the publisher and his firm were at their most perilous point since the beginning of the business. The success of *Black Oxen* and the arrival of Bennett Cerf had forestalled financial difficulties in 1923, but Liveright soon lost this income through the over-promotion of unsuccessful books and his own ventures on Broadway and Wall Street. Following the organization of a theatrical producing firm in July 1924 headed by the publisher in partnership with two others, Frank Mandel, a dramatist and the author of *No, No, Nanette,* and Laurence Schwab, already an active producer, Liveright had first presented a comedy, *The Firebrand,* by Edwin Justus Mayer.[24] This play, which featured Edward G. Robinson and Joseph Schildkraut, premiered on October 15, 1924, and enjoyed a successful run of 261 performances.[25] Considerably less popular, however, was Liveright's only production of 1925, *Hamlet in Modern Dress,* an updated version of Shakespeare's tragedy set in Newport, Rhode Island, and in which Basil Sidney, a British actor who was featured as Hamlet, appeared as a young man about town.[26] The publicity releases for the play assured prospective theatergoers that this revival was not a stunt, but an attempt to remove *Hamlet* from the ordinary trappings of costumes and sets in order to enable the audience to judge it in terms of current values. Apparently New Yorkers thought otherwise or missed the sets, costumes, and atmosphere traditionally associated with the tragedy, for Liveright's *Hamlet,* which opened on November 9, 1925, closed early the next year after a run of only eighty-six performances.[27] *Hamlet's* failure was a costly one for the publisher. Although he enjoyed two more hits during his career as a producer, there were five colossal flops as well. The theater was an expensive adventure for Liveright; in fact, after its first successful season, his production company remained in the red until its collapse. Yet Liveright might have survived his plunge on Broadway, if he had not lost so much on Wall Street.

These losses came about largely as the result of tips given him by a well-meaning friend, Otto Kahn. Kahn, a millionaire financier, was naturally more closely involved in the fluctuations of the market than the publisher far away on West Forty-eighth Street. At a time when minutes meant the difference between enormous gains and losses in the purchase and sale of securities, Liveright's position was a particularly risky one. By the time Kahn could relay news of current transactions and advice to the publisher, it was often too late for Liveright to do anything but absorb his losses. Others amassed large fortunes speculating during the flush years of the market, but Liveright appeared only to lose.

It was during this period of theatrical ventures, and even more disastrous securities speculation, that Liveright and his wife, Lucile separated. While Mrs. Liveright did not sue for divorce until March 22, 1928, a separation agreement between the two had been in effect for a much longer time.[28] To fulfill this agreement, Liveright had to repay his wife and his father-in-law large amounts of money he had almost continually borrowed from them both.[29] No unexpected best-seller or blue-chip stock fell from heaven to save him in 1925. Moreover, Cerf decided to leave the house and begin his own firm; his departure made it necessary for Liveright to buy back his partner's stock immediately, and he lacked the cash to do so.[30] With mixed feelings Liveright accepted Cerf's offer to give him the partnership stock and additional capital in return for the Modern Library.[31] With the new capital, as well as Liveright's quick sale of a more expensive vice presidency to Donald Friede, the publisher momentarily averted financial crisis for the firm and for himself. But he had unknowingly made his first great misstep in publishing, one from which he could never hope to recover. The Modern Library had been the foundation of the firm. Its loss meant the removal of the major part of the backlist. The series of reprints, which had so successfully established the house and sustained it when Liveright's earlier gambles backfired, was no longer his. In the absence of the Modern Library and the security it represented, the publisher was in need of popular best-sellers, and he needed them regularly. During the next few years he was to have haphazard success.

The book which might have saved Liveright and allowed him

to keep the Modern Library was not issued until November of the year he parted with his nest egg. It was called *Gentlemen Prefer Blondes*. Anita Loos had written the first part of it on a cross-country train trip from her home in New York to Hollywood, where she was a scenario writer.[32] In California she completed part of the manuscript and, after she returned to New York, she sent it to H. L. Mencken for possible publication in *The American Mercury*. The editor, believing it was not right for his periodical, suggested Miss Loos might be able to place it with *Harper's Bazaar*, where, indeed, it appeared serially in 1925 with drawings by cartoonist, Ralph Barton. *Harper's* readers—usually more interested in the magazine's high fashion photos and commentary than its fiction—were enchanted by the adventures of Lorelei Lee; in fact, the newsstand sales of the magazine tripled during the six months she appeared. That fall, Liveright enthusiastically endorsed Smith's proposal to issue Miss Loos' work, so she could fill her Christmas gift list in an unusual way. Publisher, editor, and author all agreed from the beginning that the work would not have much of a sale; initially, Liveright offered to publish it simply as a gesture of friendship.[33] Meanwhile, Burton Rascoe, then editor of the *New York Tribune Book Review*, having discovered *Gentlemen Prefer Blondes* in *Harper's*, ecstatically announced to Miss Loos that her work would be the most popular literary sensation of the season.[34] The three people most closely involved in its production remained considerably more conservative in their estimate of its appeal.

The humorous novel was issued in late November, and Miss Loos, Barton, Smith, and Liveright sent copies to friends in lieu of Christmas cards. The remainder of the small, initial edition of twelve hundred copies was distributed among New York bookstores.[35] But Lorelei Lee was an unexpected hit once more; the entire edition was sold out on the day it appeared, and Liveright was caught short of stock. Calls for more books jammed the switchboard at the publishing house, and a second edition numbering sixty-five thousand copies was put to press. *Gentlemen Prefer Blondes*, subtitled "The Illuminating Diary of a Professional Lady," went on to sell thousands of copies during 1926 and joined *The Private Life of Helen of Troy* by John Erskine and *The Man*

Nobody Knows by Bruce Barton as the three top-selling works of the year.[36] Two million copies of the novel were sold during the next forty years. It was translated into many foreign languages, including Japanese, was pirated for a Russian edition, and eventually earned Miss Loos a million dollars. Liveright was considerably less fortunate.

Because of the unanimous feeling that the book would fail to sell in any quantity, and in the hope of moving enough copies to cover production expenses, it was decided at a sales conference to lower the price of the novel from $2.00 a volume to $1.75.[37] However, Messner and Liveright had neglected to consult the manufacturing department, and they discovered that the costs of the thick paper and large illustrations, which Komroff had devised to make *Gentlemen Prefer Blondes* look like more for the money, were so high that the firm was losing money on every copy sold. By the time the price could be raised to meet production costs, over one hundred and fifty thousand volumes had been purchased. With the main hard-cover sale of *Gentlemen Prefer Blondes* completed, it was discovered that the author's contract contained no provision for a reduction in royalties from Canadian sales. Normally, in order to give booksellers in Canada larger discounts to cover the import duties they had to pay on American books, publishers gave their authors only half the standard royalty per volume sold there in order to balance expenses. Quite legally and logically, Miss Loos asked Liveright to pay her in full. Liveright's friendly gesture proved to be even more disastrous for him financially, after the book, which was supposed to appeal only to the author's friends and a few other sophisticated New Yorkers, had become a nationwide best-seller and found many eager readers in Canada.

Sherwood Anderson

By 1925 Sherwood Anderson had nine volumes to his credit as well as innumerable essays and short stories; yet even the publication of this sizeable number of works had not brought the older writer success or security. Liveright's accomplishment in signing Anderson to a five-year contract at that time seemed to solve the writer's constant financial worries and hold the promise of greater artistic fulfillment. The publisher had good fortune with the author's second-rate novel, *Dark Laughter*, but soon a mounting debt of unearned income seemed to end Anderson's ability to write. Financial security, peace of mind, and creative ability never came to the writer at the same time. The most lasting of his works, written during time stolen from his various jobs in advertising, were composed before Liveright attempted to support him. Of course, the well-meaning generosity of his publisher was not the reason for the failure of Anderson's artistic abilities, but combined with his periodic personal conflicts, it apparently served to stifle further greatness in an author who had written some of our most important fiction.

Anderson's letters reveal an artist plagued by debt and fearful that he might lose his artistic capabilities because of it. His first published work, a three-page story called "The Rabbit Pen," appeared in *Harper's* in 1914,[1] the year Anderson was thirty-eight. Living in Chicago and supporting himself by a job with an advertising firm, he saw little chance of ever becoming financially secure as a writer, especially when his friend, Floyd Dell, tried unsuccessfully for many months to find a publisher for Anderson's first novel, *Windy McPherson's Son*.[2] Dell finally placed the book with the John Lane Company of England; its New York manager, Jefferson Jones, influenced by Dreiser's endorsement, issued it in 1916.[3] Anderson's association with Lane lasted for two years, through the publication of a second novel, *Marching Men* (1917), and a volume of poetry,

Mid-American Chants (1918) .⁴ When the three-book contract with Anderson was completed, Jones rejected the writer's next effort, *Winesburg, Ohio*. It was, he felt, too morbid to sell, and the negligible sale of Anderson's free verse—about two hundred copies —certainly confirmed his doubt about Anderson's popular appeal.⁵ Nineteen eighteen found Anderson on the one hand unable to locate a publisher for what he thought to be his best work, and, on the other, achieving the fairly regular acceptance of his stories and articles by low-paying little magazines like *The Little Review, The Seven Arts,* and *The Dial.*⁶ Major recognition and security seemed forlorn hopes. Anderson revealed his despondency in one of his letters:

> In facing what I face now—that is to say, the possibility that I will have to give up the fight—my mind gropes about trying to see some way out. Surely I am willing to live in the very simplest way to accomplish what I want, but I do need some assured income every year. I have three children who have to be supported. In all I need from twenty-five hundred to three thousand a year to live.
>
> Do you think there is any chance at all of my interesting some man or woman of money to back me to this extent in trying to do my work? I know nothing of such things, but do know that money is constantly being invested in schools, magazines, young singers, in a thousand things of the sort.
>
> It seems to me that I have proven my ability as a writer. I know of no other man in the country who has got such recognition as has come to me. Yet I make no money. . . .⁷

Later that year Anderson found a publisher sympathetic to his work, when Ben Huebsch accepted and published *Winesburg, Ohio.* While this book increased the author's reputation, two years passed before five thousand copies of it were sold.⁸ Even when Anderson received the first of the annual *Dial* awards in 1921, and some of his best work was appearing in both magazine and book form, the sales of his volumes were disappointing.⁹ *Poor White*, a novel, was issued in 1920, and a collection of stories, *The Triumph of the Egg,* appeared in the fall of 1921. The latter had an initial sale of 4,425 copies, hardly outstanding for one of the most discussed American authors.¹⁰ Writing advertising copy and snatching time to create stories, Anderson seemed reconciled to a small audience; he further revealed his deep affection for Huebsch, the man who had issued his best work:

> He really at bottom, I suspect, doesn't know what a good book is or how to sell books, but he is a fine fellow; and at any rate you wouldn't have to, with him, go through the wearisome business of having some smart publisher tell you what to do to make your book sell.
>
> As you know, my books do not sell much, but I suppose a smart publisher could sell twice as many; at least several have come to me with the proposition that they would undertake to do something like that if I would only come to them. I've stuck to Ben because my years as a businessman cured me so effectually of any desire to make money that there is almost a satisfaction in some of Ben's inefficiencies as a publisher.[11]

Anderson was encouraged by the brief success of *Many Marriages* in 1923, before its sale abruptly stopped.[12] He expressed dissatisfaction to Huebsch, but the latter's reply that booksellers refused to order the novel, or sell it, on moral grounds appeared to satisfy the writer for a time.[13] He affirmed his loyalty to his publisher and appeared to rationalize his deplorable situation:

> As for Huebsch, one of the most sincere, lovable men I have ever known, God bless him. Behind the door I would whisper to you that I do not think too much of his artistic perception. . . . [But] all the time you grow more and more to love and respect him and to realize you would rather have him as your publisher selling 5,000 than some of the damned smart young men of the publishing world "putting you over" to the tune of 25,000.[14]

This friendly relationship did not last long. Anderson's unhappiness with Huebsch's small, one-man firm persisted, and in literary circles he announced his readiness to make a change. Of the many offers he received in 1924, Liveright's was the most inviting.[15]

In 1922, when Anderson left Chicago to live briefly in New York, he met Liveright for the first time. Their business association began when the publisher issued *Winesburg, Ohio* in the Modern Library, where it sold as many copies during its first month in print as it had during the first year of its original edition.[16] The following year Liveright paid Anderson $50 to write an introduction for Dreiser's *Free and Other Stories* in the same series.[17] Anderson was, of course, very well known and esteemed by many of Liveright's own authors. The publisher made overtures to the writer on his own and through his brother, Otto Liveright, Anderson's literary agent in New York.[18] Otto Liveright wrote the author in May 1924 regarding his brother's interest in Anderson, saying that Horace Liveright was the best publisher for the writer, should he decide to leave Huebsch.[19]

By that summer it seemed as if Anderson were ready to capitulate; he had complained to Huebsch of lagging sales and told others that he might give his next work, *A Story Teller's Story*, to another publisher.[20] Huebsch responded to Anderson's discontent by explaining at length the difficulties in selling his works: if it wasn't the character of the book which made it objectionable, it was that only a small audience for his writings existed.[21] Placated once again, Anderson rejected Liveright's offer.[22] Some doubt about his own capabilities, coupled with his loyalty to Huebsch who had issued *Winesburg, Ohio* when no other publisher would accept it, held him back; he decided to try his first real sponsor once more with *A Story Teller's Story*. Like his other works, its sale was disappointing. Long on reputation but short on royalties, Anderson was forced to turn to the lecture platform, an avocation he disliked, to supplement his meager income.[23]

Undoubtedly aware of this situation, Liveright persisted in his efforts to bring Anderson into the firm. In November 1924 he wrote to the author, who was then living in New Orleans, telling him he would make a trip South, if Anderson were interested in discussing a contract again:

> I think I can convince you that I'm your man. . . . In a short time I have built up the best book publishing organization in the country. I am trying now to limit my list of fiction rather than expand it. If I don't, in another five years I'll be no better than some of the big publishers who have become manufacturers rather than anything else. . . . I know all about your relations with Huebsch and I, too, am fond of him and don't think anyone can accuse me of ever

having played the game anything but fairly. After all, business is business.[24]

Later that month Anderson replied to Liveright at length:

>I have not wired you, because it will take nothing less than a letter to tell you how matters are with me, and I will have to answer your letter to you as a person rather than as a business man and publisher. Last year when I was up against [it] and wanted a decent offer from someone, you made it to me without hesitation. Otto is one of my valued friends and has surely done a lot for me. I want to make everything as clear as I can. It may be you will feel I'm a fool.

>The truth is I would just find it too hard and uncomfortable for me to make a change. When I started to do it last year, I felt like a dog. I wanted to do it and at the same time didn't want to. While the negotiations were on, I felt like hell. I know, Horace, that all you say is probably correct. It takes an organization to place books, and if they aren't placed, they won't be sold. The number of people who will go out of their way to get books when they must be ordered from a distance or who will wait until a dealer gets them in is small and always will be. All of these things I know and have known for a long time. Why, they haven't got *A Story Teller's Story* in the bookstore down here yet. I[t] probably never will sell much.

>On the other hand, Horace, I got out of business some years ago. Things like sticking to old friends have really got bigger to me than anything else. While Ben never has sold my books much, he has been very, very fine with me in other ways. There never has been any lack of moral support. He published me and gave me his support when no one else much wanted me.

>At the same time, Horace, I think it is fine of you to want to give me this chance. There is no question of your not doing the right thing by Ben. It was me who opened the ball with you, but, really, I guess in doing so I wasn't quite myself. . . . Usually I'm not much scared about making a living. I do it always after a fashion. And from now on I am likely to do more and, I hope, better work than I have done before.

>What I dislike most about writing you and telling you just how I feel is that I hate not to make it seem necessary for you to run down to New Orleans. It's a great town really, and you would like it. Why don't you come anyway?[25]

In December, Anderson's announcement to a friend that the

publication of *A Story Teller's Story* had marked the end of an era for him and that he needed to be subsidized like an institution was the first indication he gave that Liveright had gone to New Orleans and persuaded the writer to join his firm.[26] Many years later in his *Memoirs* Anderson rather dramatically recalled this meeting with Liveright:

> It was that strange character, much maligned, much misunderstood, the strangest man, I am sure, ever in the publishing business in America. I am speaking of Horace Liveright.
>
> He was then, and, for that matter, until the end of his life, a very handsome man, tall and erect, his hair just touched with gray. He walked with an easy swing and when I saw him that day in New Orleans, he was accompanied by a very beautiful woman.
>
> There was an absurd mistake made. Already I knew Horace Liveright, had been with him on several occasions in New York. He was the publisher of my friend, Theodore Dreiser, and of another friend, Eugene O'Neill. He was with a beautiful woman and I had seen him with many beautiful women.
>
> "Meet my wife," he said and, "Oh yeah?" I answered.
>
> There was an uncomfortable moment. It *was* Mrs. Liveright. I was sunk and so was Horace.
>
> "It may have been an uncomfortable moment for you but it was a lot more than that for me," Horace later told me.
>
> However he forgave me. He came to see me later in the same afternoon and we went to drink together and, when he inquired, I told him that I was looking for a new publisher.
>
> He made me a proposal that took my breath away. I had spoken to him of the advertising agency. "I'll have to go back there, begin again to write of toothpaste, of kidney pills, of how to keep your hair from falling out." There must have been a note of desperation in my voice and Horace, on that occasion as always with me, was very gentle. We were at a table in the little New Orleans café and were drinking. He reached across the table and put his hand on my hand.
>
> "So you are discouraged, eh? You think your books cannot be sold. What nonsense. You come with me." He made me a proposal.
>
> "For five years I'll send you a hundred dollars a week. I'll take what you write. I'll sell your books."[27]

The following spring Anderson traveled to New York, ostensibly to visit friends and discuss business with Ben Huebsch, but actually to complete his contractual negotiations with Liveright.[28] During this visit the unsuspecting Huebsch gave a large luncheon for the writer at the Brevoort Hotel. Anderson returned to New Orleans having signed a lucrative contract with his new publisher, which guaranteed him financial security and freed him from the necessity of continuing the lecturing he despised so much. Their agreement, signed April 10, 1925, was to last for five years.[29] During that time the publisher promised to give Anderson $100 a week against royalties which would accrue from the sale of his works to be published by Boni & Liveright. Anderson's royalties were to be 15 per cent on new books and 10 per cent on Modern Library reprints. Boni & Liveright further agreed "to issue a uniform edition of the author's works at such time and in such format and at such price as shall be mutually agreed upon by the author and publisher." Liveright also gave his new writer all the income from the not inconsiderable sale of foreign rights, instead of retaining the customary half share. The only difficulty with the contract, so far as Anderson would be concerned, was not even stated; it was simply a verbal agreement that the writer would annually submit one book of the character of either *Dark Laughter*, his new novel, or *A Story Teller's Story*.

Liveright promised to make the arrival of Anderson at Boni & Liveright known with great fanfare. In a letter accompanying Anderson's copy of their agreement, the publisher also appraised their new association: "I have before me our agreement with Dreiser and, just between ourselves, and, of course, not for mention to anyone, the agreement with you is considerably more liberal than the one we have with Dreiser."[30]

Although Anderson delayed advising Huebsch of his defection, he announced it to his friends almost immediately. His gratitude and relief are apparent. To John Emerson he wrote: "My own notion is that Liveright has been generous and fine with me. I intend he shall never regret it. I guess you know what it will mean to me not to be constantly driven off the job by money worries."[31]

At the same time he informed Otto Liveright of his new allegiance:

Here is some news that will surprise you. I think you will agree with me that I have gone as far with Ben as any man ever went with a publisher. Even when I left New York I was sure that a change was out of the question but the strain and uncertainty of my financial situation with Ben as my publisher have become too much for me. My work has begun to suffer.

And at the moment when I had about come to that conclusion along blows Horace and makes me an offer so fair and straight that I closed with him. The agreement covers the next five years. As a matter of fact it is for keeps. Now watch me work. I intend to do the best work of my life and make Horace glad he got me.[32]

Later Anderson wrote to Huebsch; his news was no surprise to the publisher, for Anderson's desertion had been common knowledge among New York literati since the time of his visit.[33] He explained that the returns from his last book would not carry him through the summer; he had been forced to borrow money from friends:

The time had come when I could not see my way through so I wrote a letter to Horace Liveright saying I was open to a proposition if he wanted to make me one. . . . He has undertaken to underwrite my living for the next five years, leaving me free to think of nothing but writing, knowing in the meantime where my bread and butter is coming from.

I did not take this proposition up with you because I thought it was a matter I had to settle for myself.[34]

At the same time he said farewell to his old publisher, Anderson replied to Liveright. He reiterated his belief that Huebsch's failure with his works was due to his small operation and inability to place his books:

What I want most of all to impress on you, Horace, is that in going with you I go all the way and want you to feel that if there is anything in sincere intent and loyalty I will make your gamble a good one for you in the next few years.[35]

The first new work of Anderson's that Liveright expected to receive for immediate publication was *Dark Laughter*. The novelist wrote him enthusiastically about it:

Since you were here, I have been working on it every minute of every day, in fact have kept at it so hard and long that each day when I got through, I was so exhausted I could hardly get up from my desk.

You see what I am trying to give you now, Horace, is something of the orchestration of the book. The neuroticism, the hurry and self-consciousness of modern life, and back of it the easy, strange laughter of the blacks. There is your dark, earthy laughter—the Negro, the earth, and the river—that suggests the title.

Bet on this book, Horace, it is going to be there with a bang.[36]

By May 1925 *Dark Laughter* was completed, and Anderson wrote his publisher about an idea for his next work:

I have in the back of my mind something that may develop within the next year or two and seems to me to have immense possibilities. I don't believe anyone has ever done a book on the Mississippi River, and I am going to begin to gather data and see what I can find. There is a tremendous story in the early history of the river, the wild, reckless days on the river of the '40's, the tremendous part it took in the Civil War, and afterwards its decline. The whole story is full of strange romance and interest and excitement, and I woud like tremendously to get it all. I am going to keep it in mind and see what I can gather in data to help me get what I want. Don't you think it might be made quite a tremendous book? It certainly is big enough in its sweep. Think it over and one of these days write me about it, but don't talk to many people about it, as I want the plum for myself if I can get together the material I want. This is, of course, something that would take two or three years to develop, but I believe is mighty well worth working on.[37]

Liveright immediately consulted T. R. Smith, whose advice concerning Anderson's undertaking was sensible and hard-boiled:

Please tell Sherwood Anderson to reconsider writing a book on the Mississippi River! I think it would be a most unfortunate thing for him to do as it is unlikely to have a sale. There are at least 24 books in print at the present time about the Mississippi River, its history, origin, discovery, development, etc.; no phase of it has been left untouched. . . . If this book is to be treated as fiction then it might be something different, but if treated as fact I certainly hope he does not do it.[38]

When Liveright conveyed Smith's memo to the writer, Anderson was apparently satisfied to give up his project. Furthermore, he was still attending to the details of his forthcoming novel. Liveright had written him that advance orders for over five thousand copies had arrived.[39] And when *Dark Laughter* was issued on September 15, 1925, it was greeted by an eager public. Less than a week later, the publisher told Anderson that he hoped for a sale of twenty thousand copies.[40] Heavily promoted, *Dark Laughter* sold steadily during the remaining months of 1925. Anderson's royalty statement, dated December 31, 1925, revealed that 22,297 copies of the regular $2.50 edition of his novel had been sold in the United States and Canada, and that these sales had earned the author $8,209.51 in royalties.[41] Moreover, the success of *Dark Laughter* brought great demands for articles from Anderson, and he noted proudly that "People who used to quibble about paying $75.00 for an article now want to pay three or four hundred."[42] As *Dark Laughter* climbed in sales, Anderson was full of praise for Liveright: "I can't tell you how satisfactory it is to be with such a man."[43]

Sherwood Anderson's Notebook was published in the spring of 1926, while the writer was at work on another novel called *Talbot Whittingham*.[44] In the light of what was to follow it is significant that the new work did not sell and that Anderson soon laid aside the *Whittingham* manuscript, which he never finished. Both the failure in sales and the failure in creativity marked the beginning of a decline in Anderson's writing and popularity which was to continue for several years. Neither Liveright nor his author was aware of this, of course; in fact, on the first anniversary of their agreement, when it was clear that Liveright had actually made very little on the novel, because of advertising and exploitation expenses, the author expressed his gratitude to the publisher succinctly: "Just a little note to thank you for being so nice to me. You're a white publisher. But more than that I feel you as a real friend."[45]

Following the publication of two more volumes—the autobiographical narrative, *Tar: A Midwest Childhood* (1926) and poetry, *A New Testament* (1927)—and a trip to Europe, Anderson's financial security had disappeared and what he was to call "his two years of comparative leisure" had come to a disastrous close. The writer's royalty statement for the second six months of 1927 showed an unearned balance of $1219.03.[46] Fifteen thousand inexpensive reprint copies of the two-year-old *Dark Laughter* yielded the only appreciable income of $900. Royalties from his other three books were no better than those of his pre-Liveright days. Yet every Monday morning there was a check for $100 in his mailbox.

Largely on the returns from *Dark Laughter*, Anderson had bought a farm in a valley in southwestern Virginia, where he excitedly began to build a house. As he became more and more absorbed in the plans for his home, he became more and more impatient about his writing. The new house, mounting unearned income, and the obligation to produce a book annually had utterly frustrated his creativity. To a friend he wrote:

> This idea that one must produce constantly, or starve, is terribly detrimental to any sort of freedom of approach.
>
> I was afraid of the [Boni & Liveright] proposal, but was driven into it by necessity. They have been very nice, but the situation has always been on my nerves. I cannot get over the idea of being at work for them as an employee. When a day or week comes that I do not write satisfactorily, I am beside myself.
>
> Over here the *Testament* has brought down a furor on my head. . . . My death as a writer is being tolled up and down the literary press.[47]

Many years later, writing his *Memoirs*, Anderson recalled his anxiety and frustration during the fall of 1927. He also described how he resolved his problems:

> It was all too grand. I sat in the cabin with my pen in hand and there were the blank sheets on the desk before me and down below, on Ripshin Creek, the materials for my house were being brought in.
>
> Men were at work down there and there I was up there on that hill, my pen poised in my hand, no words coming to me.
>
> "Why, I cannot write. It is too exciting down there. This is the great time in a man's life. We are all, at heart, builders. It is the dream of every man, at some time in his life, to build his own house.
>
> "And so my house is to be built and I am to stay up here, writing words on paper. How silly."

But there was that hundred dollar check. It came every Monday morning.

Horace had said, "I will send it to you every week for five years. I'll take what you write."

"I'll not bother you," he said.

Yet each week the arrival of the check was a reminder that I was not and perhaps could not be a writer while my house was building.

"But I am under this obligation to Horace." I went again into my hilltop cabin. What really happened was that I never did write a word in that cabin. It may be that the view from the hilltop was too magnificent. It made everything I wrote seem too trivial. I had in the end, after my house was built, to move the cabin from the hill, tuck it away among the trees by the creek.

But I was still up there and down below the work on my house was under way. I had to give it up. I took a train to New York.

"Please, Horace, quit it."

"Quit what?" he asked.

"Quit sending me that money."

I tried to explain how it affected me.

"But," he said, "I have made enough on the one book—I am in the clear. Why should you worry?"

I had a hard time convincing him. He even became suspicious.

"Are you not satisfied with me as your publisher? Is it that?"

It seemed, as he said, impossible to him that a writer should refuse money.

"All right, I'll quit it, but I think you are a little crazy."

And so I was released. It is true that, when my house was half finished, I had to go lecturing. It was bad enough but it was better than having the checks come every Monday to remind me that I was a writer, not a builder.[48]

No work of Anderson's appeared under the Liveright imprint in 1928, but the following year a collection of newspaper pieces, *Hello Towns!*, was issued. Anderson was enthusiastic about these sketches, essays, and editorials he had written for the two weekly newspapers he ran in Marion, Virginia, but the book was financially unsuccessful. About the time he was reading the proofs of *Hello Towns!*, Anderson received a letter from Liveright accusing him of criticizing the firm.[49] In his reply, Anderson denied the accusation and reaffirmed his affection for the publisher.

> I have never been so well-used by anyone in the publishing world as you and everyone connected with your firm. In addition to that I have thought of myself as your friend.
>
> What does it matter to me whether you sell *Hello Towns!* or not?
>
> I might go on for pages about your liberality to me, your squareness. You ought to know I feel all this.[50]

The episode was quickly forgotten by Liveright, but Anderson continued to feel guilty—not so much because of a false rumor, but because he knew he had failed to complete any extended fiction. His attempts and failures to finish his new novel, *Beyond Desire*, were partially recorded in his correspondence with the publisher. After a visit with Liveright in June of 1929, Anderson was elated by his progress on the novel; he promised to deliver his manuscript by January 1, 1930.[51] During the month before his work was due, the author wrote Liveright less hopefully that he was pushing himself to finish it:

> I may have been spoofing myself and you and Maurice [Hanline], in saying I had it about done. I did have all the scenes of the book, the people, events, etc., but it did not have any real movement. The music wasn't in it yet.
>
> I think you know, Horace, that I have to have this book right, not only on account of its chances of success, but also because of myself. I want to whip out of me this sense of defeat I have had.
>
> I wish I could say definitely that in a week, two weeks, a month, I will be through this job, but I can't. I have to take it as it flows. All I can say is that I will do nothing else, think of nothing else.[52]

Liveright responded that he was certain *Beyond Desire* would be Anderson's best work.

> If you get hard up, don't hesitate to let me know. And, above everything, don't rush the book because you think we've got to have it. We want it, of course. We want it badly for the Spring, but I know you can't work on schedule.[53]

The breakup of Anderson's third marriage, together with the death of his second wife—for whom he still had considerable feeling

—coming, as they did, while the novelist was struggling to complete *Beyond Desire,* plunged Anderson into a state of depression from which he did not recover for a long time.[54] By the end of December he knew he could not continue writing. He telegraphed Liveright:

> AM SORRY—BUT WILL HAVE TO WITHDRAW PROMISE OF THE NOVEL FOR THIS SPRING/HAPPENINGS IN MY OWN LIFE HAVE UPSET ME AND I WILL HAVE TO HAVE TIME TO GATHER MYSELF TOGETHER/ANYWAY IT IS NOT A GOOD PIECE OF WORK/FORGIVE MY BEING OVERSURE[55]

Liveright telegraphed a sympathetic reply to Anderson, concluding with the wish that the coming year might be the best the novelist had ever known.[56] When Anderson finally completed *Beyond Desire* and it was issued in 1932, Liveright was no longer connected with his publishing firm, and this work, like so much of the author's post-1925 writing, was unsuccessful. None of Anderson's books in the Thirties received special acclaim; in fact, it was not until nearly ten years after his death in 1941 that Anderson became much read again.

Hemingway, Faulkner, Jeffers, and Crane

When the manuscript of Hemingway's short stories arrived at Boni & Liveright in 1925, its author was known only to a small circle of other writers. Hemingway had, however, been published in book form on the Continent.[1] Three hundred copies of his first work, *Three Stories and Ten Poems,* had been issued by Robert McAlmon's Contact Publishing Company in 1923; it had been followed by a one hundred and seventy copy, limited edition of the thirty-two page *in our time* printed by William Bird's Three Mountains Press. Consisting entirely of miniatures, *in our time* later became the interchapters of the American edition of *In Our Time.* In the fall of 1924, anxious to find a larger audience in America, Hemingway sent a manuscript of his new work, revised and considerably expanded, to Donald Ogden Stewart in New York.[2] Stewart took it to George H. Doran, and Company which rejected it, and then to Mencken in the hope of its eventually being accepted by Knopf.[3] Nothing, apparently, came of this move either. Whether it was Stewart's copy that came to Liveright or a similar manuscript Hemingway gave to Leon Fleischman, Liveright's former partner who was living in Paris, is not completely clear.[4] It is more likely that it was the latter, since it is known that Harold Loeb brought Hemingway into contact with Fleischman, who in turn forwarded his *In Our Time* manuscript to New York[5]

The manuscript Liveright received contained the three stories from Hemingway's first volume: "Up in Michigan," "Out of Season," and "My Old Man"; all the miniatures from his second; and ten additional stories, all but three of them having appeared earlier in little magazines and in McAlmon's *Contact* anthology.[6] The new stories were "The Three Day Blow," "The End of Something," and "Cat in the Rain." Once the manuscript arrived, the reaction of those who read it was enthusiastic; T. R. Smith and Edith Stern both reported very favorably on the work of the young writer.[7] Moreover, those who were with the house at this time remember that Liveright himself showed no hesitation about acquiring Hemingway. Later, the author expressed his gratitude to Anderson and Dos Passos for their help in putting him over with Liveright, but the publisher's quick, enthusiastic response to the writer seems to support the theory that he too believed he had read the work of a very promising newcomer.[8]

In any event, while Hemingway was skiing in Austria in February 1925, he received two cables from Stewart and Loeb announcing that Boni & Liveright had agreed to publish *In Our Time*.[9] Next a cable and letter arrived from Liveright himself offering Hemingway an advance of $200 on his book of short stories. Liveright was enthusiastic about the quality of the stories as a whole, but he had reservations about two of them. There was a passage in one, "Mr. and Mrs. Elliot," which he was afraid might be held obscene, and there was one entire story, "Up in Michigan," which Liveright believed was outspoken enough to be censorable and would have to be replaced. On March 5, Hemingway cabled Liveright his acceptance, and later in the month returned the signed contract with a new story, "The Battler," to replace the unsatisfactory "Up in Michigan." In his covering letter Hemingway admonished Liveright and Smith to make no further changes in his manuscript without his approval, for, the young writer announced, the altering of so much as a word could damage a whole story.[10] Moreover, he said, he looked upon the American reception of his first effort, very unemotionally. A new novel of the first rank, like

ming's *The Enormous Room,* had not sold because Cummings' style was difficult for American readers unaccustomed to modern writing. However, *In Our Time* would not suffer on that count. It had a three-to-one chance for success. Nobody with a high-school education would find it difficult; in fact, it could be read by lowbrows, while being praised by intellectuals. Hemingway said that he was pleased to be published by Boni & Liveright, and he hoped that he would become one of the firm's regular authors, but he knew that a long-term association depended upon both of them.

Five days after Hemingway had accepted Liveright's offer,

he received a letter of inquiry from Maxwell Perkins of Scribner's.[11] Perkin's letter had been delivered to Hemingway in care of Sylvia Beach's bookstore in Paris, and its arrival had been delayed while the author was out of town. Hemingway wrote Perkins that he would have been happy to let the editor see the manuscript of *In Our Time*, but he had just signed a contract with Liveright to issue the book and giving the latter an option on Hemingway's next two works. The failure of Liveright to accept Hemingway's second book within sixty days after the manuscript had been received would mean that the publisher had relinquished this volume and forfeited his rights to the third. Should the opportunity ever present itself, Hemingway said, he would submit a book to Perkins. Indeed, Hemingway's friend F. Scott Fitzgerald suggested in his own letter to Perkins about the same time that if the new author became displeased with Liveright, he would join Scribner's.[12]

In June 1925, Hemingway received a letter from Liveright urging him to be on the look-out for new talent in Paris and direct it to Boni & Liveright.[13] Hemingway replied that he had only recently reached the point of getting *himself* a publisher, and as soon as he received enough money to look the part of a successful author, he might be better able to fulfill Liveright's request.[14]

In Our Time was published on October 5, 1925, in a modest edition of about thirteen hundred copies.[15] Its failure to sell can scarcely be attributed to Liveright or his handling of the book. The publisher had gotten Anderson, Hemingway's supporter, to write the catalogue description and a jacket blurb. Other comments on the jacket praising the volume were supplied by John Dos Passos, Waldo Frank, Edward J. O'Brien, and Gilbert Seldes. In addition to the enthusiasm for Hemingway's short stories among the readers in the office, Liveright himself looked upon the young writer as an exciting new gamble and probably lucrative investment.

In the meantime, Hemingway had completed *The Torrents of Spring*, which he promptly sent off to New York. In his covering letter of December 7, 1925, Hemingway explained to Liveright that his new book was not *The Sun Also Rises*, which he was rewriting, but a parody of Sherwood Anderson's current fiction.[16] In his opinion he (Hemingway) was a twentieth-century Fielding who had found his twentieth-century Richardson. He said *The Torrents of Spring* had been read and praised by Fitzgerald and Louis Bromfield, who thought it funny enough to become a classic American satire. The only reason Hemingway could imagine that Liveright might not accept the work was because it might offend Anderson. However, the young writer explained, it would be in the publisher's interest to differentiate between the older man and himself. Hemingway demanded certain guarantees: illustrations by Ralph Barton, who had done the drawings for *Gentlemen Prefer Blondes*; extensive advertising to compensate the author for the failure of *In Our Time* to sell; and a $500 advance, though he ought to ask for a $1,000 one. In closing, Hemingway asked for an immediate reply. He had other offers to consider, but he really wanted Liveright to publish *The Torrents of Spring*, because it was a very funny book and because its success would make them both a lot of money.

Three weeks later Hemingway had heard nothing from New York. He wrote Fitzgerald that he had no doubt *The Torrents of Spring* would be rejected by Liveright, since it satirized his current favorite and best-seller, Sherwood Anderson.[17] The popular view that Hemingway, with or without Fitzgerald's help, planned his satire deliberately as a contract-breaker—that is, on the assumption Liveright would refuse it solely for fear of offending Anderson and as a result Hemingway could move to Scribner's—appears somewhat unsound in view of Hemingway's hopeful, though heartily puffed up, description of his work and his later actions.[18] In any event, it is a most equivocal letter. If, by offering Liveright *The Torrents of Spring*, Hemingway was trying to break his contract, it seems a half-hearted attempt. Early in January 1926 came the cabled response: "REJECTING TORRENTS OF SPRING/PATIENTLY AWAITING MANUSCRIPT SUN ALSO RISES/WRITING FULLY."[19] Liveright's rejection of Hemingway's work was made after careful consideration, as the letter relating to this matter bears out. It is a model of firmness, restraint, and good sense:

> Your letter of December 7th came in a couple of weeks ago and practically everyone here in the office has read *Torrents of Spring* about which Scott Fitzgerald wrote us so enthusiastically.
> Really, old top, admitting that *Torrents of Spring* is a good

American satire, who on earth do you think would buy it? Entirely apart from the fact that it is such a bitter, and I might say almost vicious caricature of Sherwood Anderson, it is so entirely cerebral that it can't be compared with the humorous books of Don Stewart, Bob Benchley, etc. There are too few people in our benighted land interested in intellectual travesty to assure you of a sale of more than 700 or 800 copies for *Torrents of Spring*.

To get back to the Sherwood Anderson angle: it would be in extremely rotten taste, to say nothing of being horribly cruel, should we have wanted to publish it. Nevertheless, I feel that a publisher should keep an open forum and that it would be crueler to you not to publish a book we considered fine to protect one of our other authors. So you must understand that we are rejecting *Torrents of Spring* because we disagree with you and Scott Fitzgerald and Louis Bromfield and Dos Passos, that it is a fine and humorous American satire. We, of course, may be wrong, and when the book is published as possibly it will be by someone else, we may see how wrong we are. By we I mean T. R. Smith, Mr. Friede, Mr. Messner, Mr. Komroff, etc., etc.—everybody in our office to say nothing of two or three outsiders who have an entirely unprejudiced point of view, assuming that we might have one.

You say that you have made no kick about the way we handled *In Our Time*. The idea of the jacket of the book was considered by the trade as extremely valuable and was practically the only reason why the bookstores gave us any orders at all for a volume of short stories by a man whom they did not happen to know very well. You must realize that the little group in America that read some of your work in the highbrow magazines amounts to a very little in the sale of a book. That you should criticize our exploiting of *In Our Time* is ridiculous. You speak of the lack of advertising; because the book did not sell does not mean that we did not advertise it. The work we did and the money we spent in publicity before the book came out was considered unusually intelligent and aggressive. After the book came out and had its chance through the two or three advertisements we placed throughout the country, it was up to the reading public. They rejected *In Our Time* stupidly enough, but then they rejected Conrad for some 10 or 15 years, have been persistently rejecting other fine authors, some on our own list, and until we took over Sherwood Anderson, gave him a very lukewarm support. *In Our Time* will sell some day—after your first successful novel. We published *In Our Time* because we, more than any other publishers in New York, play for the long future. I am cabling you today to Austria as you requested.[20]

By rejecting *The Torrents of Spring*, Liveright had lost his option on *The Sun Also Rises*, and Hemingway was a free agent. During 1925 he had received inquiries from Scribner's, Knopf, and Harcourt, Brace.[21] Early in 1926 he left Paris for America determined to find himself another publisher. The way Hemingway had been carrying on, Fitzgerald confided to Perkins, sounded as though Liveright had been responsible for breaking up his home and doing him out of millions; actually, it was because Hemingway was young, far from New York, and knew nothing about publishing.[22] Hemingway arrived in New York on February 9 and went straight to Boni & Liveright, where he received a friendly reception from Friede, Smith, Edith Stern, and Liveright—who was gracious but firm in his rejection of *The Torrents of Spring*, but who still wished to issue Hemingway's new novel when it was completed.[23] Hemingway proceeded to Scribner's where Perkins offered him a $1500 advance on both works, and then to Harcourt to tell of the Scribner offer and see if Harcourt would do better. Harcourt declined, and Hemingway joined Fitzgerald as a Scribner's author.[24] By 1927 Liveright had come to regret his decision, and through his junior partner, Friede, offered Hemingway a contract that included advances of $3000 on any novel, $1000 on any volume of essays or stories, and the pledge to buy the rights to *The Torrents of Spring* and *The Sun Also Rises* from Scribner's preparatory to issuing them along with *In Our Time* in a uniform edition.[25] Completely satisfied with Scribner's, however, Hemingway declined the proposal; his association with Scribner's was to last the rest of his life.

During the same year that *Dark Laughter* appeared, establishing Anderson as one of Liveright's leading authors, and the short stories of Ernest Hemingway were issued at least partly on Anderson's recommendation, the older novelist sent his publisher a second obscure young writer, William Faulkner. Anderson had become acquainted with Faulkner in New Orleans. Impressed with Faulkner's talent, Anderson urged him to submit the manuscript of his first novel, *Soldier's Pay*, to Liveright in New York.[26] According to Faulkner, writing about his relationship with the older novelist thirty years later, Anderson is supposed to have told the young author that he would recommend the novel to Liveright if he—Anderson—did not have to read it.[27] Nevertheless, during June and July the book was read at the house; the readers stood two to one for acceptance, and Liveright decided to read it himself. He did not like it.[28] After Anderson continued to urge publication, Liveright gave in and accepted Faulkner's work for issuance the following spring.[29] By the time *Soldier's Pay* appeared, Faulkner and Anderson had had a falling out, but the latter continued to give the younger writer his support in correspondence with Liveright:

> I saw in the *New York Times* a very good review of the Faulkner novel. I hope you will have sales enough of this novel to encourage both Faulkner and yourself. I do not like the man personally very much, but I have a hunch on that he is a man who will write the kind of novels that will sell. He is modern enough and not too modern; also he is smart. If I were you, I would do what I could to encourage him to keep at work. If you want to do so, why don't you write him a letter telling him some of the things I have said about him, as it may buck him up, particularly if this first novel does not have much sale? You see what I mean. He may be a little bit like a thoroughbred colt who needs a race or two before he can do his best. He was so nasty to me personally that I don't want to write him myself, but would be glad if you were to do it in this indirect way, as I surely think he is a good prospect.[30]

In view of Liveright's reply, it appears that neither man cared for the Southerner:

> About Faulkner; I don't want to say much just yet. He's a peculiar man and my heart didn't warm to him when I met him here in New York. This doesn't mean we're not working very hard on his book and spending more in fact than we have on a first novel in a long time. But I don't want to write him a personal letter for a while. I want to wait until the sale gets to a certain point. Hang it all, he's not the man that I can write to frankly and intimately and whole-heartedly.[31]

In the end, the Liveright-Faulkner association lasted only a little longer than the publisher's connection with Hemingway. *Soldier's Pay* did not break even, but in spite of this Liveright accepted Faulkner's next novel and gave him a second advance.[32] *Mosquitoes*, issued in 1927, fared even more poorly than its predecessor.[33] To the publisher it meant both an increased financial loss and, more importantly, little reason to hope Faulkner would develop into a major writer with popular appeal.

The next manuscript Faulkner submitted to Liveright was a work entitled *Flags in the Dust*. While it met with a uniformly negative reaction from the readers at the house, there was a feeling that behind the disorder of the book lay great power.[34] It was finally decided that Louis Kronenberger should explain to Faulkner that to publish this work on the heels of his first two failures would be a mistake and that Kronenberger should propose that Faulkner put aside this manuscript, while accepting an advance to work on an entirely new book. Faulkner declined Kronenberger's proposal, and the association between Liveright and Faulkner was over. Two years later, a thoroughly rewritten *Flags in the Dust*, retitled *Sartoris*, was issued by Harcourt, Brace, and the first of Faulkner's Yoknapatawpha County novels was launched. While *Soldier's Pay* and *Mosquitoes* were scarcely representative of Faulkner's great talents, their publication by Liveright surely encouraged the young artist. A man is not always equipped with foresight, and had the publisher realized the potential of the young writer he might have made allowances and suppressed his personal feelings, but Liveright's flair did not extend that far.

Liveright's lists of the mid-Twenties seem remarkable today because they included so many major American novelists of the twentieth century, but there were some unusual volumes of poetry as well. In 1925, Boni & Liveright offered Richard Le Gallienne's *Anthology of American Poetry*, George Moore's *Anthology of Pure Poetry*, *The Collected Poems of H. D.*, and the first successful volume—*Roan Stallion, Tamar, and Other Poems*—by a relatively unknown poet named Robinson Jeffers. A packet of Jeffers' poems was rejected by Boni & Liveright in 1922, after it had also been declined by the Macmillan Company.[35] Discouraged by his inability to find a paying sponsor, Jeffers submitted a volume of his efforts, *Tamar and Other Poems*, to Peter G. Boyle of Greenwich Village, who printed five hundred copies of it at Jeffers' expense. Boyle, a printer, was enthusiastic about Jeffers' verse and unsuccessfully tried to place the volume with a regular publisher himself. First, Albert & Charles Boni followed by Thomas Seltzer refused it in 1924, and then Liveright rejected it once more in January 1925. While the poems were intense and rugged, Liveright wrote Jeffers, they did not contain sufficient beauty to merit publication. But after a very few, highly favorable reviews of the volume appeared in New York, Liveright reconsidered his earlier judgment.[36] At the urging of Maurice Hanline and Donald Friede in particular, Liveright wired Jeffers on June 12, 1925:

> AT EDITORIAL MEETING TODAY WE VOTED UNANIMOUSLY TO PUBLISH WITH YOUR APPROVAL ONE VOLUME THIS FALL CONTAINING ALL POEMS IN TAMAR AND ROAN STALLION FOR THREE DOLLARS/OFFER TEN PERCENT ON FIRST THREE THOUSAND AND FIFTEEN PERCENT THEREAFTER/CATALOGUE ABOUT GOING TO PRESS SO PLEASE WIRE ANSWER AND POSSIBLE NAME FOR VOLUME.[37]

Roan Stallion, Tamar, and Other Poems was the title Jeffers settled on. Later on in the fall he was alternately horrified to see his volume promoted like "baking-powder," then certainly pleased and surprised at its widespread reviews and its initial sale of over five thousand copies as well as the special limited edition of twelve copies Liveright produced for members of the firm and the poet.[38]

Following the successful publication of Jeffers' first volume with Boni & Liveright, Donald Friede seems to have become the poet's most regular correspondent at the firm.[39] The Jeffers-Friede association was cordial and lasting; in fact, Friede requested and was given several of the poet's verse manuscripts. On the whole, Jeffers' association with Boni & Liveright seems to have been a pleasant, though uneventful one. Jeffers' later works, *The Women at Point Sur* (1927), *Cawdor and Other Poems* (1928), and *Dear Judas and Other Poems* (1929) were all profitable publications for both the poet and his sponsor.[40] In 1931 Liveright visited Jeffers and his wife in Carmel, California.[41] After the firm went bankrupt in 1933, thirteen publishers tried to add Jeffers to their lists. The poet chose Random House, and Bennett Cerf took over his latest work, *Give Your Heart to the Hawks*—then in galley proofs at Liveright's—and issued it in 1933.[42]

By 1925 Hilda Doolittle had acquired considerable reputation both in the United States and in England. Liveright accepted her collected works for publication partly because of Pound's blessing and partly because the poetess' verse lent quality to a Boni & Liveright list.[43] *The Collected Poems of H. D.* sold well from the date of its appearance; it contained the major pieces from her earlier works, *Sea Garden, Hymen,* and *Heliodora.* Unlike her fellow poet, Jeffers, H. D.'s association with the firm lasted for only one volume, and her next work was issued by Covici-Friede.

With the exception of poets like Frost and Sandburg, individual works like *The Spoon River Anthology,* and poets whose verses have appeared regularly in college-textbook anthologies, the works of major twentieth-century poets have had no great popularity. Jeffers was the best-selling of Liveright's serious poets.[44] Although the publisher was to make a great deal of money on the humorous works of Dorothy Parker and Samuel Hoffenstein from 1927 to 1930, the verse of Kreymborg, Cummings, Pound, Dreiser, Anderson, and Hart Crane never achieved significant sales. Of all the true poets Liveright published perhaps the least successful was Crane.

In late December of 1916, sixteen-year-old Hart Crane left his home in Cleveland, Ohio, to begin a new life as a poet in New York.[45] His early poem, "C 33," had appeared in *Bruno's Weekly* earlier that fall.[46] It was ten years later that Boni & Liveright issued Crane's first small volume of verse, *White Buildings.* However, the young poet's first contact with the house occurred in 1919, when he was sent there by Padraic Colum to apply for a job as a proofreader.[47] He was not hired at Liveright's or at the other publishing houses where he applied, and he continued to eke out his living in various unsatisfactory ways. Meanwhile his poems had been and were appearing in little magazines both in the United States and abroad. By 1923 he had begun *The Bridge,* which he hoped to submit in completed form to Liveright, B. W. Huebsch, or Knopf to be issued along with his shorter verse in a collected edition of his writing. Waldo Frank, Eugene O'Neill, and Gorham Munson, Liveright authors, all encouraged him to proceed with his plan.[48] To his mother Crane wrote:

> Waldo Frank is very anxious for me to have that [*The Bridge*] finished, as he intends to take me up to his publisher (Boni & Liveright), and have me published in volume form. But, of course, such things *can't* be rushed as he understands.[49]

But Crane was unable to finish *The Bridge*, and the prospect of publication was delayed for a year. In 1924, Crane had decided to submit his work to Huebsch instead of Liveright, who was, in the poet's opinion, "pretty commercial and pettifogging."[50] Huebsch proved less interested in Crane's poetry and, temporarily at least, more interested in employing him as a personal assistant. Next, after the Huebsch job fell through, Crane was more than ever determined to be published in book form. In 1925 he finally found a printer, Samuel Jacobs of Polytype Press in Greenwich Village, who offered to issue *White Buildings* for $200, with his own services as compositor thrown in free.[51] But financial difficulties soon caused Jacobs to postpone his offer, and Crane's manuscript was refused first by Thomas Seltzer and then by Harcourt, Brace, who replied that they couldn't make anything out of most of the poems.[52] Then the siege of Liveright began. At Frank's urging, Liveright agreed to issue Crane's verse if O'Neill would consent to give the volume a boost by writing a short preface or foreword to it. Even with O'Neill's name and praise Crane apparently had no illusions regarding the difficulties of selling the work of a little-known poet:

> They have lost so much money on the better kind of poetry (which simply *doesn't* sell these days) that they want to hook the book up with an illustrous name and catch the public that way as much as possible. Gene is a good friend of mine and admires my work—I know that—but whether or not he feels like performing this favor I haven't yet heard. Frank thinks he can engineer the matter anyway—in time, but I don't know. He would gladly write the foreword himself if he thought his name would count sufficiently, and at any rate will write a whole page of praise for it in *The New Republic* when it comes out. This and other favorable reviews that I am sure to get from friends of mine ought to make quite a sensation for the book.[53]

Unfortunately, Crane was unable to contact O'Neill immediately, and though the playwright finally did agree to write the introduction, Liveright decided that he was no longer interested in the project.[54]

A loan from Crane's newly found patron, Otto Kahn, saw the poet through part of 1926, but *White Buildings* seemed destined to remain unpublished.[55] O'Neill wrote that there had been a misunderstanding: Liveright was not waiting for the playwright's foreword, but for additional poems from Crane.[56] On June 19, 1926, Crane, in low spirits, wrote to Frank about the fiasco:

> [O'Neill] knows that I have prepared in mss. all the poems which are to be included in the book and that all that can now hold it back is the lack of his foreword. It was hard for me to ask him to write such a thing for my book, and it has been harder and more embarrassing still for me to have kept trailing him with letters of urgence. . . . It's impossible for me [to] address him again on the subject. I'm sorry that what-ever-it-was made him feel constrained to promise the favor initially. It will be just as well for me to forget publishers for awhile, I think, though I can't forget how steadfastly you have persevered in helping me—whatever the results have amounted to.[57]

In the end the interest of Liveright's friend Kahn, in addition to the faithful support of O'Neill, Frank, and James Light (director of the Provincetown Playhouse and Liveright's own Broadway production, *Hamlet in Modern Dress*), caused the beleaguered publisher to reconsider his refusal, and he once more agreed to his original plan. Crane described how it happened:

> The way it came about is not without interest, About a month ago Liveright, Jimmy [Light] and others were at Otto Kahn's for a week-end. L[iveright] had the mss. with him at that time and on the boat coming back he said he had decided not to publish it—that he didn't care for the poems and so far as he could see nobody understood them. Then, a little over a week ago, Jimmy and O'Neill were in L[iveright]'s office on business and [my] mss. was on the table. Jimmy asked him if he had stuck to his decision and he said "Yes." Then Jimmy and Gene both told him they thought he would eventually be "proud" of having published [my] first volume, so that even if he did not care for the poems, as a publisher he was failing to take advantage of an opportunity. So finally L[iveright] came around to his old position of saying that he would publish them if Gene would write a preface. (Previously L[iveright] had said that he did not want to publish the poems at all—preface or no preface.) Gene protested some, saying that while he liked the poems he wasn't

at all sure he could tell why he liked them, that he was by no means a critic of poetry, and that L[iveright] was preparing a fine opportunity for him (O'Neill) to make a fool of himself. But finally it was decided that the preface would be written, L[iveright] phoned immediately to the printer and dictated the announcement. And I understand that the preface is already written and in L[iveright]'s hands.[58]

In reality O'Neill's introduction had not been composed, but the production of *White Buildings* moved along anyway. Crane wrote:

> It comes out sometime this fall. I have my contract and the $100 advance royalties. . . . O'Neill finally backed out on the foreword, as I thought he would. He's enthusiastic about my work, I've never doubted that, but he didn't have the necessary nerve to write what his honesty demanded—a thorough and accurate appraisal of my work. He can't write criticism, never has tried even, and I foresaw the panic that this proposal on the part of our mutual publisher would precipitate in his bosom. . . . None other than Allen Tate!, it seems, is to write the foreword. I was informed by my publisher of all this—along with the acceptance.[59]

With a critical introduction by Allen Tate and a jacket blurb by O'Neill, Hart Crane's *White Buildings* was finally issued in December 1926.[60] Crane recorded that his poems were greeted enthusiastically by reviewers in the *New York Times*, *New York Herald Tribune*, *Poetry*, *The Nation*, *The New Republic*, the *London Times*, but these good notices failed to sell many copies of his work.[61] Liveright's royalty statement to the poet showed that by April 1, 1929, out of an edition of five hundred copies, three hundred and seventy-eight had been sold, while one hundred and twenty-one had been sent out to reviewers.[62] The publisher's account did not reveal that many of the volumes he told Crane had been sold, and for which he had paid the poet royalties, had actually been remaindered.[63] It was simply the publisher's way of encouraging the young poet.

When Crane later requested publication of a second edition, Liveright asked Messner his opinion. Since the firm's loss on the first one had amounted to $200 (including Crane's advance), Messner's response was a simple "certainly not."[64] Nevertheless, Liveright ordered a second printing of two hundred fifty copies. Besides encouraging the poet in this way, the publisher sent him a $200 advance on *The Bridge*, which was finally issued in April 1930.[65] At the time of the poet's suicide in 1932, Crane's debt to Boni & Liveright had grown even larger.

Shortly after Crane's death, T. R. Smith wrote to the poet's mother:

> We should be very glad to publish next spring all that now remains of Hart's unpublished verses. Waldo Frank has kindly offered to put this material together and write an introduction to the volume. Perhaps his (Hart's) notes and writings which are now in your possession may be sufficiently interesting to add as an appendix to the book. He was a perfectly amazing human being and everything he said was of some importance.
>
> In so far as Hart's financial status is concerned he is $210 in debt to us on *The Bridge* and *White Buildings*, but this sum is being reduced gradually by permissions being granted for the use of different poems for use in various anthologies . . . [his] books won't earn much in the near future. I feel as a matter of understanding that the meaning of Hart's verse will not reach a large public for some years to come, although he has had immediate intellectual appreciation and will continue to do so.[66]

It was to be many years before the poetry of Hart Crane paid for itself, and that time was not to come during Liveright's lifetime or, for that matter, the lifetime of his firm.

An American Tragedy

Unlike serious poetry, which in this century has never been a particularly lucrative venture in trade publishing, novels make up a large part of most firms' lists. A writer of successful fiction represents a steady source of income to any house; as his reputation and popularity grow, his publisher enjoys larger profits. When Dreiser joined Boni & Liveright in 1917, he had already established himself as a major American author. Dreiser's early critics, who had held that his writings were crude, immoral, or both, while never completely silenced, had, by the mid-Twenties, been largely shouted down. Of the shouting voices, H. L. Mencken's was the loudest and most influential. Dreiser's stature as a writer, the respect in which Liveright held his work, and his value to a firm which had invested heavily in his potential popularity cannot be overestimated.

"[Where is] the big novel that is going to rub Sumner the wrong way?" Liveright wrote the author, as he awaited completion of what had been promised for so long.[1] Begun by Dreiser in 1920 and encouraged by Liveright through letter and check, *An American Tragedy* had been announced by Boni & Liveright for the fall of 1924, then the following spring, and finally for October 1925.

At the end of June 1925, the first bulky chapters of Dreiser's new novel began to arrive at the house. Liveright, Smith, and Komroff were all impressed by the promise of the work. As he was editing the novel, Smith wrote to the author: "I must tell you once again, Dreiser, that I have read the last five or six chapters of Book 2 with real agony. The slow, fatal working-up to the death of Roberta is one of the grimmest and most gripping tragedies that I have read in years. The whole idea was so powerful that I had difficulty in re-editing it for you. It is the tragedy of truth, expressed with the most skillful understanding and expression."[2]

Although he deferred to Dreiser in the end, in the beginning

Liveright was not happy about the title of the novel. Initially, the publisher wanted to call the work by the name of the protagonist; but when Dreiser stuck to Clyde Griffiths as the name of his central character, Liveright discarded the idea because Griffiths was too difficult to pronounce. Finally, Liveright urged Dreiser to change both the name of his main character and the title of the book to one he felt would be more commercial. "I feel I must once more implore you to call the book *Ewing* or *Warner* or some good representative name with the sub-title *An American Tragedy*. Commercial I may appear, but in the end it is you who will keep after me and after me if the book doesn't sell as well as you feel it should sell. Won't you think this over once more and let me know tomorrow, definitely, what to do."[3] But Dreiser steadfastly refused to make the change, and Liveright, influenced by Smith and Komroff, agreed to drop the issue. If the book succeeded, they reasoned, Dreiser would have accomplished it with that title; if the book failed, the responsibility for having changed the title would not be Liveright's, and Dreiser could not legitimately blame him for its failure.[4]

Once the matter of the title was settled, a new difficulty emerged. As the three men read the manuscript, it became apparent to them that it was much too long for publication in one volume.[5] It ran, in fact, to about four hundred thousand words after it had been cut from at least a million before its appearance at the house. Moreover, unless the novel were cut appreciably, it might run into more than two volumes. The price the firm would be forced to set on a three-volume novel would certainly lower its sales and perhaps cancel the profit. The only alternative was to cut *An American Tragedy* still further, and T. R. Smith undertook this final editing. After Smith, with Komroff's part-time assistance, had cut over fifty thousand words from the manuscript, he contacted Dreiser, uncertain of the response he would receive. According to Komroff, the following succinct exchange took place:

> "We are taking fifty thousand words out of *An American Tragedy*." Smith told the writer.
> "Who is we?" Dreiser replied.
> "Manuel and me."
> "OK. What the hell is fifty thousand words between friends?"

Apparently Dreiser was much less cavalier than this conversation suggests; almost immediately he insisted that over half of what Smith and Komroff had cut from the novel be restored.[6] Consequently, the published work amounted to about 385,000 words. With proofs to read and corrections to make, it became clear that October publication would not take place. Moreover, Dreiser wished to make extensive revisions, particularly on the section describing Clyde Griffiths' experience in the death house. It turned out, in fact, that the novelist even wished to visit Sing Sing to be certain he had achieved the proper realistic treatment. He made his visit and revised, and November passed. It was feared that the lateness of the novel would prevent it from having a good pre-Christmas sale, but at last, in mid-December, 1925, *An American Tragedy* was issued in a two-volume edition priced at $5.00 per set. Prepublication orders for over ten thousand sets appeared to promise Dreiser a popular recognition he had never received before. On the other hand, $5.00 a set was double the price of a standard, one-volume novel, so Liveright was taking a serious risk. He was also issuing a limited, signed edition of *An American Tragedy* at $12.50—a great gamble too, on a work that had yet to be received by the public.[7] The publisher was counting on Dreiser's first new novel in ten years to be a sensation. It was. On January 9 Smith wired the author:

THE REVIEWS ARE AMAZING, ENTHUSIASTIC, AND DIGNIFIED/YOUR POSITION IS RECOGNIZED/THE SALES ARE EXCELLENT[8]

During its first full year in print, plus about two weeks in 1925, *An American Tragedy* sold over fifty thousand sets.[9] Dreiser's royalties amounted to $47,647.53, and the success of his new novel—along with a $10,000 advertising campaign by Liveright—had, as expected, boosted the sales of his old novels to over twelve thousand copies during the same time.[10]

Nineteen twenty-six was a remarkable year in the Liveright-Dreiser association. During this period a successful adaptation of *An American Tragedy* was produced by Liveright on Broadway; Dreiser sold the silent screen rights of his novel to Jesse L. Lasky of Paramount Famous Players for $80,000 (he sold the sound rights for $55,000 more in 1931) ;[11] and the author signed a new contract with Boni & Liveright guaranteeing him, among other things, $500 a month and weekly advertisements promoting his work in the *New York Times*. Finally Dreiser, who had paid $40.17 to the Internal Revenue Service two years before, became, in 1926, a corporation in order to conserve his income. Despite this action he appears to have paid nearly $5,500 to the government in 1926.[12] Of course, the total sales of *An American Tragedy* for 1926 never approached those of such books as *Beau Geste* and *Show Boat* during the same time; still for Dreiser and Liveright it was a triumph. But instead of establishing trust and goodwill between publisher and author, the enormous success of *An American Tragedy* served to alienate them.

Although neither was aware of it at the time, the difficulties began with Liveright's desire to produce a dramatization of *An American Tragedy* on Broadway. The publisher's choice for writing the adaptation was Patrick Kearney, a young actor-playwright whose play, *A Man's Man*, had had a limited success in New York during 1924.[13] Early in March 1926 Liveright wrote Dreiser about his production plans.

> Patrick Kearney was out to New Rochelle yesterday afternoon, stayed for tea, all evening, all night, and came in with me this morning.
>
> I think that Kearney and I took up at least a dozen different scene plans for the play and about 1:30 this morning, after much discussion and difference of opinion, finally decided on a scenario in four acts and twelve scenes which I think is just about as fine as anyone will ever arrive at on this play. I'm honestly bubbling over with enthusiasm about it. I like very much two scenes which Kearney has already written in the rough.
>
> I am perfectly willing now to make a contract with you and Kearney to produce the play in early autumn on the basis of what Kearney has drawn up with me. . . . As I told you in the office the other day, I have two of the best actors in America who will sign contracts to play in *An American Tragedy* providing I can assure them right away that the play will be produced. Otherwise, they will, undoubtedly, get other engagements because they are very much in demand. Glenn Hunter is, unquestionably, the only Clyde Griffiths. No one can compare with him. I wouldn't even at the same price swop him for John Barrymore. June Walker makes an idea Roberta. It is true that they both get big salaries, but that's my money and my worry, not anyone else's.

I made excellent terms with Kearney. He is willing to take 45% of the royalties instead of 50%, and on the motion picture end of it he will take as little as 35% of what you get, instead of the usual 50%. You know, of course, that the producer of the play always gets 50% of the motion picture rights. I'm frank to say that my deal with him on the motion picture rights doesn't mean so very much because it's extremely doubtful that *An American Tragedy* can even be done on the screen. Tremendous pressure would have to be brought on Hays to let him pass it, and then the theme is such that it's rather unlikely that any company who would make a good picture out of it would care to go on it.

Well, old boy, I've worked pretty hard, and quick on this, and I think things are in fine shape. Will you call me up tomorrow morning and let me know if you can have lunch with me, or what time tomorrow you'll see me so that we can get the thing in shape to go ahead with it? Naturally, I wouldn't expect you to sign a contract with me unless I give you the usual advance and guarantee against the option to produce it this year.[14]

Within the week the publisher sent his author a contract covering the rights of production accompanied by a letter of explanation.

I'm enclosing two copies of the contract which I have signed and which Mr. Kearney will explain to you at full length.

You will note that I am giving you, too, an advance of $1500 against the usual advance of $500 to $1000. You will further note that the scale of royalties I am giving you is better than the usual one . . . I am taking only 45% of various rights instead of 50%.

The clause regarding the motion picture rights I think covers everything that we talked about. When I first dictated this clause, I specified that I was to receive 1/3 of these rights in case the play ran for ten weeks in New York to an average business of $12,500, or better. However, I don't want to hold up the contract because I feel that if it is not signed before I go to Cincinnati, that we will be in great danger of losing Glenn Hunter and June Walker who are being approached on all sides for parts in the fall. I have left this whole matter to the arbitration of John Emerson, present President of the Actors' Equity Association, who frequently acts in matters of this kind. Emerson is an author himself whose plays have been produced in New York and he understands the business inside out.[15]

Through the interest of his friends, Jesse Lasky and Walter Wanger of Famous Players, Liveright soon learned that more than one Hollywood studio was indeed interested in the possibilities of Dreiser's novel as a movie. The prospect of its appearance as a play may have increased their enthusiasm. Accordingly, on the morning of March 19, 1926, Liveright and Dreiser met in the publisher's office and signed the contract for the production of the play. The publisher had already arranged to meet Lasky and Wanger for lunch at the Ritz-Carlton to talk about the possibilities of a motion-picture version of *An American Tragedy*, and he invited Dreiser to come along, unwittingly gathering together the principals for an impromptu drama.[16]

That morning, when he signed the contract with Dreiser to produce a stage version of the novel, Liveright agreed to waive any percentage due him as Dreiser's agent from the sale of the film rights, if they were sold before the play was presented and totaled $30,000 or more. Furthermore, on the way to the Ritz from the office, Liveright asked Dreiser if the author planned to "take care" of him at lunch. Dreiser answered affirmatively, and Liveright later recalled that the writer had promised him everything over $60,000 that the rights brought. Apparently Liveright entered the Ritz dining room with Dreiser believing that the author, now flush with success after so many lean years, would repay his publisher's generous sponsorship with a sizeable share of the proceeds from the sale. Liveright hoped for as much as a half or a third of the profits. Then, during the luncheon with Lasky and Wanger, when Liveright stated that the price of the movie rights to *An American Tragedy* was $100,000, to be split between author and agent 70-30, Dreiser smiled but said nothing. Liveright next excused himself and left the table so that the three remaining men could settle on a price and conclude the bargain without the presence of the agent who had brought them together and who, of course, expected to share in the proceeds.

For his part, Dreiser apparently always believed that the luncheon at the Ritz had been staged by Liveright in order to cheat him. Dreiser's characteristic attitude toward Liveright had been one of suspicion: perhaps because Liveright was a publisher who was too flamboyant for Dreiser's taste, perhaps because of Dreiser's anti-

Semitism perhaps because of Dreiser's personality. However, Dreiser, whether he planned to or not, seems to have given the publisher the very definite impression that he would receive a handsome reward when the sale was completed even though Dreiser himself believed that Liveright was trying to cheat him. Once Liveright mentioned the selling price, the proposed split, and left the table, Dreiser, Lasky, and Wanger began to dicker. Verbally they settled on $90,000 with $80,000 going to Dreiser and $10,000 to Liveright. The publisher returned and was told of his $10,000 share on a $90,000 deal. He immediately protested to Dreiser that the author had promised to take care of him, that he had been assured that he would receive everything over $60,000 or 30 per cent of the final price. Dreiser replied that he had made Liveright no explicit promise at all. "You're a liar!" Liveright asserted. Dreiser leaped up and commanded Liveright to rise. When the publisher remained seated, Dreiser hurled a cup of hot coffee in his face and walked out.

One of the problems in this story is that Liveright seems to have forgotten he was dealing with Dreiser, not one of his easier authors. Also, it seems clear that the publisher truly felt he had earned this cash after so many years of advances and concessions. The letters of Liveright and Dreiser on this matter indicate the major sources of confusion and a good deal about the thoughts and actions of each man, although they by no means clarify the affair completely. Dreiser initiated the correspondence.

> The facts connected with the *American Tragedy*-movie transaction are a little too drastic to be dismissed with a "sorry." I feel that I am entitled to a written apology based on the facts and the following are the facts.
> You will recall that just before leaving your office at noon of that day [March 19, 1926, is the date on the contract] in order to meet Mr. Lasky and Mr. Wanger I had signed a contract with you for the dramatization by Patrick Kearney of *An American Tragedy*. A very vital part of that contract reads as follows.
>> "In consideration of the fact that *An American Tragedy* is a play made from a successful novel written by Theodore Dreiser, the manager (Horace B. Liveright) agrees that the terms on the division of the motion picture rights shall be as follows:

No share of the motion picture rights is to be received by the Manager, providing *that before the date of production* (of this dramatization) *the picture rights shall have been sold by Theodore Dreiser for a sum of $30,000 or more."*

You will also recall that in a supplementary clause or letter to a four-year general publishing agreement dated Jan. 1, 1923 between yourself and myself, it is stipulated that in case you, as agent, should at any time sell or cause to be sold for dramatic or picture purposes any one of my books, you were entitled to a commission of ten percent. Yet in arranging for the dramatization of this play by Mr. Kearney you were anxious to exact from me a half and latterly 30 per cent of the moving picture rights of the book before production, regardless of whether the play planned by you was a success or not. When I took exception and refused to allow that the clause above quoted was inserted.

Now preliminary to your remarks at the luncheon—and to which I took and still take most violent exception, I wish you to recall that before I had signed the above contract between yourself, Mr. Kearney and myself, you were urgent in your assurances that the moving picture rights could not be sold for more than $35,000; that you had consulted with Mr. Lasky about this book; that he was not interested in the least and could not be until you had explained to him that you were about to do it as a play—whereupon he had said that only in case it should be done as a play would he be interested. Also that I should be glad to get $35,000 and that if I would accept that sum you still might be able to close with him. Afterwards, however,— but only afterwards, and after I had exacted that until the play had been produced and proved a success and not before—should you claim a third interest in the moving picture rights (feeling from the start that I could sell the book as it was without a play being made from it), and had then signed the contract, was it that you announced that what you had said concerning Lasky's attitude was not true—that, as a matter of fact, he was anxious then and there to sign for the rights without waiting for the play and that for three days he had been trying to get in touch with me (which, afterwards, Mr. Lasky himself confirmed), and that for that same day at one o'clock you had an appointment with him at the Ritz to discuss terms—yet apparently without consulting me. You also said that if I would go along and would take a determined stand in regard to such price as I might have in mind he would pay it, you were sure.

Then and only then was it that you asked what I really would take—and I said $100,000 and gave you my reasons for it, although you personally suggested $60,000. You then and there agreed that if I would go to the luncheon and affirm my determination to take no less that you were sure Mr. Lasky would pay it. And then and then only was it—and that in the face of just having tried to get me to sell for $35,000 (and also in the face of the agreement just drawn and signed in which you waived any interest in the proposed sale price) you announced that I was "to take care of you"; that you were sure I would; but just how you did not say. And only when I finally inquired what you meant by "take care of you" you announced that I should take 70 per cent of whatever was paid and you 30—at which— in view of the contract just signed and the sharp practice so openly confessed, I merely smiled—said nothing at all. Later, on the way over, and to your assertions that you were sure that I would take care of you, I merely replied that I would do so. But certainly not according to your proposed division since by the clause inserted in the contract before it was signed, and which is quoted above, this had been excluded. There was no such thought in my mind at any time.

Now let us be quite frank. In view of what took place in your office and that luncheon afterwards, I consider that I have been most outrageously insulted and sharply dealt with into the bargain. Neither commercially or socially have I ever lied to you. On the contrary I have been of immense commercial and literary aid to you and you know that. From time to time you have talked bravely of what you would like to do for me. I have just clearly seen what you would like to do for me. And I shall not soon forget it.

But to return to this matter of that luncheon. When at the table at the Ritz—before Mr. Lasky and Mr. Wanger—you announced that it was agreed between yourself and me that you were to have 30 per cent and I 70, you know that you were lying. I had not said so. As I explained to Mr. Lasky and Mr. Wanger then and there—it was all news to me. Next, when later you announced that I had agreed to sell the movie rights for $60,000 and that you knew that I would double-cross you—you were lying. I had no intention of double-crossing you—was actually seeking to persuade them to pay you fifteen or twenty thousand and finally did insist on the $10,000 you are about to receive. It is due to my insistence and to none other. Get that straight.

Under the circumstances the least that can be done or accepted by me is that you acknowledge these facts either in writing or by OK-ing this letter. I have done you no wrong. I have merely protected myself against you who have insisted over and over that you were seeking to protect me.[17]

Liveright wrote two letters in reply; in the first, March 26, 1926, he explained his own position:

> So far as your letter is concerned about our quarrel, I think the less said the better. I can only say that about two or three weeks ago, Jesse Lasky and I walked out of this office and up the street to The Crillon and at that time he told me he wasn't the slightest bit interested in *An American Tragedy* for the pictures, and although even then I wanted it very much for a play, I rather shared his point of view. To my best recollection, both you and I had several drinks before we left the office and walked around the corner to have lunch at the Ritz with Lasky and Wanger. They had no idea until I telephoned Lasky (I think in your presence) that you were coming along. It was no "set up." I may have had too much to drink—you could decide upon this, but at any rate my memory is that you told me all over $60,000 was mine. When I asked $100,000, $70,000 for you and $30,000 for me, I thought you were pleased; at least you made no comments to the contrary. Please again believe that there was no price mentioned between me and Lasky, and that there was no staging of this affair. I left the table thinking that when I came back you would have gotten the $100,000, which would have let me in for $30,000. I left the table so that you might speak unconstrainedly. Well, at any rate, you got $80,000 which I think is the top price for all time. I congratulate you on it, but still I think, considering what I did in the matter, unobtrusive as it may have seemed, I was entitled to $20,000. True, I should never have been able to do anything at all if you had not written a great book, but the fact remains that it was my engineering of sentiment through my conversations with Lasky and through my eagerness to purchase the play rights that made the motion picture rights to *An American Tragedy* seem to be eminently desirable. After all, in spite of my absolute loyalty to the Famous Players, I played the cards for you. My paramount desire was to see that you got everything possible out of this book. You don't think that my buying the producing rights made any difference. I assure you that this factor made quite a difference. I think that when we talk things over, I can convince you of it.

In the second letter, April 2, 1926, Liveright capitulated to Dreiser's demand for an apology:

I have had a long talk with Friede since his luncheon with you yesterday. It's a darn shame that now that fortune is, after so many years, spilling gold into your lap, instead of merely reaffirming its pronouncement of many years, that you are our great literary figure, that what has happened between us should have arisen. These are the days when we should be riding around together in band-wagons with champagne flowing and beautiful slave girls fanning us with peacock feathers.

You are proud and I am proud but as Friede has said to me again how deeply hurt you feel at what I said at the table at The Ritz that day, my appreciation of your feeling overcomes my pride, and I want you to know how sorry I am, that no matter what might have provoked my display of temper, I should not have said what I did. One gentleman should not talk this way to another, particularly in front of comparative strangers. So I hope you will accept my apologies.

If you like, I should be very glad to send a copy of this letter to Mr. Lasky and Mr. Wanger, or possibly we might all have lunch again some day and close the incident, because, Dreiser, the incident should be closed so that as we work along together in the future, it doesn't prove a thorn in the flesh of either of us. I want to make a tremendous success of my production of *An American Tragedy* and must count on you to help me in this in many ways.

We are planning another comprehensive advertising schedule on *An American Tragedy*, I having received permission from Famous Players to speak about the sale of the picture rights to them at one of the highest prices on record. I hope that this sort of advertising will help the book reach a new audience. The advertising manager of the Famous will be over here at 3 o'clock to talk to Mr. Schneider so that we can work intelligently together on advertising and promotion. In our new campaign for the book, we mean to stress not all your books, though we will say we are publishing them all, but we want to take five of them and feature them, closely watch results, and see just what this campaign does in the way of sales increase for the particular books featured. Let me assure you that I, personally, am going to write the copy and closely supervise the campaign.

While it is clear from their letters that neither Dreiser nor Liveright really understood the other's position—or, perhaps, was willing to understand it—it soon became apparent to Liveright that Dreiser was ready to quit him once more. In a long letter to the author on June 1, 1926, the publisher outlined a new proposal he offered to the writer which was to replace their 1923 agreement.

> Over the Decoration Day holiday, we have had time to very carefully consider our past, present and possible future relationships with you.
>
> The crux of the matter seems to be that you have been fairly well satisfied with the way we have handled your books, and so far as *An American Tragedy* is concerned, have been thoroughly pleased with our exploitation of it. *An American Tragedy* and the reprint of *The "Genius"*, as you know, are the only opportunities you have given us to really lay ourselves out. We have sold aproximately 30,000 copies of *The "Genius"* at $3.00 a copy which we claim could only have been done by intelligent and aggressive advertising and general exploitation and sales methods. *An American Tragedy,* a two-volume book selling for $5.00 is now approaching the 30,000 mark. . . . This represents a sale since publication date of about 15,000 sets. Our advance sales of nearly 15,000 sets was considered phenomenal by the book-trade. You can prove this by talking to such people as Mr. Margolies of Brentano, Fred Hood of Baker and Taylor Company, etc., etc. I am enclosing a sheet of the sales of your books since we have had them with us. We feel that no firm could have sold as many copies as we did of *The Color of a Great City.* In this particular instance, it may interest you to know that we lost, not counting any overhead expenses, considerably over $1000 because we advertised it so generously.
>
> Of course your propositions from Harper & Doubleday are extraordinary ones. It would be foolish for us to consider that you will remain with us unless we convince you that staying with us will, in the long run, prove profitable to you. I think that you admitted, yourself, on Friday morning, that no publishing firm can pay you your present royalties, do a lot of advertising, and then give you either a part or all of the profits that your books may make. Of course, if they advertise outrageously, there will be no profits for you to get. They may do this advertising, which all of us honestly think will hurt the Dreiser reputation, rather than help it, for a stated period of time, and then after that they may get a bit sick of their bargain and decide to do very little advertising. Frankly, Dreiser, I think you would make a big mistake in tying up for ten years with anyone except Boni & Liveright. You have been with us; you know

what we can do, what a fine, intelligent organization we have, and how tremendously we have grown in the last few years. I should say that our organization is more solidly established than almost any other publishing house in New York City, and that we are distinctly on the up-grade. But, even assuming all of this for ourselves, I think it would be a mistake for you to make as long a contract as ten years with us.

Our idea is that you should sign up with us for three years with a renewal of two years on the following basis: In the fall of 1927, we launch the limited edition of the "great Dreiser set" (in this connection I make the assertion that we can sell this limited edition better than anyone else in the country and that you will make more money on it through us than through anyone else in the country). It will take a year to properly market this set, which brings us to the fall of 1928; or, roughly speaking, this brings us to the end of the three year term. Then if by that time we have paid you full royalties for the sale of the entire set, you are to renew the contract with us for two years, giving us the opportunity to conduct a huge mail-order campaign on "the library edition of Theodore Dreiser" printed from the same plates as the limited edition. I should say then, that if at the end of this two year renewal term, we have not proven to you that we are as able merchandisers as any concern in the country, you should, of course, leave us.

So far as the regular Dreiser books are concerned, entirely apart from the question of sets, we feel that up to the publication of *An American Tragedy*, we did everything that was possible from a sane, business standpoint to make the name of Dreiser well known and the books of Dreiser popular. Now, of course, things have changed because of the phenomenal success of *An Amerian Tragedy*.

Our books will show you that our advertising expenditure on this set has been most generous. We will agree, though, that we will spend on this one book, *An American Tragedy*, during the balance of this year, a sum not less than $10,000. We, furthermore, agree that if during the course of the renewal of our contract with you, you give us a full length novel to publish, we will spend on it, in advertising, a sum equal to that spent on *American Tragedy* in proportion to its retail price.

As regards your general books, both the new and those we now have on our list, we believe that the plans we want to talk over with you regarding institutional advertising, so to speak, (meaning Theodore Dreiser as an institution) will greatly please you. Please believe,

Dreiser, that too much money spent in advertising is going to react immediately against you and make you instead of what Harper, I believe, said, they were going to make you, America's greatest author, which you are, an author more in a class with some whom we could mention, who are supposed to contribute largely to their own advertising campaigns. You whose sense of essential values is so keen and so just can quickly appreciate the point that we have just made.

When you were here the other day we suggested that you become a member of our Board of Directors. You quite properly said that would be a fine thing for Boni & Liveright, but not such a fine thing for Theodore Dreiser. This would have placed upon your shoulders part of the responsibility for the running of the whole business. Intead of doing this, I would suggest that we put in our new agreement a stipulation that there is to be a monthly meeting between you and our sales, editorial and advertising staffs, at which meeting you are to give your views and plans regarding advertising and publicity for your books and your name, we on our part to present all of our plans to you for your approval or disapproval. In this way you truly become a contractual partner so far as your own work here is concerned.

You made some remarks about wanting to feel a sense of absolute security in renewing any contract with us. Whatever security you want, we will gladly embody in our contract. It is up to you, of course, to tell us what this security would consist of. I realize that you favor a ten year contract because it would take the matter of the business end of your books off your mind for that length of time. Naturally, we would be happy to make this ten year contract. I still say, though, that I think your best interests are served in making a shorter term contract.

P.S. In reading this letter, it has occurred to me that something else of great importance to you has been omitted. In the fall of 1927 we will issue a one volume $3.00 edition of *An American Tragedy*. The advertising appropriation for this edition will, of course, be a large one. Besides that, there would be the normal appropriations for such books of yours as we would issue each season, so that the total advertising on all your books will, unquestionably, pretty closely approximate, and, possibly, exceed some of the figures mentioned to you by other publishers as being extremely large.

P.P.S. It goes without saying that our books are always open to the inspection of you or any of your agents, as they always have been.

Liveright immediately submitted a formal contract to Dreiser which embodied the main points in his letter.[13] The contract was to remain in effect until 1932. In addition, there were provisions to give the author a $500 per month drawing account, to advertise Dreiser or one or more of his books each week in the *New York Times Book Supplement* and to extend this institutional Dreiser promotion to other papers and other cities if it proved successful, and finally, to initiate steps to make the writer a director of Boni & Liveright. It is hardly surprising that Dreiser signed immediately and remained a Liveright author.

Having settled with his recalcitrant writer, Liveright turned his attention in the fall to the stage production of *An Amercian Tragedy*. Glenn Hunter and June Walker proved unavailable for the leading roles; nevertheless, with a cast that included Frank Morgan as Asa Griffiths, Miriam Hopkins as Sondra Finchley, Morgan Farley as Clyde, and Katherine Wilson as Roberta, the Liveright production opened on Broadway on October 11, 1926.[19] The Liveright flair worked once more. Worried by the competition of a Theater Guild production scheduled to premiere on the same night, Liveright and his theatrical manager, Louis Cline, hired a seventy-five man claque to appear at their opening applauding and shouting vociferously.[20] The critics fell for the trick, and the next morning, while they had some reservations about the play, they duly reported that it had elicited cheers and an ovation from the audience. Dreiser himself was pleased with Kearney's work and was moved by the production. Donald Friede, who took the novelist to see the play, later reported that Dreiser would not talk during intermission, but just sat in his chair in silence. Only after the curtain fell on the death-cell scene did he speak. With tears in his eyes, Dreiser said, "The poor boy! The poor bastard! What a shame!"[21]

The costs of mounting so large a production as *An American Tragedy* were high, and Liveright actually made very little profit during its 216 performances on Broadway. Of course he had also failed to clear as much as he thought he deserved when he helped Dreiser sell the movie rights of the book to Hollywood. Apparently, *An American Tragedy* brought the publisher more prestige than cash.

In 1926 Liveright was involved in presenting two other plays: *The Best of Us* and *Black Boy*. Liveright's first effort, *The Best of Us*, was a total disaster and closed out of town. Later, the publisher wrote to Francis Hackett about this play and about his equally unprofitable speculation in the stock market.

> I'm too lazy to write you about the business. Publishing has been pretty good. I haven't produced anything since my terrible flop in March with *The Best of Us*, which cost me over $25,000, but I have three plays and possibly more that I'm putting on in the fall and winter. Just where I'm going to get the money for all of them I don't know, but somehow or other I do seem to get it when I have to. The stock market has been a little better. I got terribly burnt in that, you know, because my friend Otto wanted to make a millionaire of me. I may have written you about this before. At the present figures I'm only out about $10,000 or $15,000 whereas at one time I was out almost $50,000. Believe me when I can get out whole I'm through with Wall Street for a while at least.[22]

On July 23, 1926, Liveright received the title and decoration of Officier d'Academie from Maxime Mongendre, the French Consul-General of New York.[23] Liveright was the first American publisher to receive the honor conferred on behalf of the Ministers of Public Instruction and Fine Arts in France; it was given him in recognition of the work he had done to popularize French authors in America. While the recognition undoubtedly pleased Liveright, it was of less importance than his financial status which seems to have worsened significantly. In the course of a letter to a friend Liveright asked, "Can you suggest how I can make $250,000 in a hurry? I need it."[24]

The publisher must have secured part of the quarter million he said he needed, for on October 6, 1926, his first fall production opened on Broadway. This was *Black Boy*, a play about a Negro boxer by Frank Dazey and James Tully, and featured Paul Robeson in the leading role.[25] Robeson, who had already become nationally known as an actor and who had appeared as the Emperor Jones in London, seemed like a sure bet to carry this otherwise mediocre vehicle, and determined to appease the critics as well as avoid antagonizing the audience, Liveright hired a Negro actress to play opposite Robeson in a part that had been originally intended for a white performer.[26] The drama received only lukewarm reviews, however, and closed after thirty-seven performances.

The premiere of *An American Tragedy* followed the *Black Boy* opening by only five days, and after this Liveright was out of Broadway production for nearly a year. In February 1927, however, he prepared to go to Europe in search of best-sellers and dramatic hits. To a friend he wrote about his noncommercial activities:

> You have no idea how ridiculously busy I have been and I don't believe that Rome was ever madder than New York is now when it comes to the question of parties. People nowadays aren't content with telephoning or writing to ask you places, they send telegrams and special messengers. Soon I believe they'll employ carrier pigeons. This afternoon, for example, there are four cocktail parties to which I have been invited. And fool that I am I guess I'll go to all of them.[27]

About the same time the publisher discovered that a heavy investment in International Combustion Corporation stock was proving very costly, for instead of increasing in value after Liveright bought it, it began to decline. Liveright's broker urged him to hold on to it and predicted that it would rise, but a wiser business associate advised him to get out of the market entirely.[28] He said that the broker's judgment had proved faulty in the past, and the market was putting too great a strain on the publisher physically and economically. The man who gave Liveright this sound advice, which the publisher ignored, was Alfred Wallerstein, the same man who ran the advertising agency where Liveright and Albert Boni first met. Throughout the Twenties, Wallerstein's agency held the Boni & Liveright advertising account, and it was Wallerstein, apparently, to whom Liveright turned repeatedly, first for advice and later for additional capital.

Liveright returned from Europe with various projects, but *Dracula* by John Balderston and Hamilton Deane was the only play he optioned there that he ever produced. He needed money and first he tried to gain the backing of an heiress.

> I'm taking Delphine Dodge Cromwell out tonight. She is a

rather attractive married woman and an only daughter of the late Mr. Dodge of Dodge Brothers fame. I think she's got ten millions or more but she's very intelligent and shrewd and it would be hard to get her to back any play; that's my game tonight.

Everything I've done in the market since I got back to New York has been pretty bad. I sold 500 shares of Baldwin Locomotive short trying to make the price of a $3000 automobile. To make a long story short, the darn thing cost me $13,000. International Combustion closed tonight at 47, Colorado Fuel at 95. You can imagine how sweetly I feel about it all.[29]

Mrs. Cromwell was not immediately interested in Liveright's ventures, for on July 28, 1927, the publisher telegraphed Wallerstein to ask for an $8000 loan to cover a note coming due to his wife. Early the next month Liveright wrote a long letter to Wallerstein touching on most of the major facets of his life.

I have been meaning to write to you since I sent you the wire about the $8000. Thanks ever so much for your loan which will only be needed for a very few days. You know I wouldn't have asked you for it unless it was a question of very temporary assistance, because I realize you want to keep yourself in liquid shape. Of course I heartily approve of this.

Let me take up my life since I've seen you last, subject by subject.

Publishing business: Since I saw you last, Bennett Cerf and Dick Simon asked me to put a price on the business, Bennett having offered me $250,000 and I believe that he could be gotten to pay $300,000. I wrestled with my soul a good deal and I have come to the definite conclusion that publishing is a pretty fine vocation, that there is lots of chance of doing good in it, and that with proper management, while we won't make a fortune, I should have a good steady safe income here. I am getting no younger and if I cut adrift from publishing, it might not have a good spiritual effect on my life. I've let everyone around the office know that and I'll see that the publishing world at large learns it too. I'm thinking pretty much now in publishing terms, although, of course, the theatre does occupy some of my time and thoughts. When you get back I'll tell you about an idea I have for you becoming a director of the company.

Producing: The casting of *Dracula* is coming along nicely and we go into rehearsal on the 29th for three weeks, then a week on the road, three days lay-off for patching up, 3 more days out of town, and then opening in New York October 3rd. . . . Contracts have been signed all around on the musical version of *The Firebrand*, the title of which will be *The Dagger and the Rose*. . . . As you know, putting a musical comedy together means a lot of work, and although we don't open in New York until Christmas week, we are already doing quite a little on it.

The stock market: In spite of the tremendous bull movement, my stocks have done very little as you know. I have a profit on my 600 Hudson but intend to hold it for par or over but I am following it up with stock orders so I can't fail to make some profit. My Chicago and Great Western Preferred is a dog. Combustion has acted pretty well the last couple of days . . . it may be in the long pull, I'll make a great deal of money on it if I can hold it. I am watching my account very carefully and although I am still bullish on the market, I think it's a dangerous one.

Life and habits: I have really not been quite as good as I should be since I saw you last. I have been mixing up a little too much with Delphine Dodge's Long Island crowd, and they are pretty heavy drinkers and I have been having too many parties at my apartment and at their places. If it weren't for the lure of the game which even ascetic you may understand, I'd cut them all out and I guess I will soon. Of course, it's possible that I may be shot or beaten up before I decide to quit. . . . This week-end I'm taking a crowd down to Otto Kahn's; Heywood Broun, Tom Smith . . . Dorothy [Peterson] and some girls you don't know. I always love his acres and I am amused at the vast elegance of his menage, but I'd rather go up to Storm King with Dorothy which I think we'll do the week following.[30]

Two Censorship Trials

In 1928, Maxwell Bodenheim's *Replenishing Jessica* plunged Liveright into probably the most outrageous court case of his publishing career. Four years earlier Bodenheim had approached Liveright for a loan.[1] He was working on a novel, he said, and needed additional funds not only to finish it but to live. The publisher agreed to pay him $1,000 in twenty weekly installments of $50 each, even though he did not know the contents of the proposed work. When Liveright received Bodenheim's manuscript early the following year, he read it and found it to be clearly obscene. Calling in the writer, the publisher and Smith discussed with him what should be deleted. At first Bodenheim claimed artistic license for his creation, but finally relented when Liveright told him the book was not of sufficient literary merit to fight over and that he refused to argue about its contents. *Replenishing Jessica*, the story of a girl for whom the simple feat of keeping her legs crossed was a behavioral impossibility, was the first novel by Maxwell Bodenheim that he had ever issued, and, Liveright vowed, it would be the last.

As soon as the story of Jessica and her ceaseless struggles to fulfill herself appeared in June 1925, the New York Society for the Suppression of Vice, led by John Sumner, brought the novel, its author, its editor, and its publisher before the New York Grand Jury on charges of obscenity. The Jury quickly decided that Bodenheim, Smith, and Liveright had violated the Penal Law by "unlawfully manufacturing, preparing, selling, and giving away copies of *Replenishing Jessica*."[2] A few hours later Smith and Liveright with their lawyers, James J. Walker and Arthur Garfield Hays, appeared before Judge Rosalsky in General Sessions court to enter pleas of not guilty and to be released on bail pending trial. That evening the publisher announced that "the indictment would be fought to the finish," that Bodenheim was "a great author and poet," and that the novel was both highly moral and of literary significance. Unaccountably, motions to bring publisher and writer to trial were not made at that time. In fact, it was not until March 1928, nearly three years later, that the case was prosecuted. Following the Grand Jury verdict, Liveright had withdrawn the book. The only reason it ever made news again was directly due to the publisher's dedicated fight against censorship of all kinds.[3] Bodenheim's novel was not, however, the work he wished to save from mutilation; rather, it was a controversial play with which Liveright had no prior connection that caused the *Jessica* case to be reopened.

Early in February 1927, three Broadway plays—*The Virgin Man, Sex,* a Mae West vehicle, and *The Captive,* a drama dealing with lesbianism written by Edouard Bourdet—were raided by the police.[4] *The Captive* had premiered on Broadway on September 29, 1926 at the Empire Theater.[5] It had received lavish praise from the New York critics, who emphasized Bourdet's delicate, wholly inoffensive handling of a subject that was new to the American stage.[6] Moreover, this play had been produced first in Paris in March, 1926, where it was still running, and had also been presented by Max Reinhardt in Berlin and Vienna. The critics at all four of its premieres had noted the complete absence of sensationalism surrounding the drama; but the quality of the play and the determination of the New York producer, Charles Frohman, not to exploit its theme were apparently lost on the local district attorney, Joab Banton, who closed the show and took the members of its cast, including Helen Mencken and Basil Rathbone, to court. Just before the formal hearing on February 16, Frohman announced that he intended to close the play to avoid further prosecution. During the actual proceedings, Liveright rushed into court demanding the opportunity to buy the rights to the drama and produce it. At the judge's direction, the publisher was first warned and then ordered to return to his seat. Liveright was undaunted, for that evening he announced that he would indeed reopen the show, and offered a statement signed by every member of the cast, all of whom had agreed to act in his production.

We, the undersigned members of *The Captive* company, feel that the principle involved in the suppression of *The Captive* is more important than our personal interests. The play has been acclaimed by the intelligent public as a masterpiece of dramatic literature. Critics all over the world have paid tribute to the author. Far from feeling that we have been engaged in the commission of a crime for the past six months, we feel that we have been privileged in using our talents in a play of the highest merit and social value. Commendation has come from people of all walks of life, including the ministry; and the Play Jury, which considered the play at the request of the District Attorney, found in it nothing objectionable.

Our counsel advises us that we are violating no law. We owe it to ourselves, our profession and to our public to refuse to be intimidated. We expect to act and receive the protection of the courts against unjust persecution.[7]

Later, Liveright was able to obtain the rights to the play and applied for a permanent injunction to prohibit the mayor, the district attorney, or the police from closing the production when it reopened.[8] After reading the work, however, the judge from whom Liveright sought the injunction denied his petition.[9] *The Captive*, which had offered a serious treatment of the problem it depicted, was to be heard from no more.[10] Acting Mayor Joseph V. McKee, who was engaged in a vigorous clean-up campaign of New York City, was infuriated by Liveright's typical Barnum tactics. In revenge, McKee ordered an investigation into the long-standing indictment against the publisher for issuing *Replenishing Jessica*.

The *Jessica* trial opened in General Sessions Court before Judge Charles C. Nott on March 19, 1928.[11] On hand for the State were Sumner himself, Charles J. Bamberger, an investigator for the Society (whose *nom de metier* was *ECIV DETACIDARE*), and Assistant District Attorney James G. Wallace who acted as the prosecutor. Arthur Garfield Hays was the Chief Defense Counsel for Liveright; Bodenheim was absent, reportedly on a lecture tour, and was represented only by his lawyer. On March 20, directed by Judge Nott, the jury acquitted the author on the grounds that he could not be held accountable since he had received no royalties from the sale of the book and therefore had no interest in the book's distribution.[12]

Following this action Hays succeeded in obtaining Judge Nott's consent to having the entire novel read to the jurors and thus into the record.[13] Reporters who had followed the early stages of the trial with a minimum of interest soon gave the courtroom activities their complete attention. In the *New York Evening Sun* of March 21 it was reported that after the dismissal of charges against Bodenheim, "the jury settled down in its chairs to listen to Assistant District Attorney Wallace read the 272 smoldering pages of *Replenishing Jessica* aloud in the courtroom. The general impression was that *Jessica* would be too much for Mr. Wallace in one session and that her adventures would trail along through most of tomorrow morning." The only incident recorded during the District Attorney's recitation was Hays' objection to Wallace's placing an improper emphasis on certain passages in the book. However, Judge Nott ruled that the reading and emphasis might "properly be left to the honesty of Mr. Wallace."[14]

Newspaper coverage of the following sessions reveals that other reporters had taken their cue from the *Evening Sun*.[15] *The Evening Post* headlined its report, "BODENHEIM JURORS NOD OVER JESSICA," and related that Wallace had given out on page ninety, called for a relief reader, and "rushed into a sunny corridor to 'replenish' his lungs." *The Evening Telegram* caught one juror napping, another holding his head in his hands, and the remainder looking "resigned." As Prosecutor Wallace continued his reading in a dull monotone, reporters carefully counted the glasses of water he consumed and continued to sketch the reactions of the jury. Everyone, including the jurors, the lawyers, and the reporters, had difficulty staying awake. Once, when Liveright asked and received permission to leave court for the day at noon, it was recorded that the jurors, compelled to remain, made no attempt to conceal their desire to follow him. Wallace, taking a brief respite from the text, described Bodenheim's heroine as a woman who went through a series of "adventures" with one man after another; between each one she philosophized on philandering, wondering whether she was being replenished. Then, having exhausted all the normal men of her acquaintance, she married a cripple. When Hays interrupted hurriedly to point out that Jessica had married the cripple to replenish herself "spiritually," reporters were delighted.

On March 22, Wallace finished his reading, and Liveright was called to testify.[16] The publisher said that he had bought the manuscript of the novel from Bodenheim, then he had marked certain passages for deletion, and that he could only recall in a very general way the events that led up to its publication. He believed that Smith and Bodenheim had worked together revising the manuscript, and that the published volume differed considerably from the original manuscript. When the Prosecutor began to question the publisher about another one of his publications, *Poetica Erotica*, Smith's compendium of amorous and bawdy verse, Judge Nott broke in to announce adamantly, "I'm not going to have another book read at this trial." Following Liveright's testimony, Nott directed the jury to acquit Smith, since it appeared that he, too, had made nothing from the sale of Bodenheim's book. Finally, the Judge directed the jury to retire to consider only the State versus Horace Liveright. After fifteen minutes, they returned with a verdict of not guilty.[17]

Within a week of the trial, *Replenishing Jessica* was in the bookstores. Despite the novel's soporific effect on the twelve jurors, it sold nearly thirty-three thousand copies in the next two years.[18] Meanwhile, Liveright wrote the following letter to each member of the jury; with it he enclosed three of his latest, most popular publications:

> When you rendered your verdict last Friday afternoon, I was a bit too nervous to express to you my proper appreciation of what I sincerely believe to be your contribution to a free press in these United States.
> I do want you to know that Boni & Liveright do not publish many dull books. I think the three which I am sending you will prove this. Any time you happen to be in this neighborhood, won't you drop in and see what a respectable establishment we run?[19]

The replies the publisher received were all friendly and favorable. One juror went so far as to invite Liveright to lunch in order to tell him exactly what went on in the jury room.[20]

The final absurdity climaxing the *Replenishing Jessica* trial occurred over a year later when Liveright received the following poetic effusion from a stranger and admirer, Louise Heald. Dedicated "To Horace Liveright an Apostle of Beauty," Miss Heald's ode was entitled *"A Modern Knight"*:

How brave you are to wage our war for us,
To fight Propriety, reveal her shames,
Puncture her stupid bourgeois blunderbus,
Reveal the shams in banal bourgeois games.
You fight for Art; you have no other creed;
Hypocrisy you loathe, detest, despise.
You champion Beauty, her quick cry you heed.
You are superior to compromise,
The Puritan Art's deadly enemy,
A vandal every artist must condemn.
I praise you for the war you wage for me.
I grave your name on Beauty's diadem![21]

In spite of the ludicrous aspects of the trial, both the publisher and Bodenheim made money on the strength of it.

The correspondence between Bodenheim and Liveright before and after the trial reveals the writer as alternately amiable and quarrelsome, grateful and hysterical. The early letters, for example, were friendly ones asking for various sums of money. On November 11, 1926, Bodenheim wrote the publisher:

I have commenced my fifth novel, entitled *Georgie May*, but since I am penniless and hounded by a million scarecrows, I do not see how I can complete it, much less carry it to a successful termination, unless you can possibly rescue me as you did in the case of *Replenishing Jessica*. If you will pay me fifty dollars a week until an advance-royalty of five hundred dollars has been exhausted, I will guarantee to have my fifth novel ready for you by March the 15th at the very latest. Of course, the five hundred would be exhausted before that date, but I am hoping that *Ninth Avenue* will also aid me with a good press and a large sale.

Liveright paid, and *Ninth Avenue*, Bodenheim's latest effort, appeared. The following August came a smaller request.

The world being an idiotic travesty in G Minor, and my kid's school rent having piled up, much to my confusion I need $75 like a baby needs moral support.

Mr. Pell has a heart remarkably like New England granite. I have just handed in my fifth novel, and as a result of my exhaustion thereafter, I think that the firm of Boni & Liveright might be lenient.

With incredible sincerity,
MAXWELL[22]

Liveright sent the money immediately.[23]

The association of Liveright and Bodenheim seems to have been a stable one, as long as the publisher helped support the writer on demand. Once the reports of the *Jessica* trial proceedings began to reach Bodenheim in Chicago, the writer became abusive. To Messner he wrote:

> You failed to answer my wire for money, sent when I felt that I might be compelled to return to New York. No one connected with B & L wired me of my acquittal, of the successful termination of the case, or any details and assurances I might have wanted to know. Also, though I was told that *Georgie May* would positively appear in March, it is now the very end of March and I have not received the slightest news concerning what may be happening to this novel. These attitudes of BOORISH REMOTENESS have wearied me, especially since I know that they would not have been given to a Dreiser, or an Anita Loos, under the same circumstances. Frankly, you and the entire B & L staff have treated me cavalierly for just about the last time. Also, accounts of the trial in New York newspapers have disgusted me. . . . I am tired of this endless campaign of calumny, ridicule, and distortion waged against me . . . Letters of suave, dodging "explanation," and efforts to smooth me down, are not going to work this time. The entire trial was so handled that it was bound to reflect on my creative importance—my being released on the FALSE assertion that I had received no royalties from the sale of the book gave thousands of people the impression that the novel was so negligible that nearly everybody ignored it. On the other hand, every care was taken not to bring belittlement or ridicule on the name of Horace Liveright. . . . To say that I am disgusted with the whole mess is to put it mildly. . . . The sooner I get out of America and away from the whole curious pack of you, the better it will be for my work.[24]

To this outburst Liveright cabled the following reply:

HOW COULD WE SEND YOU NEWS OF TRIAL WHEN WE HAD NO IDEA OF WHERE TO REACH YOU/NATURALLY PRESUMED YOUR LAWYER KEPT YOU POSTED/YOU ARE ONE OF THE MOST UNGRATEFUL MEN I HAVE EVER KNOWN/I CONTRADICTED SUMNER'S TESTIMONY IN EVERY DETAIL/IF THE CONDUCT OF TRIAL DISGUSTED YOU YOU ARE A DARN FOOL/I AGREE THAT THE SOONER YOU GET OUT OF AMERICA THE BETTER.[25]

Determined to press the issue, Bodenheim in his next letter to Liveright maintained that real injury had been done to him.

> When I thought I might have to come back for the trial, having received no news of it beyond the fact that it was in progress, I wired Mr. Messner for fifty dollars. He failed to answer in any way. Your telegraph states that you people had no idea of where to reach me. The moment I arrived in Chicago, I sent my address to both Mr. Pell and the phone-girl, who has been forwarding mail to me, so I simply cannot understand your statement about not knowing my address. . . . Also, I have received no word concerning *Georgie May*. It was scheduled for March at the latest and the month of April is now at hand. . . . Concerning the trial, I have had no way of knowing what happened save through the newspaper reports, which were highly unflattering, to say the least. I still believe that my being acquitted on the false assertion that I had received no royalties on the book must have given people the idea that the novel was negligible and met with general indifference. . . . Again, I am one of the most ungrateful men you have ever met. I'm quite sure that you'll retract that assertion when your blood cools down. It is true that your firm has been lenient in the matter of advance royalties, but I couldn't begin to count the hard-luck stories, hour-long pleadings, threats, stormy sessions, and what not, which are necessary to insure this leniency. Let neither of us masquerade as perfect, Horace. . . . It is imperative that I have a conference with you, since we cannot get along in the present atmosphere of misunderstanding and dissension. Other reasons also dictate my return to New York. Please wire me one hundred dollars, or, if you do not much wish to do this, please return a prompt answer. Things in general simply must be cleared up.[26]

The check from Liveright was dated April 2, 1928, but the requests for money continued, though the tone of Bodenheim's letters became considerably less harsh as the amount he asked for became greater. In June the novelist wrote his publisher once more.

> Please read this very carefully and realize that very real and grim finalities have come into my life. I am well over thirty now, and the role of a struggling, defiant vagabond—renegade, which I've hugged for some twelve years, can no longer be continued. Complex responsibilities are taking command of my life. I gave five hundred

dollars to my wife, who is now on the ocean and sailing to France on the steamer Paris. The poor kid, only twenty-seven now, had worked for several summers without the hint of a vacation. My "babe," a bright boy of seven, is at a summer school and I'm his sole support. My mother, who had been supported by a wealthy uncle of mine, has now quarreled with him and hasn't a penny on which to live. I happen to be her only child, and while she misunderstood and maltreated me in my youth, I certainly cannot see her in the not always mythical poor house. All this, dear Horace, does not include my own needs, which are desperate enough in themselves, God knows. I am not Atlas and if I must hold up a world, it's imperative that I secure some permanent and substantial rescue. I have been "dissipating," philandering, and somehow carefree in spite of everything, but the last act has been reached. It must be apparent to all of you now that most of the critics are determined not to give any novel of mine anything remotely resembling a square deal. They had some semblance of an excuse in regard to *Ninth Avenue* and *Jessica*, which were above the average and yet filled with descensions from my very best, but their conduct regarding *Georgie May*, an indisputable masterpiece from every angle, has been incredibly mean and disgraceful. Somehow, I have become an entirely personal figure to them—a taunting, red-raggish, brilliant, disreputable Count Bruga —and, from the depths of their respectability and "sanity," they are determined to demolish this specter with invective, grudging praise followed by spiteful contradiction, and a general campaign of belittling distortion. That most of them are *entirely unconscious* of this malicious unfairness does not alter the mournful situation. Naturally, *they would have to tell themselves* that they are right and justified. With most of them in blind opposition to me, no matter what I write, I can't go on. My novels would have to sell twenty thousand or more to keep alive those dependent on me, and myself. My work has no ultimate ingredients of popularity in it, and only the loyal support of at least a few prominent critics could make it sell. I've been working on a really wonderful novel—three hundred pages dealing with the last minutes in the life of a man about to die in the electric chair—but I can't continue it unless a miracle happens. The hopelessness of the general situation; three people, mother, son, and wife, needing money constantly; and my own physical demands —these make a truly impossible situation. Remember, I am saying this not with a beginner's cowardly impulse but as a man with twelve books already to his credit. If you can send me five hundred dollars immediately, I'll be barely able to struggle through till September—*barely indeed!*—and write a novel fully equal to *Georgie May*. If you can't do this—and I know that you must be a business-man as well as an appreciative friend—I intend to give up writing *permanently* and sell myself to the most legally dishonest and well-paying job that I can find. A novel—at least the kind that I write—demands months of grim, complete immersion—and I've got to make an immediate decision. Won't you please answer instantly, and won't you always believe that, in spite of the angers and disagreements which I've sometimes given you, I have not been entirely unappreciative of your loyalty?[27]

By August, Bodenheim needed $300 more. Along with his request to Messner for this additional sum, he said:

The thing that cut me the most was an account in that MORAL TOILET, the *Graphic*, to the effect that one of their reporters had called up Liveright and that Liveright had said that he was washing his hands of me and cared to have no more connections with me of any kind. I know that this must be a lie—I certainly hope so—and I wish that you would ease my mind about it.[28]

Bodenheim's anxiety produced an immediate telegram from Liveright.

PELL IS WIRING YOU THREE HUNDRED TODAY/THE GRAPHIC NEVER GOT ME ON TELEPHONE AS I REFUSED TO DISCUSS YOUR CASE WITH ANY NEWSPAPER/WE ALL FELT IT BETTER FOR YOU IN EVERY WAY FOR US TO MAINTAIN COMPLETE SILENCE RATHER THAN DIGNIFY CHEAPLY SENSATIONAL TABLOID STORIES BY ANY STATEMENT[29]

And so, apparently, it went from month to month.

Bodenheim needed publicity to sell his books; Dreiser did not. The failure of the defendants to win in the *American Tragedy* case the next year climaxed a period in Boston history during which the "sensitive emotional mechanism" of the Watch and Ward Society, led by the Methodist minister, Reverend J. Franklin Chase, "determined what Bostonians might or might not read."[30] As outspokenness in sex matters became more common in writing, Boston censors made self-righteous grasps for greater influence. The Massachusetts statute they used to further their aim was included in Section 28 of Chapter 272 of the Massachusetts General Laws:

Anyone who imports, prints, publishes, sells or distributes a book, pamphlet, ballad, printed paper or other thing containing obscene, indecent or impure language manifestly tending to corrupt the morals of youth, or an obscene, indecent or impure print, picture, figure, image or description manifestly tending to corrupt the morals of youth . . . will be liable to criminal punishment.[31]

Following a gentleman's agreement that evolved under the cosponsorship of the Watch and Ward Society and Richard F. Fuller, a prominent Boston book-dealer, the Vice Society, the booksellers, and the police quietly cooperated to prevent this law from being violated and simultaneously protected members of the trade from prosecution.[32] The method of their operation was quite effective: once Chase or another member of the Society discovered a work that he believed to be actionable, he submitted the book to a committee of six, the so-called Boston Booksellers' Committee, consisting of three members of the Watch and Ward and three booksellers. If the committee agreed that the book was objectionable, Chase informally notified the trade of their opinion: that they took no further responsibility in the matter, nor would they give advice, and that local booksellers had forty-eight hours to remove the volume from circulation. If the committee failed to agree on the status of a book, it was turned over to a municipal judge or the district attorney and both sides accepted the decision of this outsider without exception. The entire operation was accomplished without publicity for either the committee or the book it suppressed. In fact, the Boston book-market cooperated with the committee enthusiastically and unanimously. Booksellers acquiesced so readily to the warnings because local suppression and prosecution involved them— not the author or the publisher of a work—most directly. The Watch and Ward threatened Boston book-dealers, not New York publishers, and few booksellers could afford a court fight; besides, Chase had won 98 per cent of the cases he had carried to court. The most notable exception to this astonishing record was the *Hatrack* case involving H. L. Mencken.

The editor of *The American Mercury* temporarily became a Boston bookseller on April 5, 1926, traveling to Massachusetts in order to sell the April number of the *Mercury* to Chase, who had masterminded the suppression of that issue because it contained "Hatrack," a story by Herbert Asbury.[33] Mencken completed his transaction at the foot of the Boston Common, when Chase paid him fifty cents for the magazine. (The editor reportedly bit the coin.) Arrested at once on the charge of selling obscene literature "manifestly tending to corrupt the morals of youth," Mencken was defended by Arthur Garfield Hays and acquitted by Judge James P. Parmenter the next day. Since Chase had been made to appear foolish, it was hoped that the strangle hold of the Methodist minister and his associates on contemporary literature would be relaxed.

Within the next year, however, events moved in the opposite direction. Chase died, and no one emerged to continue his work. Then the Boston Police Department joined the battle, and seemed to become the sole custodian of Boston morals. In any event, the gentlemen's agreement was soon swept away. By March 12, 1927, the Boston police had suppressed nine books and their activities were proclaimed nationally by the press.[34] The police asserted that the works either contained "obscene, indecent or impure language" or manifestly tended "to corrupt the morals of youth." Among the nine volumes attacked were Percy Marks' *The Plastic Age*, which was three years old, and a Liveright publication, *The Hard-Boiled Virgin*, by Frances Newman. (In the case of Miss Newman's novel, a poorly chosen title obscured what was really a serious book.) When asked by newsmen for a statement, Superintendent of Police Michael Crowley said: "I have read these books, and I think they are bad. I have a duty to protect the morals of the people of this country, so far as I am able." Only Liveright, however, took any immediate steps to challenge the actions of the police. He immediately sent Arthur Garfield Hays, the firm's attorney, to Boston to investigate. On his return Hays pronounced the activities of the police "ridiculous" and "tyrannical," but he advised Liveright against fighting the ban.[35]

It was Mencken, however, who received the most publicity when he characterized Boston as a city in the grip of "frenzied moralists whose authority meets no resistance from the civilized element of its population." "The most recent suppression . . ." he continued, "is nothing to be alarmed about in a city where fanatical moral tyranny is unchallenged and where objections have been so stifled that they are no longer heard."[36] However, there was cause for alarm. Bostonians had the reputation for spending more money per capita on books than the residents of any other large city, and there was public speculation that local would-be censors outside of New England might follow the successful example of the Boston super-moralists.[37]

On April 12, *Elmer Gantry* was officially banned, and it was announced that several other volumes were under scrutiny, one of them *An American Tragedy*.[38] The Boston Booksellers' Committee met and decided to turn over a considerable number of modern works—about fifty—to the District Attorney's office in order to determine whether or not they might be sold. But William J. Foley, the Suffolk County District Attorney, returned the package of the works to the committee unopened. He officially revoked the tacit agreement which had worked so smoothly for twelve years among the booksellers, the Watch and Ward, and the police. In a letter to the trade that accompanied the bundle, Foley stated:

> I am writing you to state that any arrangement now existing between you and this office under which you have been able to procure the opinion of this office in advance as to any given book is at an end.
>
> You gentlemen probably can tell better than this office whether or not a book is an improper book for you to sell.[39]

In addition, Foley ominously warned that notification would not be sent to dealers when a new volume had come under the ban; there would, however, be a speedy prosecution.

An American Tragedy had not been among the books returned by District Attorney Foley.[40] Rather, it had been considered by the police earlier, but never officially acted upon. Still it was hinted that Dreiser's novel should be removed from circulation, for it was about to be suppressed by the police. The reaction in New York was immediate. While other publishers were content merely to protest this high-handed action, Liveright determined to be the first to challenge the ban. It was a matter of principle and publicity, and he sent Donald Friede and Hays to Boston to sell the novel and be arrested.

If Mencken's coup could be repeated, Friede reasoned, a "grand stunt" would both increase the sales of *An American Tragedy*, which had been on the market for sixteen months, and show up the other publishers who were too frightened to act.[41] Consequently, in order to determine the status of Dreiser's novel, while protecting the Boston booksellers from fine or jail at the same time, Friede and Hays arrived at Police Headquarters in Boston on April 16, 1927.

Followed by an entourage of reporters they first approached Captain George A. Patterson, Head of the Liquor, Narcotics, and Vice Squad, who had reported that the book contained obscene language.[42] But Patterson refused to buy a copy of *An American Tragedy*, so the three of them consulted with Superintendent of Police Crowley, who said: "The police have no feeling in this matter. We want to be fair and if you want to make this book a test case, we will do so. We will buy the book, submit it to the court, and apply for a summons." Finally, it was decided that neither Patterson nor Crowley, but a third officer, Lieutenant Donald J. Hines of the Vice Squad, would buy the book. After Hines had done so, Hays asked Crowley to buy copies of *The Scarlet Letter* and the Cambridge edition of the complete works of Shakespeare, but Crowley declined. Captain Patterson and Lieutenant Hines then applied to Judge Murry for a warrant to arrest Friede. When the judge asked them whether they thought the work would corrupt the morals of the buyer, Captain Patterson answered that he was certain that his would not be corrupted and was equally convinced that Lieutenant Hines' "could stand the strain." In the end, however, the warrant was issued and a date fixed for the trial.

The case was heard on April 22 by Judge James H. Devlin of the Municipal Court.[43] During the hearing, Richard F. Fuller, chairman of the Booksellers' Committee and testifying on behalf of the novel, stated that the price of the book had limited its sale to the mature and those able to pay for it. He had sold about 300 sets of *An American Tragedy*, he said, "about 98% was [sic] purchased by persons more than 25 years of age, who are of mature mind and readers of the finest literature. The other 2% was [sic] bought by Harvard students, who are required to read the book in their literature courses." Hays himself argued ably in the novel's behalf:

It would be impossible to write a story truly showing the gradual deterioration and disintegration of the principal character in Dreiser's book without depicting his relations with women. The point of the novel depended wholly upon that portrayal. In a two-volume book of many hundreds of pages, none but a curious kind of human animal would thumb through it to find the few particular passages that would arouse sex impulse. And no book is violative of a Massachusetts statute unless it is "manifestly corrupting to the morals of youth."[44]

Despite Hays' defense, Judge Devlin found Friede guilty and fined the publisher $100. After Liveright agreed to withdraw all copies of *An American Tragedy* from Boston bookshops, though it remained for sale across the Charles River in Cambridge, the State offered to file the case "without imposition of penalty." But Hays, acting for Dreiser, Friede, and Liveright, refused this offer and appealed the decision, because "the principle involved warranted taking the chance of even a jail penalty."[45]

The appeal of Judge Devlin's decision was not heard until two years later. In the meantime, Boston book-dealers "voluntarily" withdrew *Oil!*, and its author, Upton Sinclair, proceeded to the Boston Common, where he held forth on the absurdities of censorship, unsuccessfully tried to get himself arrested, and almost caused a riot.[46] The upshot of Sinclair's crusade was the "fig leaf" edition of *Oil!* in which the nine pages (of the 527 pages in the book) that were alleged to contain impurities had been cut. The author himself appeared in Boston to sell it wearing a large fig-leaf-shaped sandwich board.[47]

By January 1928 there were approximately seventy modern books banned in Boston, although by this time no single group wished to claim credit for the wholesale suppression.[48] Neither the District Attorney, the Police Department, nor the Watch and Ward Society accepted responsibility for the action; in fact each accused the other of perpetrating it. The sale of very popular novels like *An American Tragedy*, *Elmer Gantry*, and *Oil!* had been stopped, and other works—some of equal literary importance—were also unavailable in Boston. Along with *Kept Women* and *Loose Ladies* were *Count Bruga* by Ben Hecht, *What I Believe* by Bertrand Russell, *Blue Voyage* by Conrad Aiken, *Mosquitoes* by William

Faulkner, *Dark Laughter* by Sherwood Anderson, *Manhattan Transfer* by John Dos Passos and *The Sun Also Rises* by Ernest Hemingway.

On April 16, 1929, Dreiser, Friede, Hays and Clarence Darrow arrived in Boston for the beginning of the trial, to be held before Justice Hayes of the Superior Court in Suffolk County. Author, defendant, and attorneys were all confident that the earlier verdict would be reversed. The presence of two colorful, astute lawyers, and the prospect of a jury trial appeared to substantiate their belief.

At the beginning of the trial, Frederick T. Doyle, the district attorney, entered as evidence the first of those passages from *An American Tragedy* which he considered to be objectionable.[49] Hays reacted to this procedure immediately, on the ground that what Friede had sold to Lieutenant Hines was a two-volume work. "There might be a difference," Hays said, "as Your Honor will realize, between a mere sale of pages from a book that may have a certain effect and selling a whole book, and while I realize the District Attorney can found his charge upon part of the book, I don't believe he can put in parts of what was sold and leave out the rest."[50] Hays' objection, however, was overruled, and Doyle continued to present selections, from a paragraph to a page or two in length, out of context and in a most disconnected manner. When he finished reading these to the jury, Doyle had completed his case. Hays continued to object to this method, but his objections were overruled. Hays then tried various means to enter the whole work as evidence, but his efforts were denied at every point. First, he urged Judge Hayes to consider the author's intention:

> It seems to me quite clear that the question whether material is obscene or not depends upon the motive and intent of the entire work, what the author is trying to prove. Now, in volume two is shown what happens to Clyde Griffiths. He is a youngster of very weak character who gets into this trouble with Roberta and he finds no way out of his predicament.
>
> I have always been taught that the test of the value of a novel was the inevitability of its development. Here you have Clyde Griffiths, whose counterpart was taken from the case of *People against Gillette* in New York City. Clyde Griffiths, a young man of weak character, entwined in this web of fate, he gets into trouble with

Roberta, he loses his love for Roberta, he becomes fascinated by another girl, he gets into a difficult situation, doesn't see how he can extricate himself, and finally he resorts to crime; the crime is discovered; there is a trial at law; Clyde Griffiths is responsible for the death of Roberta; he is found guilty of murder in the first degree; and he is finally electrocuted.

In our judgment if there was ever a moral story this is it. It shows what happens to people in circumstances of this sort and that when unable to extricate themselves they go to these extremes and violate the law. . . . How can anybody tell whether this book is corruptive to the morals of youth or not without knowing what finally happens to Clyde Griffiths?[51]

While he remained unsuccessful in his primary objective, Hays was eventually given the opportunity to read to the jurors the complete chapters containing the disputed passages, but he soon found this was entirely unsatisfactory. He asked Judge Hayes:

Doesn't Your Honor see, if I just read chapters no one can tell whether this book is corruptive to youth or not, unless you show the effect of all this on Clyde's life? I am not asking to read the whole book, but I want the jury to get the fact that it is the basis of our claim that it warns youth of danger and that it is not corruptive to youth.

Unless Your Honor permits me to do it I can't even tell this story to the jury. I can't tell the jury that it isn't corruptive to youth but helpful to youth. . . .[52]

Since he had had no luck in placing the passages in the context of the entire novel, Hays turned to Dreiser. "I think I should be permitted to read the entire book," the attorney said. "Your Honor has ruled against me. Now I ask to have Mr. Dreiser tell it. I promise you it won't take long."[53] But the creator of *An American Tragedy* was not allowed to discuss its contents outside of the passages that had been mentioned by the prosecution. Finally, Hays reminded the judge of an earlier case, *Commonwealth v. Buckley* (1908), which might be taken as precedent.[54] In this trial involving Elinor Glynn's novel, *Three Weeks,* the whole book had been entered as evidence and considered by the jury, although only specific passages had been found objectionable. But Judge Hayes held that in the Glynn case the original complaint had been lodged against the whole book; the current complaint was against specific passages. Hence, only sections of the book could be entered as evidence and be considered by the jury. With that discouraging decision, the first day of the trial ended.

That evening found Darrow, Dreiser, Hays, Friede, and seven hundred others gathered at a forum and banquet in Ford Hall—a gathering organized to dramatize and protest suppressive conditions in Boston.[55] Darrow, Hays, and others spoke on book censorship and free speech, while Margaret Sanger, seated at the speaker's table with them, had her mouth covered by tape symbolizing the silence enforced upon her by Boston authorities because of her advocacy of birth control. During the evening the Watch and Ward Society, the Police Department, and the District Attorney were ridiculed in skits and speeches, and a telegram from Upton Sinclair was read to the audience. The author said: "I would rather be banned in Boston than read everywhere else, and that isn't as bad as it sounds, because you will be read everywhere else." Naturally, this meeting of spokesmen for "indecent doctrines" received thorough newspaper coverage by reporters who called it the "Ford Hall Frolic."[56] Moreover, the program served to link birth control and dirty books in the minds of many readers, including members of the *American Tragedy* jury whom Hays had ridiculed before the gathering.

In court the following day, Hays called on Clarence Darrow to help him convince the judge to enter Dreiser's complete novel in evidence. The jury was retired while Darrow spoke. "Supposing," Judge Hayes asked, "the person reading it should be 17, 18 or 19 years of age?" To the judge's question Darrow replied:

> There are precocious boys and girls, and a precocious boy or girl, of course, means just what the word implies, older than the almanac says. Of course, there are people who have lived, according to the almanac, fifty years that are not ten years old; and there are some seventeen or eighteen that know more than most people would know if they lived forever, and that is the condition that must be considered by the statute. It is the condition of the individual,—the mental condition.
>
> But let me go farther than that. If I were to concede that one or two or three young people might take a bad meaning—might! You can't make all the literature of this world for the benefit of three-year-old children, or ten-year-old children, or fifteen-year-old

children. It is utterly absurd. . . . We cannot print all our literature for the weakminded and the very immature.[57]

Darrow's point was ignored. Judge Hayes remained adamant in his refusal to allow either the book or a synopsis of it to be given to the jurors. Following this defeat, the jury returned and Hays began his summation. Working within the limits imposed on him by the court, Hays suggested to the jurors that there were hundreds of passages in the Bible which went far beyond *An American Tragedy* in frankness of expression. "What book of the ages which has stood as literature would stand up under the tests which have been applied to Dreiser?" he demanded.[58]

When Doyle's turn came to address the jury, the District Attorney declared that Hays had dragged in "everything but Texas Guinan and her troupe" to win.[59] He, on the other hand, had merely selected excerpts—most of which he managed to repeat during his final argument—from only twenty-four pages of *An American Tragedy* as the basis for the jury's decision. After rereading Dreiser's description of Clyde's initiation into the world of a brothel, the district attorney interpreted the moral of this passage for the jurors: "Well, perhaps where the gentleman published this book, it is considered not obscene for a woman to start disrobing before a man, but it happens to be out in Roxbury where I come from."[60] Doyle's closing remarks left the jury only one direction:

> Well, I know not, Mr. Foreman and Gentlemen, where they get their notion of obscenity; I know not, sirs, from whence they derive their sociology or philosophy and what not; I know not whether they are going to bring you to the jungles of Africa; but I got mine, and I know you got yours, sirs, at your mother's knee when she prayed that you would be pure in thought, pure in word, pure in actions.[61]

When Judge Hayes delivered his charge to the jurors, he directed them to consider only those portions of *An American Tragedy* which had been read to them in court. The theme, the lesson, and the whole tone of the novel, he explained, were immaterial.

> The only question before you is "Are the pages read to you and set forth in the amendment to the complaint impure, indecent,

and obscene and manifestly tending toward the corruption of youth?" If that is so, it is not necessary to find that the words alone are indecent. You must determine if the thoughts aroused by those words are offensive to morality and to chastity and manifestly tend to corrupt youth.[62]

Arthur Garfield Hays left Boston immediately, but telegraphed Liveright his forecast of the verdict to come; it was likely, he said, that the jury consisting of laborers and mechanics would vote Catholic.[63].

On April 18, on the third ballot, the jury upheld the banning of *An American Tragedy* and Friede's conviction.[64] But behind the judgment on novel and seller was an existing law—in many ways very much like the bill that had been offered by the Clean Books League in New York—as well as a precedent.[65] No other outcome was perhaps possible in 1929. Thomas D. Lavelle, who had assisted Hays during the trial) moved to have the verdict set aside as soon as it was announced. Lavelle explained that the jury might have been prejudiced against the defense because of the forum meeting the attorneys had all attended two evenings before. But Judge Hayes denied the motion, and Friede was given the choice of a $300 fine, ninety days in jail, or further adjudication.[66] After consultation, Hays Dreiser, Friede, and Liveright, who was of course paying for the whole thing, agreed to proceed with an appeal to the Supreme Court of Massachusetts.

The issue raised in the *American Tragedy* case was a major one, one which has been a point of contention in censorship cases of the past and present. It was simply "whether or not one can put into evidence the whole book, so as to show the background in which the 'obnoxious' passages occur."[67] Could a two-volume novel like *An American Tragedy* be banned because a few brief excerpts were considered by some to be "objectionable?" Moreover, were a judge and jury not entitled to consider the complete work rather than selected portions before making their decision? The Massachusetts statute involving censorship contained no provisions relating to this question. The defendants in the *American Tragedy* case and their attorney decided to seek clarificaton of the law and entered their appeal.

In his brief for the *Commonwealth v. Donald S. Friede*, submitted to Justice Pierce of the Supreme Judicial Court for Massachusetts, Hays set forth two major points.[68] First, the defendant had the right to enter the whole novel in evidence, since he was charged with having sold the entire book of two volumes to Lieutenant Hines. He had been tried as though he had sold certain paragraphs from twenty-four pages out of about a thousand. Whether *An American Tragedy* was corrupting could only be determined if the complete work was entered as evidence, but not even the theme of the book or any material in general contained in the novel had been allowed. It is impossible to judge the "obscenity" of the excerpts without knowing the context in which they occur. Should the procedure by which the prosecutor had selected and presented only isolated passages prove constitutional, sellers of the *Bible*, the classics, the dictionary, the encyclopedia, and Shakespeare would be liable for prosecution.

Hays' second argument concerned the class of persons likely to purchase Dreiser's novel. No children, he submitted, would buy a $5.00, unillustrated book by Theodore Dreiser called *An American Tragedy*. Moreover, all the literature in the world could not be made to conform to the standards of the immature. The attorney concluded his brief with a motion to reverse the earlier conviction: "The verdict of the jury imports that *An American Tragedy* manifestly tends to corrupt the morals of youth and that this is so beyond a reasonable doubt. It is submitted that no twelve men could reasonably come to this conclusion."[69]

Judge Pierce thought otherwise, however, and on May 27, 1930, he upheld the decision of the lower court.[70] In his opinion Pierce stated that it was impractical to read a work the length of Dreiser's novel to the jury. Moreover, there had been no error in Judge Hayes' direction to the jurors or in the handling of the case.

Although he had been unsuccessful in defending *An American Tragedy* against censorship in the courts, Liveright gained added respect in literary circles. Edward A. Weeks, Jr., of the *Atlantic Monthly*, writing about the practice of censorship in Massachusetts, praised the publisher for his courageous action: "Under the absurdly strict terms of the existing law no publisher other than Horace Liveright has felt justified in exposing his book and himself to a test case."[71] In 1929 Weeks became chairman of the Massachusetts Citizens' Committee for the Revision of the Book Law, a group devoted to achieving the liberalization of the Massachusetts obscenity law.[72] The reformers were modest in their aims, and by the spring of 1930 they succeeded in convincing the state legislators to eliminate the reference to obscene language in the old law, while retaining the passage alluding to the morals of youth.

With this small but important modification, the state of the law remained as it was in the *Commonwealth v. Friede* case until 1945. At that time, in *Commonwealth v. Isenstadt,* the court set forth the standard Massachusetts definition of obscenity.[73] The relevant test was the effect of a work on probable young readers. Any book was to be judged in the light of its audience and the customs and usage of the times; its value as a work of art had no relation to its "corrupting" effects. The court stated, however, that the 1930 Statute had to be interpreted to treat any book as a *whole* in determining whether it violated the statute: ". . . the book is within the statute if it contains prohibited matter in such quantity or of such nature as to flavor the whole and impart to the whole any of the qualities mentioned in the statute."[74]

In 1945 the old Section 28 was repealed by the State Legislature and a new Section 28 was introduced applying to sellers and publishers who introduced obscene materials to minors, into families, or into schools. Under the new law, obscenity action was to be brought against the book itself, not against the bookseller.[75]

The Massachusetts approach to the concept of obscenity was further changed in *Attorney General v. Book named "Tropic of Cancer"* handed down by the Supreme Judicial Court in 1962. At that time the Court held "that the First Amendment protects material which has value because of ideas, news or artistic, literary or scientific attributes. . . . We conclude, therefore . . . that with respect to material designed for general circulation, only predominantly, 'hard core' pornography, without redeeming social significance, is obscene in the constitutional sense."[76]

In 1927, Liveright courageously protected the booksellers from prosecution by the district attorney of Boston, but it was years before a firmly entrenched habit of mind was legally changed.

Eugene O'Neill

The Liveright-Eugene O'Neill association, extending from 1918 until 1930, illustrates the kind of serious, friendly cooperation between publisher and author which proves rewarding for both. O'Neill's extant correspondence with Liveright testifies to this as do the firm's catalogues, which annually included important new plays by the dramatist.[1]

During the existence of his house Liveright published thirteen volumes containing one or more new O'Neill dramas, several limited editions of his more popular writings, a set of the playwright's works, and countless reprints of his various plays. With the exception of 1923, at least one new O'Neill drama appeared every year during the Twenties:

Beyond the Horizon	March 10, 1920
The Emperor Jones, Diff'rent, The Straw,	April 7, 1921
Gold	September 10, 1921
The Hairy Ape, Anna Christie, and The	
First Man	July 24, 1922
All God's Chillun Got Wings and Welded	April 17, 1924
Desire Under the Elms	April 11, 1925
The Great God Brown, The Fountain, and	
The Moon of the Caribbees and Six Other	
Plays of the Sea	March 15, 1926
Marco Millions	April 23, 1927
Lazarus Laughed	November 11, 1927
Strange Interlude	March 3, 1928
Dynamo	October 5, 1929[2]

The regular publication of his plays in book form both here and abroad substantially increased the dramatist's income and, more significantly, enormously enhanced his reputation. The playwright often spent days going over each manuscript meticulously before publication—editing, revising, or restoring speeches and even whole scenes which had been cut during production.[3] O'Neill was intensely aware that the published volumes of his plays would be the versions to endure. In fact, he made so many corrections in the proofs of *Strange Interlude* that Liveright discovered it was cheaper to reset the whole work.[4] Aside from his acute, but natural concern that his published plays represent his final intentions most completely, O'Neill—in contrast to many other Boni & Liveright authors—never complained to his publisher about lagging sales or about the kind or quality of advertising his works received. Only once was there a serious misunderstanding. It involved the title sheets of a limited edition of *Desire Under the Elms*, which had been sent to O'Neill to autograph.[5] According to Liveright's plan, the edition was to consist of 1250 copies, but O'Neill believed that 1700 or 1800 sheets had been sent to him. He further suspected that Liveright planned to sell the "extra" volumes without paying him his regular royalty, and in a letter to the publisher the dramatist called him a crook. Liveright, quite naturally angered, was innocent; a careful printer had sent the extra sheets to the playwright as a margin against spoilage. The matter was immediately cleared up, and O'Neill apologized.

Although O'Neill was practically unknown in 1919, he had found a reading public of considerable proportions by the mid-Twenties; with Broadway successes such as *Desire Under the Elms* and *The Great God Brown,* Liveright could count on immediate sales of at least ten thousand copies for an O'Neill play. From the publisher's viewpoint it was of less importance that the dramatist had developed into the best-selling playwright of the Twenties; it was far more to the point that O'Neill had become one of the firm's most popular authors. For example, when a $10 limited edition of the seven-year-old *Emperor Jones* was issued in 1927 with illustrations by the then unknown Alexander King, the entire publication was quickly exhausted.[6] Moreover, when O'Neill made the national best-seller lists the next year with the appearance of *Strange Interlude,* both author and publisher were surprised. That this nine-act drama became a national success was the result of O'Neill's talent, the extensive promotional treatment Liveright gave the work, and the popular appeal the play had for an audience which both of them had developed.

The success of *Strange Interlude* brought unexpected problems to the dramatist and his publisher. On the basis of its great success, two other writers charged that O'Neill had used or was using their works in the composition of his own plays. These two authors, Alice E. Parsons and Gladys "Georges" Lewys, threatened to take action unless immediate redress was made to them on their own terms.[7] Liveright himself dealt with Miss Parsons and eventually succeeded in eliminating the threat she represented, but Miss Lewys persisted until a plagiarism suit involving O'Neill, Liveright, and The Theatre Guild began in May 1929. Although neither woman was ultimately successful in her efforts, each appeared to be a serious menace to the reputation of the dramatist and the integrity of the publishing firm.

Of the two writers, Alice Parsons urged her cause, to see her work published by Boni & Liveright, the longest; she sought the Liveright imprint for ten years. In 1919 the publisher first refused to accept her dramatic trilogy for publication. She submitted it again in 1925 with an accompanying letter asking that her manuscript be reread and the earlier decision be reviewed.[8] When Liveright returned her plays once more, he wrote that he was not prepared to accept the plays of unknown writers, "that failing Broadway production, our policy is not to publish."[9] Nearly a year later, following the appearance of O'Neill's *The Great God Brown* and *The Fountain,* Miss Parsons renewed her efforts. In a letter to Liveright she said she was convinced and prepared to prove that O'Neill had used her trilogy in the creation of his two latest works. The new O'Neill plays "marked a change in style of the dramatist. The similarity of his new method," she asserted, "expressing the same thought, with identical use of phrase," impelled Miss Parsons to address her statement "to Mr. Horace Liveright, and through him to Mr. Eugene O'Neill."[10] While she carried on about Eugene O'Neill's use of "her" plays, Miss Parsons did not offer to take any direct action. Liveright did the sensible thing and ignored her. In 1929, after Miss Lewys had successfully instituted her own plagiarism suit, Miss Parsons made herself felt more strenuously. She insisted that Liveright see to the production of her plays by The Theatre Guild and their subsequent publication by his firm, first, as an "answer" to O'Neill's *Strange Interlude,* and second, as "the simplest step toward compensation" for her grievances." With the assistance of Arthur Garfield Hays, Liveright drafted his reply to Miss Parsons' ultimatum: "I have your amazing letter of September 17. Our records show that the plays were received by us on October 2, 1925, were read by Mr. Maurice Hanline on October 5, and returned to you express collect, on October 8, 1925. During that period they were not out of our hands; neither we nor any third party made use of them."[12]

Miss Parsons pressed on but with considerably less vigor. Would Liveright, she asked, "be interested in considering the publication of the trilogy as an answer to *Strange Interlude?*"[13] The publisher responded that he had refused her plays in 1919, 1925, 1926, and as of October 17, 1929, he still did not want them.[14] Miss Parsons then submitted to anonymity but not without the last word in the matter: "You will make good to me, I know. Life has ordained us to light as well as shadow and there comes a day when we must seek it."[15]

Liveright's decisive handling of this example of publishing blackmail probably went unnoticed by O'Neill; but the second authoress, apparently buttressed by money and evidence, was a more serious threat.[16] On May 27, 1929, Miss Lewys instituted a suit against O'Neill, The Theatre Guild, and Horace Liveright in which she demanded a million and a quarter dollars in damages as well as an injunction against *Strange Interlude* both in its acted and published forms. Miss Lewys charged that the playwright had stolen his drama from her novel, *The Temple of Pallas-Athenae,* which had been rejected by Liveright in 1924 but later published by another firm. With her complaint, Miss Lewys' attorneys filed copies of both the play and the novel in which many points of alleged similarity had been carefully marked by the plaintiff. In addition to the texts they also submitted a detailed comparison of the two works showing similar ideas, characters, situations, and even lines. O'Neill, in France, chose to remain there, but he anxiously wrote to Liveright regarding the suit. It was blackmail pure and simple the playwright said, yet he was alarmed by the suit and its attendant publicity. What did Liveright's lawyers think? What did the publisher himself think?[17]

Liveright, who had been in consultation with Arthur Garfield Hays, as well as Harry Weinberger, O'Neill's counsel, replied to the playwright that he was satisfied Miss Lewys' efforts would fail.

> The plagiarism business simply nauseates me. I've had talks with several lawyers about the introduction of some law that will make it necessary for the plaintiffs in plagiarism and libel suits to post bond covering all legal expenses of the defendant in case the judge in his charge to the jury makes it clear that the suit had no legitimate basis. On the other hand, if the plaintiff wins the suit, the defendant, who has posted a bond, must pay the plaintiff's legal charges, the fairness of these charges to be determined upon by the judge in the case. Of course, it will take a long time to get any such idea across, but I think it is bound to come some day. I have no recollection of ever having met Georges Lewys. Tom Smith here knows her and it seems that we did reject four of her books, but have no record at all of *The Temple of Pallas-Athenae*. I know I don't remember ever having seen it. It's hell, isn't it, to take up a lot of time and spend a lot of money both of which could be used to some constructive purpose.[18]

After the intial hearing and its attendant publicity, Lewys versus O'Neill, the Theatre Guild, and Liveright was continued for almost two years.[19] During this interval *Strange Interlude* completed its seventeen-month run on Broadway, won the author his third Pulitzer Prize, and was banned in Boston.[20] The published version of this drama sold one hundred thousand copies to become the best-selling play of the Twenties and one of the most popular dramas in American history. O'Neill's financial share in the success of *Strange Interlude* has been estimated at over $250,000.[21]

Three months before Miss Lewys began her suit, O'Neill's new work, *Dynamo*, was produced on Broadway.[22] Following, as it did, the dramatist's great success, Liveright was eager to issue a printed version immediately after the play's opening; he had advance orders for eighteen thousand copies.[23] After *Dynamo* received negative reviews upon its premiere, the publisher was even more anxious to get the book out. O'Neill, however, said that the adverse criticism of his play did not bother him, for many critics had not liked *The Great God Brown* or *Desire Under the Elms*. Besides, the playwright felt *Dynamo's* chance for a lengthy Broadway run was good, since the subscriptions of thirty thousand Theatre Guild members entitled them to see it.[24] Writing to O'Neill less than three weeks after the *Dynamo* premiere, Liveright warned the playwright about waiting.

> I've been working terribly hard at the publishing game and, of course, have been tremendously pleased by the huge success of *Strange Interlude*. It has unquestionably far outsold any other play in bound form in our generation. In this connection, Gene, the proofs of *Dynamo* will be sent you by the fastest steamer we can reach tomorrow or Saturday. I beg and urge you to correct these proofs as quickly as possible. We are getting a very good advance sale on the book in spite of the rotten reviews, but I feel that the play is going to slip at the Martin Beck. Last week I understand it did $17,000 whereas capacity there is about $23,000, and last week was a very very good week on Broadway and around the country. As an example, my lousy little play, *Dracula*, played to $17,800 in Newark. So the quicker we can get the book out, the better it will be for all of us.
>
> I do wish, Gene, that you had been here when *Dynamo* was in rehearsal. I feel you would have done a great deal with the third act to clarify it, pep it up, make certain cuts, etc., etc. The first act is magnificent, the second act good, and when I see you in April or May, I'll tell you just how I feel about the third act.[25]

Theatre Guild subscribers did not show up for performances of *Dynamo* as they had for *Desire Under the Elms* and *The Great God Brown*.[26] Moreover, O'Neill announced that he wished to revise the entire play prior to its publication. Frantically Liveright cabled the dramatist:

> THINK YOU ARE COMMITTING FINANCIAL SUICIDE SO FAR AS BOOK PUBLICATION DYNAMO IS CONCERNED/DONT WANT YOU TO FEEL OR OURSELVES TO THINK ONLY OF MONEY BUT POSITIVE UNLESS DYNAMO PUBLISHED EARLIEST POSSIBLE DATE ADVANCE ORDERS NOW OF FIFTEEN THOUSAND COPIES WHICH HAVE BEEN CUT FROM TWENTY FOUR WILL BE CUT IN HALF AGAIN/MAKE QUICK AND FULL REVISION PROOFS AND WE

WILL GUARANTEE NO MISTAKE IN PAGES/OF COURSE PLAY IN BOOK FORM MUST STAND ON ITS OWN REGARDLESS OF PRODUCTION/EITHER YOU OURSELVES OR SOMEONE ELSE WRITE EXPLANATORY FOREWORD IF YOU SO WISH/FEEL THIS IS VITAL FOR FINANCIAL SUCCESS OF BOOK BUT WILL ABIDE BY YOUR FULLY CONSIDERED DECISION[27]

Soon after this O'Neill's new drama closed, after a run of only fifty performances.[28] The playwright himself proposed to delay the publication of *Dynamo* even longer. Liveright was unhappy, but, apparently, resigned to the delay.

WHILE I DO NOT AGREE THAT LONG POSTPONEMENT WILL BE GREAT COMMERCIAL GAIN ALL CONCERNED IN LONG RUN CHEERFULLY AND UNDERSTANDINGLY ABIDE BY YOUR DECISION ON DYNAMO/PLEASE CABLE WHEN YOU THINK WE CAN COUNT ON HAVING COMPLETE REVISED MANUSCRIPT TO SET UP AND WHAT DO YOU THINK BEST EXPLANATION FOR POSTPONEMENT OF THIS EAGERLY AWAITED BOOK SHOULD BE TO TRADE AND PUBLIC.[29]

O'Neill's thoroughly revised manuscript meant the additional expense of resetting the type for the play, along with a further loss in orders, but Liveright agreed that the drama must be printed as the author intended it to stand. O'Neill was apologetic for the trouble he was causing, and Liveright replied:

Of course, I'm disappointed that we have to send you another set of proofs but I get your point of view. Our sales department feels that once again our orders will be cut in half. Originally, we had an advance sale af about 18,000 copies. This was cut to between 9,000 and 10,000 copies because of the very long postponement and partly, too, I think because of the reception of the play. Now postponing the publication again from August 2nd, which we had liberally advertised, to some time in October, is pretty tough. Usually when the trade gives very generous advance orders, they display the book in windows, heaped tables, etc. and the public being a lot of sheep buys things that are shown in large quantity. Do your very best to get the revised proofs back to us the quickest way a few days after you receive them.[30]

By the end of July 1929, O'Neill had finished correcting the last *Dynamo* proofs and had returned to work on his new play,

Mourning Becomes Electra. He suggested that Liveright include the playwright's own drawings for the sets in any special limited edition of *Dynamo* the publisher might plan.[31] O'Neill thought that despite its failure on Broadway, the novelty of a dramatist's own attempts at scenic design might make the published *Dynamo* successful. In addition to worrying over the plagiarism matter, which was still hanging fire, the playwright was feeling a strain on his finances. A very large offer from a Hollywood studio for the motion picture rights to *Strange Interlude* had been withdrawn after Miss Lewys had instituted her suit. Hence O'Neill asked Liveright his opinion about an offer he had received from a Harry Marks to buy his play manuscripts; their sale, O'Neill said, would clear up his financial obligations. Liveright's reply concerned both the possible sale of the manuscripts to Marks and the coming publication of *Dynamo.*

> You can't imagine how eager I am to read *Dynamo* in its new form. I would not worry at all if I were you about the plagiarism suit; I am in it just as deeply as you are and I rarely give it a thought.
> What is the new play all about? This is a pretty big question to answer, isn't it? Tell me what you can. Will it be ready for 1930? And will you be able to give me a chance at producing it? I assure you that I could have done *Dynamo* a lot better than it was done—I do not mean scenically but I could have interpreted it so much more truly.
> About Harry Marks—he is a pretty wise dealer in books, but I am of the distinct opinion that you should do nothing further about the manuscripts at this time, at any rate I would not make any offers or talk to anyone about them. I should say that since the production of *Dynamo* the market is a little bit off; wait for your next big triumph and then let them come to you begging. Of course if you need the money that is a different thing. If this is the case, let me hear from you and I will sound out the market again.
> In this connection, I have gotten your drawings for *Dynamo* from the Theatre Guild, and though they are very interesting they should not go in the limited edition of the book, and in this the sales department agrees with me. The public does not expect this sort of thing from you and your work and I believe the inclusion of the drawings would make you a little less mysterious and interesting a figure. Don't let us have them see the wheels go round.[32]

As a result of Liveright's well-meaning advice, O'Neill did not sell his manuscripts. A few months later the stock market crashed and with it, of course, the demand for limited editions and orginal manuscripts by prize-winning authors.

In 1930, Liveright went to Europe in the hope of uncovering several best-sellers. There he saw O'Neill, who was still concerned about the suit. Liveright promised the playwright to look into the matter again, and upon his return home wrote to O'Neill.

> I had a very exhaustive and interesting talk with Harry Weinberger [O'Neill's lawyer] about the grand plagiarism suit and feel about it just as I did when I talked to you in Paris. To all of us here it's just a grand joke. I doubt that the case will come to trial although, of course, in her efforts to get publicity the lady may persuade her lawyers to push the case. And if business is bad enough with them maybe they will.
>
> At any rate, I believe the matter is in the hands of excellent attorneys. To my mind calling in any other lawyer at this time would be a confession of fear and weakness on our part. We'd immediately get into the newspapers, prejudice the public against us, and we might also prejudice the judge or judges sitting on the case. This opinion is concurred in by everyone around me and by the lawyers for all parties concerned. Do please, Gene, try to forget the matter. Harry Weinberger has most painstakingly studied the whole history of plagiarism suits in this country, Arthur Hays is one of the best trial lawyers I know....
>
> What a lovely day we had together. I've had nothing but headaches since I got back to New York what with the dollar book-war, one of the worst general business depressions the country has had in years, to say nothing of heat and gloomy faces all around me. I, myself, never felt in better health and spirits.[33]

The old bravado was there, but the trip abroad had simply been a prelude to Liveright's swan song as a publisher. The next month he wrote O'Neill that he was on his way to Hollywood and, though he didn't admit it, no longer the playwright's sponsor.[34]

On March 11, 1931, the *Strange Interlude* plagiarism trial finally began.[35] O'Neill did not appear. Instead, the dramatist's statement was read by a proxy under the direction of Weinberger.[36] O'Neill absolutely denied ever having read *The Temple of Pallas-*

Athenae. His diary, containing a synopsis of *Strange Interlude* and written in 1923—the year before Miss Lewys' novel was submitted to Liveright—was entered as evidence. Lawrence Langner and T. R. Smith both testified that they had not read the Lewys work. Three weeks later, Judge John M. Woolsey dismissed the novelist's suit and directed her to pay all the defendants' counsel fees.[87] When Judge Woolsey wrote that Miss Lewys' claim was "preposterous," the defendants' victory was nearly complete. The plaintiff, however, was able to delay paying the assorted lawyers until 1933, when she had herself declared bankrupt. Naturally, this placed the burden of payment on the innocent defendants. Despite the costly losses borne by O'Neill, the Guild, and Liveright, they had the satisfaction of knowing that Miss Lewys' defeat in court was a deterrent to others.

Liveright was not present for the trial, nor was he connected any longer with his firm. In 1932, after Saxe Commins, who had replaced Manuel Komroff as O'Neill's editor at the house, advised the playwright that the firm was in financial difficulties, O'Neill asked for and received an agreement from Arthur Pell stating that in case of bankruptcy all contracts between the house and the playwright would become void and all rights the firm had to his work would revert back to O'Neill.[38] The next year, when the firm did fail, O'Neill signed with Random House and took Commins along with him. The new association with Bennett Cerf lasted until the playwright's death in 1953.

Horace Liveright, Inc.

From the mid-Twenties until his retirement from publishing in 1930, Liveright appeared to devote less and less of his energy to discovering and promoting new writers, preferring to rely on the works of his established authors. Along with the regular publication of books by Van Loon, Bodenheim, Adams, Mrs. Atherton, and their literary superiors, Liveright issued a number of volumes which can be most simply classified as examples of "jackpot" writing, that is, works of popular and topical appeal with little promise of enduring for more than a season or two.[1] *Broadway Racketeers* by John O'Connor and *The Road to Buenos Aires* by Albert Londres were just such works; the first dealt with prohibition and gangsters in New York, while the second promised the inside story of white slavery in South America. Both volumes appeared, and quietly disappeared in 1928, a year which saw the publication of a third work that had the same kind of appeal, but was promoted in a way suggesting the publisher expected it to capture the public's fancy and set a new record in Liveright sales. It was called *Doomed Ship* and was written by Judd Gray in the Sing Sing Deathhouse. The advertisements for this volume promised something special:

> Probably no murder case in the history of our country has been so exploited, falsified and sensationalized, as that of Ruth Snyder and Judd Gray. The vilest of human emotions were aroused: on the one hand a hideous blood lust, on the other a maudlin sentimentality. Decent public opinion revolted: some of it against the press, some against the institution of capital punishment, most against the two sordid figures in the center of the stage.
>
> The autobiography of Judd Gray is one of the most biting pieces of debunking ever offered to the much debunked American public. In place of lurid melodrama it gives the reader tawdry reality.

In place of jazzed-up fiction, it gives him artless truth. By this very contrast the naive narrative becomes in the hands of the intelligent reader a scorching exposure of sensationalism.

For whatever the press might say, Gray had no illusions about himself, either as hero or as devil. "All this is very average," he writes early in his book, "and very average I considered myself in the brief moment I spent in introspection. As I take my daily walk in the gray concrete pen that is my only chance to drink the sun and air, I realize how set apart an average man can become." And later he speaks of himself as "one of those average Americans that Mencken laughs at."

Every reader will make his own estimate of the author. Gray's unhappy marriage, his relations with Ruth Snyder, and her almost hypnotic influence over him, the intense religious fervor which seized him after his arrest and carried him through the last black months of his life—all these can be variously interpreted, and a final verdict is almost impossible. Some readers will regard Gray's life as absolutely drab and normal, suddenly hurled into melodrama by an odd twist of circumstance. To others the story will serve as an unconscious revelation of abnormal tendencies, running underground for most of a lifetime, to emerge to the surface in unusually spectacular form. To the psychologist this is a priceless document.

On the whole people will read Gray's life, not to condemn or to condone, but as a study in human nature. It is as such that it is offered to the public.

PUBLISHERS' NOTE

The publishers issue this book only after confirming its authenticity beyond the shadow of a doubt. It was composed in the death cell at Sing Sing, and finished less than an hour before execution. Gray gave it to his sister, who arranged it for publication. It remains as he wrote it, except for the omission of a few repetitions and occasional incoherent passages.

Despite this kind of flashy copy, *Doomed Ship* did not catch the fancy of a million readers. Rather, it had a perfectly respectable initial sale of about twenty thousand copies and then stopped. Still, Liveright, Smith, and Messner all responded favorably when Liveright's secretary, Ida Goldman, suggested that some member of the firm contact Mrs. Edmund Wheeler Hall about writing her memoirs prior to her execution for the murders of Reverend Hall, her husband, and Mrs. Eleanor Mills; however, Mrs. Hall rejected the offer of literary fame.[2]

When Liveright turned to the sensational and the lurid in the hope of quick, high sales, he revealed how much he missed the steady income he lost when Cerf took over the Modern Library. Its replacement, the Black and Gold Library, was begun in 1927 with a dozen volumes including *The Dialogues of Plato, Tristram Shandy, The Confessions of St. Augustine* and, in 1928, *The Shorter Novels of Herman Melville*—marking the first publication of *Billy Budd* in America. Despite this substantial beginning, the Black and Gold series did not have the popularity of its predecessor and was never particularly successful.[3]

However, in 1927 and 1928 Boni & Liveright had the highest gross profits in the firm's history. The house had on its list ten books which accounted for nearly a million volumes in sales.[4] Two, *Gentlemen Prefer Blondes* and *An American Tragedy,* were holdovers from 1926. The others included O'Neill's *Strange Interlude,* Mrs. Atherton's *The Immortal Marriage,* Adams' *Revelry,* Emil Ludwig's *Napoleon* and *Son of Man,* Dorothy Parker's *Enough Rope* and *Sunset Gun,* as well as Samuel Hoffenstein's *Poems in Praise of Practically Nothing.* In one month, July, 1928, Liveright had six of the best-selling books in the United States.[5] This achievement marked the first time in the history of publishing that six best-sellers had come from one house simultaneously. Even more remarkable was the fact that two of the volumes were light verse and another was a play.

During these two years Liveright offered other books that were popular enough to sell at least twenty thousand copies apiece and often more.[6] These were mainly novels: *The Crystal Cup* and *The Jealous Gods* by Gertrude Atherton; *Replenishing Jessica* and *Georgie May* by Bodenheim; *God's Stepchildren* and *Mary Glenn* by Sarah Gertrude Millin; *The Hard-Boiled Virgin* and *Dead Lovers are Faithful Lovers* by Frances Newman; *Unforbidden Fruit* by "Warner Fabian"; *But—Gentlemen Marry Brunettes* by Anita Loos; a biography, *Meet General Grant,* by W. E. Woodward; and two autobiographies, *My Life* by Isadora Duncan and *Doomed Ship.* Several of these writers were relatively new to the Liveright list. Well known in England, Mrs. Millin wrote about her native country of South Africa and its people. Frances Newman was the librarian of the Georgia School of Technology in Atlanta.[7] She had begun her writing career by publishing reviews in the *Atlanta Constitution*, and had progressed to the *New York Herald Tribune*, the *Saturday Review*, and *The Smart Set*. One of her early short stories won the O'Henry Memorial Prize in 1925, and the next year her first book, *The Short Story's Mutations*, was issued by Ben Huebsch. Though her titles were flashy, Miss Newman's writing ability was considered quite respectable by the critics. Woodward's treatment of Grant, like his earlier volume on Washington, followed the vogue of debunking biographies.

In addition to Mrs. Parker and Hoffenstein, other members of the Algonquin Round Table who appeared in Liveright catalogues were Margaret Leech and Heywood Broun.[8] Dreiser was represented by a revised edition of *The Financier* and *Chains*, as well as *Dreiser Looks at Russia*; Anderson by *Hello Towns!*; Masters by *Kit O'Brien*; Mrs. Atherton by *A History of California*; Van Loon by *America* and *Man, the Miracle Maker*; Freud by *The Future of an Illusion*; Darrow by *The Prohibition Mania*; Mary Heaton Vorse by *Second Cabin*; Djuna Barnes by *Ryder*; Bodenheim by *Returning to Emotion;* Rose Macaulay by *Daisy and Daphne;* Bertrand Russell by *The ABC of Relativity*; Frank Sullivan by *Innocent Bystanding*; Cummings by *Him;* Dr. Morris Fishbein by *The New Medical Follies;* Horace Kallen by *Why Religion?* and *The Frontiers of Hope*; and George Moore by *Celibate Lives* as well as a limited edition of fifteen hundred signed copies of *Aphrodite in Aulis* which sold for $20. There were, finally, another edition of Smith's *Poetica Erotica*—this one limited to 1250 numbered copies and retailing for $15—plus a popular trade edition of *The Satyricon* of Petronius Arbiter.[9]

Authors who were new to the public, or who appeared on the Liveright list for the first time in 1927 or 1928, included John Colton and Randolph Clemence with *Rain,* a dramatization of Maugham's story; Sutton Vane with *Outward Bound*, another play; Aimee Semple McPherson with *In the Service of the King;* Art Young with *Trees at Night* and his autobiography, *On My Way;* Philip Barry with his play, *White Wings; The Songs of Paul Dresser*; Percy

MacKaye's autobiography, *Epoch*; Kathleen Millay's verse, *The Evergreen Tree;* Helena Rubenstein with *Feminine Beauty*; Isidor Schneider with *The Temptation of Anthony and Other Poems*; Arthur Garfield Hays with his account of contemporary censorship cases, *Let Freedom Ring*; and two thousand sets of *The Plays of Aristophanes* priced at $25 each.[10] In addition to this cornucopian promise of the later Twenties, Liveright began to offer the reading public a new volume by a writer who is better known today. It was called *The Devil and Cotton Mather* by Katherine Anne Porter.

Miss Porter had arrived at Boni & Liveright in 1927 with little more than a sketch for her book, which was to be a biography of Cotton Mather.[11] The thirty-three-year-old author was, as yet, unpublished. Liveright liked her Mather idea and offered to advance her $300 which she said would enable her to complete her research and deliver the manuscript in time for fall 1927 publication. With the aid of an outline explaining what she intended to do, Liveright's advertising staff composed the following description of Miss Porter's biography. It appeared in the Fall 1927 Liveright catalogue, although the book itself was postponed:

> This study in sadism is one of the most remarkable psychological portraits in the whole field of biography. Miss Porter's chief concern is with the prolonged emotional debauch that was Cotton Mather's hidden life, expressing itself outwardly in the cruelty, superstition, and intolerance which made the old divine famous as a savage witch-burner of colonial history.
>
> Luckily he kept a diary. One page of this amazing document reveals—all unconsciously—more than a psychoanalyst can ever draw from a reluctant patient in six months of daily sessions. To so shrewd a student of human nature as Miss Porter, this diary is a rich mine of material for treatment in the modern biographical manner. She discovers in Mather a life long death obsession and the secret practice of diabolism. She explains his witch burning orgies, comparing them with the outbursts of religious revivalists in our own day.
>
> As a narrative of religious ecstasy and righteousness, the bigotry and superstition of the Salem witchcraft mania, as a psychological study of a morbidly diabolical figure, and as a portrait of a conscience that found cruelty a means to self-approbation, this biography of Cotton Mather challenges the imagination, and pro-

vokes the thoughtful mind to speculate a little longer on the mystery of human nature.

This was as much of *The Devil and Cotton Mather* as the public received. Moreover during the next two years Liveright himself saw nothing of either Miss Porter or her manuscript, but he heard from her occasionally. The writer, it appeared, had become involved in considerably more research than she had at first anticipated and needed additional advances. In June 1929, she wrote Liveright from Bermuda asking for an extra $250; she had earlier received a second advance of $300.[12] Miss Porter explained that she had been working on the manuscript for eleven months, had read four hundred and nine books for background material, but had been forced to stop her research in order to earn money from literary hackwork and translations. She further promised to send the publisher two chapters every week until the complete text of her book was in his hands—probably by August 1. Liveright replied:

> Once more you ask for money on a book that should have been published long ago and which has been in our catalogue, counting this coming issue of the Fall catalogue, three times. In the meantime, another book on Cotton Mather has been published, the one which you reviewed, and which, naturally, is going to hurt the sale of our book. For example, I spoke about your book, yesterday, to the Literary Guild, and Carl Van Doren said he wasn't in the least interested in considering it, because a very satisfactory life of Cotton Mather had recently been published.
>
> Nevertheless, we want the book and want to be sure that we're going to get it in time to publish it this Autumn. Therefore, I am enclosing a check for $250. which you must understand is absolutely the final payment, until sufficient royalties have been earned to write off your advance of $850. Originally we agreed to give you $300 and now we have almost given you three times that much.[13]

Two weeks later Miss Porter wrote to thank the publisher for his generosity, and she sent him the two chapters she had promised earlier. She was certain her work would proceed on schedule and that she would not need further financial support.[14]

Before September 1929, however, the installments had ceased to appear, and Liveright wrote Miss Porter to ask about her progress.[15] The writer did not reply until December. She asked him to stop announcing the book. She could not finish it because of the demands of her other work. She thanked him for his patience and friendship, saying she hoped he was encouraged enough by what he had seen of the manuscript to be patient a little longer.[16] Puzzled, Liveright responded immediately:

> Naturally, I am surprised, shocked and chagrined to learn that there is as yet no definite date from you for the delivery to us of the balance of the manuscript of *The Devil and Cotton Mather*. Can't you give me some sort of idea when we will have the book? Can't you say that we will surely have it for publication in the Fall of 1930?[17]

Whether Miss Porter replied cannot be determined, since no other correspondence between the writer and Liveright, her prospective publisher, has survived. Although she is reported to have taken up *The Devil and Cotton Mather* from time to time, the completed work has never appeared in book form.[18]

Besides a number of unknown American writers new to the Liveright list, the 1927 and 1928 catalogues contained announcements of more Continental authors than the publisher had previously offered. In nonfiction there was Dr. Wolfgang Kohler's *Gestalt Psychology*, a work which had only a limited success.[19] Two other leading German writers, Hermann Sudermann and Jacob Wassermann, were each represented by novels. Sudermann's *The Mad Professor* was that author's first new fiction since World War I, but it failed to find a sizeable audience in the United States.[20] Equally unsuccessful were Wassermann's *Wedlock, World's End, The Triumph of Youth*, and *Caspar Hauser*; the first three novels sold very poorly through 1928; yet Liveright continued to publish Wassermann and offer the novelist praise and generous advances.[21] Replying to a letter from Liveright which included a contract and an initial payment of $2000 for the American rights to still another one of his books, the German replied: "I have always considered you as more of an artist than a book-publisher, possessing imagination and feeling, together with the determination and skill of a man of the world."[22]

At least part of the reason for Wassermann's failure to catch on in the United States, according to Liveright, was attributable to economic conditions in the country during the latter part of the Twenties. For example, on June 3, 1929 the publisher wrote Wassermann that it had been absolutely impossible to issue *The Maurizius Case* that spring, principally because of the inept translation the firm had received from Wassermann's translator. In fact, Liveright said that he was having the whole book retranslated by Eden and Cedar Paul at his own expense. In addition to the faulty manuscript, however, the general business depression could only have affected the sales of the book adversely.

> You may say that a business depression does not affect a book like *Maurizius*. This may not be the case in other countries, but it certainly is in this country. We published this spring Francis Hackett's *Henry VIII*. It was adopted as the choice for the month of April by the Book-of-the-Month-Club. It has been the best-selling book in the country, not only for non-fiction but also including fiction for the last three months. In any normal season, the best-selling book in the country would have sold at least 50% more than *Henry VIII* has sold. So you see, we have an absolute check on how the general depression has affected the book business.
>
> In conclusion, let me say, my dear friend, that our interests are mutual. We consider you one of our most distinguished authors, and we believe that we have done everything that any good publisher could do to further your reputation in this country and to sell as many copies of each and every one of your books which it has been our privilege to publish. You must admit that we have always met every one of your requests or suggestions regarding money matters.

The failure of Wassermann to become popular in America—he was at one time regarded as second only to Thomas Mann in the field of fiction—was a surprise and a disappointment to Liveright. However, the astonishing success of Wassermann's fellow countryman, Emil Ludwig, more than covered the firm's losses on the two German novelists.

In January 1927, T. R. Smith prevailed upon Liveright to pay Ludwig's American agents $1,000 for the American rights to the German's biography of Napoleon, which he then turned over to Eden and Cedar Paul for translation. Soon after publication Liveright sent the German another $1,000 as an expression of admiration for his work and as an inducement to the writer to consider Boni & Liveright as the publishers of his future books.

> As you know, we contracted through the literary agents, Brandt & Brandt, with your publishers for the English speaking rights to *Napoleon* for which we paid $1000. First let me say that I cannot adequately voice to you my great admiration for your magnificent achievement in this book. My firm is truly honored by its publication.
>
> You must know that it is unusual for a publisher either in this country or elsewhere to depart from the contractual arrangements arrived at with an author to the extent of doubling the price originally agreed upon. Nevertheless, we feel that it is only due you that we send you the $1000, which we are enclosing not as a payment to you, but as an expression of our admiration for your work and, let us say, frankly, as an example, of our fair dealing which we feel may lead you to consider us as the publisher of your future work. The sale of *Napoleon* to date has been a very good one, and we feel that it will have a steady and increasing appreciation from American readers. Won't you carefully consider the idea of making some arrangement with us for the publication of your future work on a royalty basis? We will, of course, on each work give you a substantial advance against royalties. Or, if you would prefer, we would be willing to consider an outright purchase of each book as we did with *Napoleon*.
>
> We should be glad to have your reactions about making a definite contract with us for say a period of two or three years.[23]

Ludwig's biography sold well as soon as it came out, so well, in fact, that it soon developed into one of the most popular books Liveright ever published.[24] Once its success was established and it reached the top of national best-seller charts, Liveright offered Ludwig a contract which featured $1,000 advances on all the German's major works and $500 ones on his minor writings.[25] Ludwig refused this agreement, countering with a demand for advances of $2,000 as well as the immediate publication of his novels. Since Ludwig had become popular here for a biographical work, and as fiction by Wassermann and Sudermann had not sold, Liveright's enthusiasm for German novels had diminished.[26] For these reasons, he refused to yield to Ludwig.

Following his failure to sign the author to a long-term contract, Liveright paid him $25,000 for the American rights to his life of Christ, entitled *The Son of Man*. After Ludwig accepted this offer, he insisted that the publisher issue his verse novel, *Tom and Sylvester*, immediately, and he further demanded that Liveright pay him more money for *Napoleon*.[27] Replying to the German in November 1927, Liveright refused the novel, saying it would lose too much in translation to have any sale here, and he rejected Ludwig's demand for additional money on his successful biography.

First let me tell you that I have read the preface and the first three chapters of *The Son of Man,* and I am genuinely enthusiastic. The third installment came to my desk last Saturday and I took it home that afternoon. When I finished it I felt absolutely cheated that the rest of the book was not ready at hand to read. . . . You have written another masterpiece and I assure you that the exploitation we do for the book will meet with your genuine approval. By the time you get to New York, I will have read all your book and we can then discuss it.

Relative to *Tom and Sylvester*: My dear Mr. Ludwig, how on earth do you expect this book to be translated and preserve anything like the beauty and essence of the original. You have written your book in verse. It would take another poet to even adequately translate it, and in another language I fear that it will lose much of its poignancy and significance. I know that you will damn me from the Italian Lakes to the Suez Canal when I tell you that here again I urge you not to publish this book in the English language. We would rather wait for another and more characteristic book.

Now to the disagreeable part of my letter. I want you to know that I feel very much hurt at your attitude regarding *Napoleon*. As you know, we bought this book not from you or your German publishers but through your accredited agents in New York for $1000. At this time there were several books by you on the market. You were practically unknown to the American reading public. We bought *Napoleon* and started to advertise it in the trade journals at $5.00 a copy which is certainly a fair price for the book. Then, on having the opportunity to have it made "The Book of the Month," which would give it great advertising and your name a quick and sensational impetus with our reading public, we reduced the retail price of the book from $5.00 to $3.00. Our transaction with the Book of the Month gave us very little profit indeed. But because of their being unable to offer a book for more than $3.00, we were obliged as above stated to make our general price $3.00. As you know, both *Bismarck* and *Kaiser Wilhelm* are priced at $5.00 retail and their sales are correspondingly very very much smaller than that of *Napoleon*. In addition to a very small profit at $3.00, we have advertised *Napoleon* at least five times as heavily as any of your other books have been advertised; I should say ten times as heavily would be nearer the mark. Do not misunderstand me. We have not done this from a purely altruistic standpoint. We have regarded Emil Ludwig as a property and the money that we have spent on *Napoleon* we believe will be returned manyfold in the success of *The Son of Man* and your subsequent books. In this connection, by the way, it must amuse you to see how Little Brown & Co. in *Bismarck* have exactly copied every detail of our manufacture of *Napoleon*—jacket, cover, type, paper, etc.

To continue: As soon as the Book of the Month arrangement was made, we sent you an additional check without any obligation on our part, of $1,000. May I quote from your letter of February 6th in answer to my letter telling you that we were sending this check? You said, after expressing your pleasure: "I shall not refrain from spreading out the news of this rarity amongst your German colleagues. I was especially pleased to note that there were no conditions hanging to your cheque and you will therefore find me readier to go with you in the future." You may remember that when I was in Ascona [Switz.], I said that before the end of the year I would send you another $1,000 if the sales of *Napoleon* continued well, and inasmuch as they have done very well indeed, I am sending by this mail with a copy of this letter, this check made out to your order, to Rowohlt [Ernest Rowohlt, Ludwig's German publisher].[28]

Considering the $25,000 Liveright had paid him for *The Life of Christ*, as well as the publisher's generosity after the success of *Napoleon*—which had sold over two hundred thousand copies after its acceptance by the Book-of-the-Month Club—Ludwig's response was singularly ungrateful. He was returning the check, he said. It was an insult following the enormous success of *Napoleon*. Moreover, Ludwig asserted, he, as its creator, had the moral right to share much more fully in the proceeds from the sale of his biography. Finally, he demanded that Liveright publish his verse novel as well as similar books that followed it.[29]

Since Liveright appeared to be making no progress with the writer in their correspondence, he decided to write a new contract. The agreement he sent Ludwig the following January reaffirmed his intention of issuing *The Son of Man* at the original $25,000 fee and called for the author to deliver a biography of Woodrow Wilson within the next three years.[30] As an extra inducement to accept, Liveright promised to pay Ludwig a 10 per cent royalty on each copy of *Napoleon* sold in America from January 1928 on. Ludwig signed this contract immediately. But when the publisher proposed bringing out a three hundred and seventy-five copy, limited edition of *The Son of Man* and offered the writer $1.50 per autograph, Ludwig returned to his earlier, money hungry stand. His price, he announced, was $2.50 per signature. Liveright explained that a small limited edition of the kind he proposed was done only for prestige and not for profit, but the German merely offered to reduce his fee to $2.00. This still made the cost of the volume too high to manufacture, so Liveright was forced to drop the idea.[31]

Upon the publication of the costly biography of Christ, Liveright cabled Ludwig in Germany:

BOOK PUBLISHED JUNE 12TH/ADVANCE SALES ABOUT 15,000 COPIES/ PRESS SO FAR NOT FAVORABLE BUT MANY IMPORTANT REVIEWS TO COME/ TOO EARLY TO JUDGE PUBLIC OPINION/WE ARE ADVERTISING AS AGGRESSIVELY AS WE DID NAPOLEON/WILL KEEP YOU POSTED[32]

Neither the serial appearance of Ludwig's book in *The Pictorial Review* nor the sign Liveright had erected at the corner of Forty-second Street and Fifth Avenue touting its virtues created enough public interest to put *The Son of Man* into that prestigious circle of works which sold over one hundred thousand copies.[33] By August 1928 Liveright had had enough of the bickering, unsatisfied author. At this time Ludwig was bargaining with a rival house over the rights to a biography of Lincoln he proposed to write. In correspondence with Liveright he asked permission to substitute an analysis of the political situation prior to World War I for his biography of Wilson—a replacement that would have been commercially inadvisable for the publisher to accept. At the same time Ludwig accused Liveright of doing him out of part of the money

The Pictorial Review had paid the firm for the serial rights to his life of Christ.[34] Before Liveright replied and ended his association with the author, he sent Messner Ludwig's letter with the following memorandum: "Please note what Ludwig has to say about *Review*. He's a swine you know." On it Messner simply replied: "Noted!"[35] Then Liveright wrote to Ernest Rowalt, Ludwig's German sponsor.

> Why you or Ludwig think that we are such babes in the woods, as to accept a book on European politics concerning the events immediately preceding the declaration of war in August, 1914—a book made up in half of quotations from official papers—in exchange for a biography of one of the most interesting and distinguished Americans in the last generation, is beyond our comprehension.
>
> We feel that both you and Ludwig are acting in a most unfriendly manner considering the fact, whatever Ludwig may have said to the contrary, we have been largely responsible for his great success in this country.[36]

In addition to the four German writers, three French authors appeared in 1927 and 1928 in Boni & Liveright catalogues. There were de Gourmont, represented by *A Dream of Women*; Laforgue by *Six Moral Tales*; and François Mauriac by *Thérèse*, the first volume of his early trilogy. Like Roger Martin du Gard, whom Liveright issued for the first time in America in 1925, Mauriac had come to prominence after the War. In 1926 he was awarded the French Prix de Roman, and, under the sponsorship of Donald Friede, Liveright's vice president, Mauriac was first published here in 1928.[37] However, neither Martin du Gard nor Mauriac became popular in the United States, and both were dropped by the house.

Usually once a year, Liveright or one of the editors went abroad to visit authors, agents, and publishers in the hope of securing new books for the house to issue. During most of the Twenties, T. R. Smith made these annual trips because of his numerous Continental contacts. In 1927, Friede went abroad. His main purpose in going was to sign James Joyce to a Boni & Liveright contract.[38] Everyone at the firm was excited about the prospect of capturing the Irishman. Portions of *Ulysses* had, of course, appeared in *The Little Review* before the book itself had been banned in the United States. Despite this defeat, Joyce's reputation had been established among writers here, though they were able to read his later works only in pirated or mutilated versions. Both Liveright and Friede were anxious to fight for the right to publish *Ulysses* in America. Since to do so would involve considerable expense, they hoped to protect themselves by first signing the author to a contract and publishing his new work, *Finnegans Wake*.

Before he left New York, Friede had fifteen volumes of Joyce's *Work in Progress* (a fragment of *Finnegans Wake*) privately printed in order to prevent piracy and secure the American copyright for it.[39] With a copy of this very limited edition, a contract offering the writer sizeable monthly advances on his next work, and an introduction to the author from Elliot Paul, who had published *Work in Progress* in the little magazine *transition*, Friede arrived in Paris to meet Joyce. Friede offered the author a $2000 advance and 15 per cent royalties on his latest book. But when Joyce saw the copyright on the volume Friede showed him (it was in Friede's name), the writer at once concluded that the Liveright firm was trying to hoodwink him into signing away the rights to his work.[40] Despite Friede's protestations and his honest explanation that the copyright had been taken out in his name only to protect Joyce's interests in America and would be transferred to the writer immediately, Joyce continued to be suspicious. He absolutely refused to have anything to do with Friede or Boni & Liveright.

Shortly after Friede's unsuccessful trip, he left the Liveright house and eventually joined Pascal Covici in founding Covici-Friede, Inc., in 1929. The vice president's departure from Boni & Liveright was precipitated by his disagreement with Liveright over the financial responsibility for a number of unsuccessful books that Liveright maintained had been issued only on Friede's guarantee. Surviving memoranda show that Messner and Smith agreed with Liveright on most of the eleven disputed volumes, and this had increased the friction between the partners.[41] When Friede decided to leave to pursue his own enthusiasms, Liveright was forced to obtain the funds to buy back his partner's stock. To accomplish this, the publisher had to borrow heavily from Arthur Pell and others on his own share in the business.[42] Beside his uncertain financial involvements in the stock market and on Broadway, the added burden of purchasing Friede's holdings in 1928 left Liveright's personal solvency, his control of the firm, and even the stability of the house itself in a more hazardous state than they had ever been in before.

The publisher's inveterate gambling on Wall Street and in the theatre seemed always to fail. There was a dichotomy between Liveright's handling of authors and his management of money. Where he was daring and successful with the former, he was foolhardy and wildly unsuccessful with the latter. The chances Liveright took on writers supported the company and his own way of life for a decade, but the publisher needed more best-sellers than he could possibly produce to support him through the reversals he was to suffer in 1929.

"I'm surely a Jonah when it comes to the stock market," Liveright wrote a friend.[43] Later, in another letter, he explained a little more fully.

> I've just been rushed to death since I wrote you last, and my desk is crowded with work now. I have an important lunch engagement with a lawyer, one right after lunch with someone who may put up some money for plays, and later on in the afternoon I am going to hear two new applicants for the prima donna role in *The Dagger and the Rose.*
>
> I'm really not exaggerating when I say that International Combustion has aged me five years. I've been stubborn, it's very true, but on the other hand, with all the information I got on this one stock, I was always afraid that the minute I would get out, up it would shoot into the sky.[44]

The Dagger and the Rose, a musical version of Liveright's first Broadway success, *The Firebrand*, by Edward Elison, Gene Berton, and Isabel Leighton, had been scheduled for production during the winter of 1927–1928 but had been postponed. At the same time Liveright had been preparing this abortive venture, his London import, *Dracula*, had opened on October 5, 1927.[45] Featuring Bela Lugosi as Count Dracula in a role he was to become identified with for the rest of his career, Liveright's play was an immediate hit. It ran 261 performances, closed, and went on tour. Meanwhile, the delay of *The Dagger and the Rose* tied up a considerable amount of his money. Besides these ventures and further losses on the market amounting to $40,000, the publisher was drinking heavily. He confided as much to Alfred Wallerstein.

> Now for a little confession: I'm *not* on the wagon. Don't think that this means that I'm really drinking. But I find that when I sit around all night with a crowd that is drinking, unless I take one or two gin and gingerales, I seem to give nothing; but with a drink or two I'm much more my real self. This may sound like an awful bit of sophistry to you. It's really true. Everyone can tell you that since you've left I've been an angel, so don't worry that the occasional drink is going to develop into any more. I'm simply lost when I feel that I can't do something.[46]

Though the situation was far from favorable, Liveright decided to change the name of the business from Boni & Liveright, Inc., to Horace Liveright, Inc.[47] He was not aware that the course of his fortunes was to change, too. Within two years, the publisher had left the house, forced out of his executive position. Within five years, the firm was bankrupt, the victim of mismanagement and rival publishers.

1929–1930

When the last three catalogues assembled by Liveright in 1929 and 1930 are compared with the earlier lists he had offered in the Twenties, the disparity is startling. Some of the writers he had developed into best-selling authors were still publishing at the end of the Twenties, but their new works were largely second-rate. This failure of established popularity, supplemented by Liveright's inability to discover any new talent of great promise, appeared to point to the firm's demise. The stock-market crash in October 1929 all but assured it. Liveright and his house might have survived the Wall Street disaster had their publications sold well, but this was not the case. For example, Gertrude Atherton's new novel, *Dido*, sold fewer than twelve thousand copies, over one hundred thousand fewer than her great success *Black Oxen*. In addition, the sales of Van Loon's *Rembrandt*, Adams' *The Flagrant Years*, Millin's *The Fiddler*, Bodenheim's *Sixty Seconds*, O'Neill's *Dynamo*, Hoffenstein's *Year In, You're Out*, Dreiser's *Gallery of Women*, and a reissue of Huneker's *Painted Veils* were slow and disappointing. Moreover, lower sales and smaller royalties seemed to signal the departure of some of the publisher's most successful authors. Following the poor reception of *Daisy and Daphne*, Rose Macaulay switched from Liveright to Harper's early in 1929.[1] Emil Ludwig and Lewis Mumford had ended their associations with the publisher the year before.[2] Samuel Hopkins Adams left the firm in 1930 complaining of inattention, while Dreiser tried, unsuccessfully, to break his contract about the same time.[3]

By the end of 1929 unearned advances paid out by Liveright during the preceding years amounted to over $100,000 and the gross income of the house had fallen off badly. There were very few signs of possible financial recovery; only one volume, Francis Hackett's *Henry VIII*, had been issued with any substantial success.

Liveright's initial association with Hackett began during the winter of 1922–1923, when the publisher suggested that the journalist write a biography of Henry the Eighth.[4] Under contract to Harper's for a novel as well as being an editor of *The New Republic*, Hackett accepted Liveright's proposal, and resigned his job to concentrate on his books. Liveright wrote him enthusiastically in February 1923:

> I'm tickled to death that you're going to do *Henry VIII*. Maybe you'll have it finished by the Spring of next year. By all means let the $500 stand against *Henry*, and if you get along well with *Henry* and he's going well, I may be able to give you some more when, as, and if you find yourself in a tight place.[5]

In the same letter Liveright explained that he was not interested in issuing a book on socialism Hackett had recommended to him.

> We're not the slightest bit interested in Guild Socialism and darned little interested just now in anything that's the slightest bit theoretical or speculative. Nothing on Economics or Sociology is going. Fiction, Autobiography, Biography, Parody, and even some drama and poetry go. Stunt books like Van Loon's *History*, they're the thing, my boy! I know perfectly well that you understand what I mean when I say stunt books. Something new, something new. That's the cry these days.

By fall, Hackett was full of plans for a third book and, not surprisingly, in need of money—for he had still to produce his first volume. Liveright replied to his request.

> You ask what is so monotonous as the money troubles of the small-tradesman author? My answer comes not tripping to my lips but rushes out like a cataract: The money troubles of a rapidly growing book publisher. And this in spite of all sorts of successes. Of course, my troubles don't concern themselves much with paying tailors' or butchers' bills or even for gasoline and concert tickets. But it's just as monotonous to talk to Presidents and Cashiers of banks and to explain to a hundred and one different tenth rate authors why you cannot support them for a year or so while they're writing God-awful drivel, as it is to stand off the collector from the gas company.
>
> *Harry Juniper in the Land of Promise* is a good title and I

like the idea. By all means serialize it in Mencken & Nathan's new magazine which you've very likely heard all about by this time. Knopf is going to publish it. But if it comes to the Knopf scouts trying to wean you away from your legitimate father who has nursed you at his breast so long, although so unnourishingly, I'll send you a marked copy of *Aesop's Fables.*

Why not start on *Henry VIII* right away so that you can have it for the fall of 1924. I'm sure it will go.[6]

Late in 1924 Liveright obtained Hackett's release from Harper's by repaying the firm the money it had advanced the author.[7] Added to the sums he had already sent Hackett on *Henry VIII*, the writer's debt to the firm totaled $1500, but the prospect of Hackett's novel *That Nice Young Couple,* seemed to lessen the gamble. When the manuscript of the work arrived at the house in September, however, Liveright became uneasy. The best thing about the book appeared to be its title. Along with a detailed explanation of what he felt was wrong with the novel he wrote to Hackett:

> I am confident that you are going to make this book a fine one. . . . You understand, of course, that the book will be published just as you think it should be published. I will do all I can to urge you to make the book better but the decisions rest with you. When I am convinced that you are satisfied with the book as you want it to go to the compositors, you will find me the same enthusiastic co-operator that you have always found me.
>
> As I write I have an open mind about this and assure you, Francis, that if you are not too provoked with me because of what you might consider my lack of literary taste and publishing sense, because of my opinion of *That Nice Young Couple,* we will have no trouble so far as our financial relations are concerned. I think it is better to leave this open a bit until you digest this letter.
>
> I have one suggestion to make. Suppose I show Clarence Day the manuscript as it is now or Harvey O'Higgins, with whom, by the way, I was out to lunch the day before yesterday. I would value either of these men's opinions very highly.
>
> My dear boy, you don't know what a difficult letter this has been for me to write but I can't say any more now. . . . Please believe that I am always your very faithful friend.[8]

Hackett was opposed to the prospect of having Day or O'Higgins read his manuscript, but he did revise about sixty pages of the work. Once the revision arrived at the house, Liveright still had reservations about the future popularity of Hackett's book. On March 13, 1925 he wrote the author and enclosed a check for $500.

> First and foremost as you say, the price of *That Nice Young Couple* is going to be $2.00 not $2.50; so set your fluttering heart at rest. But what's more serious is the fact that the trade absolutely won't buy the book in advance. They say it's another first novel. That (to quote them) the few people who do know you in this country know you as a critic, etc., etc. I am enclosing a copy of a letter that I am sending out to all the book trade. Please believe that I'm going to do my level best on the book. $1500.00 advance is an unquestionably large one against any novel by a person who hasn't had a very successful novel already published. The average first novel sells about 1200 copies. I simply give you these facts so that you can prepare for the worst. The book will be published about April 15th.

On May 7, 1925 he wrote the author once more:

> Instead of sending you the rough proof of the advertisement, I am attaching the finished proof. I wonder if you realize that this advertisement in the *New York Times*, *Tribune*, and *Evening Post* Book Sections, the *New York World* Broun page, The *Philadelphia Ledger*, *Boston Transcript*, *Post* and *News* in Chicago, costs $550. This means 20¢ a copy on 2500 copies and, of course, before this we have done a lot of trade advertising and also ran two announcement advertisements in three of the New York papers which I think you've already seen. Thirty cents a copy is just about the limit on a $2.00 novel if the publisher is to break even.
>
> You will notice that the advertising reads "second edition before publication." So that you don't get too much cheered up by this, the facts are as follows: Our first printing was 2000 copies and right before publication we found that our advance orders DUE TO DARN HARD WORK IN PUTTING OVER A FIRST NOVEL TO THE TRADE WERE 1478 copies. One hundred nine were sent out for review to various publications throughout the country and approximately 250 were sent to the trade itself with my compliments, a total of 1837 copies. So, naturally, we reprinted 1000 copies immediately to be sure to have books in stock, when, as, and if reorders come in. Up to present writing I am thoroughly satisfied with the course and progress

of your first child. I intend to reprint in editions of 1000 right along now should the book catch on.

But Liveright did not have the occasion to reprint *That Nice Young Couple*, for, as he informed Hackett the next month, the reviews were "ugly."[9] Moreover, the book Liveright had suggested —and still very much wanted—seemed no closer to completion. In an attempt to spur on Hackett, the publisher sent him a revised contract for the biography on June 3, 1926. With a check for $500 in the envelope, Hackett's advance on *Henry VIII* amounted to $2200; another $500 would be sent once the first twenty thousand words of the manuscript appeared. For his part the author promised to deliver the first twenty thousand words by September 15, 1926 and the final completed work in time for publication in February 1927. While Hackett, in Europe, often mentioned Liveright's "characteristic and shocking liberality" and kept promising to deliver the manuscript, it was not until nearly three years later that Liveright received it. But the publisher's patience was rewarded when the Book-of-the-Month Club expressed an interest in offering *Henry VIII* to its subscribers.

As Liveright soon discovered, the Club's proposal was a mixed blessing: for Hackett it offered prestige and a much larger audience than he might have expected to achieve, while to his publisher it meant higher sales and lower profits.[10] The gross profit for Liveright on Hackett's biography at its original retail price of $5.00 a copy was $1.07. However, in order to meet the requirements of the Book-of-the-Month Club, Liveright was forced to cut the price of the work to $3.00. The gross profit for the house at this figure was only 64 cents; hence Liveright in effect lost 43 cents of profit on every copy he sold at the lower price. But with heavy advertising as well as distribution by the book club, nearly one hundred sixty thousand copies of *Henry VIII* were soon sold, making it the second best-selling work of nonfiction in 1929.[11] At the height of the book's popularity, however, Erich Maria Remarque's *All Quiet on the Western Front* was issued, and within a few weeks the public was reading about the War instead of the life and passions of the English monarch. Even Hackett did not make an enormous amount of money, since a considerable part of his royalties went back to the firm to settle his large advances. Nevertheless, the author appeared to be extremely grateful to Liveright, for during the success of *Henry VIII* he wrote the publisher that without him the book would not exist. Liveright, Hackett said, had asked him to write about Henry and had helped him when no one else was willing to. Hackett signed himself "your collaborator."[12]

When Liveright learned that Hackett would be unable to finish his next book in time for spring publication, he wrote the author:

> Business is so dull now that I feel sure some of the morons in America who are thinking of nothing but the radio and golf now, will take to reading again in October. And I see no reason why *Henry* shouldn't carry over into the Fall as a big-seller, although, of course, by then some non-fiction will, undoubtedly, have appeared that will displace it as the best seller, or No. 1 on the list. I believe, for example, that *All Quiet on the Western Front* will beat us this month. It is the book-of-the-month for June and starts off with a tremendous press, though the advertising to my mind doesn't compare with ours on *Henry*. And to the Baker & Taylor Company, *Henry* was the biggest seller in the country during May, not only of non-fiction, but of any book being sold during that period including fiction. Unfortunately for *Henry*, it was published during the worst season the book-trade has known in fifteen years. This opinion is concurred in by not only most of the publishers to whom I have talked, but was stated flatly in several speeches at the American Booksellers Convention in Boston a couple of weeks ago.
>
> All sorts of explanations are given for this condition, but few people seem to realize that the speculative mania which has spread through the country is at the root of the whole matter. From bootblacks and barkers and elevator boys and Jap valets to society women, Cooper Union students, college boys, etc. etc., the getting something for nothing hysteria has spread like wild-fire. If people read at all now, they read financial pages. I've been so impressed with this state of affairs that I've gotten Arthur Train to write a novel on the subject which is to be called, *Nothing for Nothing*. There has been a terrible shakeout in the market during the last month which I think has sobered people up a bit. They may find consolation in reading about Henry and getting away from themselves.
>
> How I find myself going on in spite of a desk piled with

detail work! I'll wind up now by saying it would be a big mistake not to have *Harry Juniper* for publication by February 1st. Naturally, following Henry we want to make a big preliminary campaign on it, so the manuscript should be in my hands for careful reading not later than September 15th. And really, this should be the deadline.

The big historical novel interests me tremendously. I am frightfully eager to know what the subject is going to be.

It will interest you to know that up to June 1st, the approximate figures on the sale of *Henry* were 63,000 copies to the Book-of-the-Month Club, and about 43,000 to the general trade. I think if the season had been better, the book club sales would have been up about 12,000 copies and our own 15,000 to 20,000. However, we can't sneeze at this.[13]

Hackett's gratitude was apparently of short duration. In the fall of 1929, he wrote Liveright that he had abandoned *Harry Juniper*; in addition, he set forth to the publisher the terms on which he would deal concerning the book he proposed to do next. Liveright was amazed at the sudden change in tone, but made his offer.

Your cable which I received a few minutes ago comes as a great shock to me. After all of our correspondence on *Harry Juniper*, including your definite promise to deliver the manuscript to us in time for publication, and the advance work we have done with the trade on this book, I am frightfully disappointed, to say the least. No less of a shock is your cool wiping out of all of our past relationships with the offer of a book in place of *Harry Juniper* at such and such a price. Don't you feel in your heart, after all that has been done for *Henry*, which took into consideration, to some extent, the fact that we were going to have your next two books, namely, *Harry Juniper* and *The Lives of the Saints*, that you should simply say: "I feel *Harry Juniper* is not my book, but in place of it, I am doing for you a *Life of Francis 1st*. And what additional in the way of advance could you afford to give me, Horace, because of the great success of *Henry*?"

I am terribly cut up by the whole matter. However, I don't want to enter into any sort of business or legal dispute with you as to our rights. We have a contract and you have received an advance on *Harry Juniper*. Please believe me when I write in this fashion that I am not trying to enter into a quarrel of any kind. It is likely that *Francis* will be a great book and that it is the sound kind of thing for you to do after *Henry*, rather than *Harry Juniper*, but [i]t is anything but friendly of you to simply say you are not going to do *Harry Juniper* and that if I don't accept your terms on *Francis* you'll offer it elsewhere.

You say that *Francis* will be ready for publication by the Spring of 1931, but you thought *Henry* would be ready years before it was. Granting that $10,000, by date of publication is not too exorbitant an advance, though it is very very stiff, how is the money to be paid so that we can have some measure of security about the delivery of the manuscript? Suppose we enter into a contract for *Francis* which will carry the option on another one or two of your books. Suppose we are willing to pay you on the signing of this contract $5000. the remaining $5000. to be paid to you by us on receipt by us of the finished manuscript of *Francis*? Do you honestly feel that this original payment of $5000. will carry you along so that you won't want to draw on us again until the manuscript is finished? I certainly feel that with the continued sales of *Henry* this should be all right. I would like your assurances on the subject. Let me hear from you about this right away.

You ask for 50¢ royalties on the $3.00 work. In the first place, we don't know whether *Francis* would be a $3.00 book. Naturally it depends to some extent upon its length. But say it's around 100,000 words. Then we should get anywhere from $3.50 to $5.00 for the book and sell as many copies at $3.00. Naturally if it is a Book-of-the-Month choice, it will have to be $3.00. It is extremely unlikely that they will as early as 1931 pick another book of yours no matter how glorious it is. I feel that we will have a better chance with the Literary Guild, presuming that the book clubs will be as flourishing by that time as they now are. I think it only fair to ask you to keep the royalties, apart from any deal with the book clubs, at 15% of the retail price. You may say that 5¢ a copy on a $3.00 book means very little, but I am sure that this amount spent in advertising will do you more good than the royalty, itself. If you could look over our books and see the immense amount spent per copy on *Henry VIII*, you would get my point.

There can be no doubt that a book on Francis 1st covering Calvin and Rabelais, Marguerite and the beginnings of Modern France would be a magnificent companion volume to *Henry VIII* and that after a year or so they could be sold together in a set. In fact, I have plans in mind already for this.[14]

Hackett was far from being pleased with Liveright's proposals. In reply to another letter from the writer, Liveright wrote on October 17, 1929:

> I have just read for the third time your letter of October 7th. My answer to you is going to revolve around one sentence in your letter which reads as follows: "My feeling is that you make a mistake in accusing me of not acting in a friendly way." I'll leave it to any jury of absolutely unprejudiced minds . . . to pass on the whole matter. I want you to understand that I am not talking in business terms at all. I am talking to you now as man to man, not as publisher to author. I don't want to get sentimental nor do I want to say anything that isn't logically sound. After the tremendous success of *Henry VIII* which after all, as you say, was a sort of a stepchild of mine, I am going to feel deeply humiliated if you publish *Francis I* with someone else. You definitely say in your letter that you would not take my acceptance of your original terms. Nevertheless, I formally put myself on record as being willing to accept your terms. You also say that I don't seem to know real friendliness when I see it. But time is bound to disclose the full history of my efforts. Naturally, Francis, I realize that if *Henry VIII* had not been the great book it is, no efforts of mine would have been worth very much. Now I make the flat statement that no one can sell as many copies of *Francis I* as I can. Unless you are already definitely committed on the book, do stop and think.

Liveright was too late. Hackett had joined another firm—for security he said—and he wrote the publisher a long letter setting forth his reasoning in great detail.[15] First, Hackett asserted that he stood by his original demands, which were, he felt, not unreasonable in the light of the success of *Henry VIII*. Then he accused Liveright of haggling with him and announced that he had found a London publisher who was willing to subsidize him for a five-year period while he wrote *Francis I*, and who had also promised him 20-25 per cent royalties when the book appeared. Third, Hackett admitted that he was greatly indebted to Liveright, who had, of course, advanced several thousands of dollars to the writer over the past seven years; but Hackett complained that the publisher was insensitive to the humiliating position he (Hackett) had had to endure. In fact, in a lengthy diatribe directed specifically against Liveright's treasurer, Arthur Pell, but indicting Liveright as well, Hackett listed his most recent grievances: unpaid hotel bills in Copenhagen, Christmas presents he could not buy, a poor impression he had made on a relative, and his wife's present illness from anemia. Pell, he said, was most directly responsible for his "anguish"—the treasurer had deducted the publisher's advances to Hackett before sending the author his earnings from *Henry VIII*—but, Hackett implied, Liveright must share the blame as well. While there was nothing illegal about Pell's method, Hackett did not now wish to live on his *Henry VIII* earnings while writing *Francis I*. Therefore, he found Liveright's offer of $5000 now, $5000 on delivery of the manuscript, and 15 per cent royalties insufficient for his needs. Though Hackett gave Liveright credit for his fantastic success in publicizing and selling *Henry VIII*, the author could not forgive what now appeared to him as a loss of faith on the part of the publisher. Hackett ended the letter by saying that his decision to leave the firm was the most painful business decision he had ever made because he felt that he and Liveright had found a common bond and because of Liveright's *joie de vivre* and talent in publishing. But Liveright had sold out, become callous, and so their relationship must end; on the other hand, Hackett held himself blameless.

Liveright's reply was a good deal shorter and simpler.

Rather than write you a long letter in answer to yours of December 4th which I got, by the way, about the 20th, I'm merely enclosing a memorandum that I asked Mr. Pell to draw up for me. Mr. Pell says in the first paragraph of his explanation to me that every deal and payment between you and our firm was made with my knowledge. As a matter of fact this is not exactly so as I have divested myself of practically all the financial parts of the business.

I really feel too deeply about the whole thing to say much. I smile a little cynically when I read your lovely inscription in the copy of *Henry* which you sent me. And I grit my teeth a bit when I think that *Francis I* will be written quickly because of the vast amount of research work you did on *Henry* and which equips you so well to do the *Francis*. You say you think I have hardened since we first met. You are entirely mistaken. And I am sure that practically every author on my list would disagree with you.

Well, at any rate, a happy New Year to you and Signe. I'll be in London in March. Maybe we'll run across each other and have a drink in spite of the change in our status.[16]

Deserted by both new and established best-selling authors, Liveright put his hope in the success of several less prominent figures and concentrated on attentive treatment of those popular writers who remained loyal to him. Four new authors seemed to show promise of good sales. They included Will Cuppy and S. J. Perelman, whose early works *How to Be a Hermit* and *Dawn Ginsberg's Revenge* appeared in 1929; Peter Arno, whose two volumes of cartoons, *Parade* and *Hullabaloo*, sold a total of over thirty-five thousand copies combined;[17] and, unlike the preceding in practically every way, Mike Gold, then editor of *The New Masses*.

Gold's letter of inquiry to Liveright in July 1928 clearly indicates the publisher's continuing impact in the New York literary world of the Twenties. Having finished his autobiography, which dealt with growing up on New York's lower East Side, Gold wrote that he felt he was ready to be discovered. He was approaching Liveright because of the publisher's known genius for gambling on new talent and developing unknown writers of promise. What did Liveright think, Gold asked, of adding him to the publisher's list of trophies?

In his reply Liveright offered Gold a $400 advance on his autobiography; if the firm did not accept it for publication, Gold was to keep $150 for his inconvenience: "You need the money and I need to do just as little work as I can for the next week or so, so I am enclosing the check for $150, and when I get around to it I will send you the usual contract."[18] Despite its appearance during the worst publishing season in years, Gold's memoirs, *Jews Without Money*, had a highly respectable sale in 1930 of over thirteen thousand copies.[19]

In the spring of 1929 Liveright heard from Ezra Pound, who wanted him to issue the poet's translation of Fr. Fiorentino's *Manual of Philosophy*.[20] In addition, Pound wished to know Liveright's reaction to a small "translation factory" he proposed to start.

The poet's idea was to have amateurs translate French and Italian works of biography and fiction to which he would add the finishing touches. Whatever Liveright thought was commercial, Pound would be willing to supply. It was not of course, the poet stated, in the mainstream of his literary career—just a way to make some extra money. Finally, Pound was concerned with the political situation in the United States and wanted to know Liveright's opinion as to the advisability of debating Upton Sinclair here on the virtues of socialism. Sinclair's books appeared to be on every newsstand in Germany and in Russia too, Pound volunteered, but his own point of view would follow the capitalistic, or as Villard called it abusingly and ignorantly, the "fascist" philosophy. Liveright refused Pound's translation proposal. In responding to the poet, however, he asked to be kept informed of any other works or writers Pound considered worthy of recognition.

> It is very interesting to know that you are about to start a small but chaste translation factory. But first let me say nothing doing on Fiorentino's manual of philosophy. According to my information, which may be wrong, I am told that this is a rather formal manual and I don't think it would have any sort of sale these days particularly having been done by a continental. If my facts are wrong, let me know.
>
> Upton Sinclair's position in the United States is a peculiar one. Everyone knows him but unless some special stunt publicity comes out at the time of publication of his books, they don't sell. I've published a couple of his volumes that have done fairly well. Then we rejected *Oil!* but due to the tremendous publicity it got through being suppressed in Boston, and the way the whole thing was arranged, it had a very fine sale and his subsequent two-volume work, *Boston*, largely concerned with the Sacco-Vanzetti case, has also done well. I'm afraid, my friend, that the socialist idea is dead as a doornail in America and will be so long as the country is prosperous.
>
> We'll keep thinking about the translation idea, but I must once again revert to the fact that my idea to you about the novel is the hot potooty.[21]

Whenever a letter from Pound arrived at the firm, the personnel gathered in Liveright's office to hear what the poet had to report or castigate.[22] Unlike Pound, whose correspondence and enthusiasms were sporadic and vehement but whose literary judgment Liveright respected and whose suggestions he invariably considered carefully, Gertrude Atherton maintained a steady flow of letters to the publisher—letters which besides being constant were newsy, filled with gossip about food and people "too stupid to talk to," and, from time to time, quarrelsome or indignant. Like Ezra Pound, however, Mrs. Atherton was never dull.

After the success of *Black Oxen* in 1923, Gertrude Atherton had produced no other sensational best-seller, though her later works, *The Crystal Cup*, *The Immortal Marriage*, and *The Jealous Gods*, were by no means failures. The novelist had become somewhat dissatisfied by the fall of 1928, particularly after her latest effort, *The Jealous Gods*, had slipped off the popularity charts almost as soon as it had attained them. She wrote to Liveright complaining of the lack of publicity her book was receiving and went on to protest the apparent inattention from which she had suffered lately: "I don't see how you could think I would not be angry with everybody . . . and only two ads in three weeks. If you had explained the situation in the beginning and told me you thought it was not to advantage to advertise until shortly before Christmas, I shouldn't have said a word for I am always reasonable."[23]

Though satisfied that he could answer Mrs. Atherton's questions about the promotion of her novel, Liveright could not understand the lack of attention from his staff. He sent the author's letter, along with a memo, to two of his associates, Aaron Sussman and Natalie Hankemeyer, and inquired about the matter. Sussman replied that "Mrs. Atherton in one of her letters to us definitely asked us to keep reporters, etc., from her. We did as well as we could under the circumstances—feeling that she did not want to be troubled. We are now giving her the works! I don't think she'll complain again."[24]

Miss Hankemeyer's report revealed something of what "the works" entailed. After reminding the publisher that, following a tea he had given for Mrs. Atherton, the author had announced that she had not really wanted a party, simply a few days rest, Liveright's assistant listed the schedule she had set up for the novelist:

I am arranging interviews with Harry Salpeter, a young lady from the *Post*, Mary Rennels from the *Telegram*, a writer from the

Philadelphia Ledger syndicate, Mrs. Leland from the *Brooklyn Eagle,* and I think I can get someone from the *Tribune.* This just about covers all the worthwhile mediums in town. . . . I can arrange for her to talk over the radio whenever she is ready.[25]

By January 1929, Sussman and Miss Hankemeyer had arranged for Mrs. Atherton to speak in Boston, to be interviewed by a writer from the *Boston Herald,* and to have an artist sketch her portrait for a *New York Times* book advertisement.[26]

Liveright himself contacted Isabel Paterson, editor of "The Bookworm" in the *New York Herald Tribune,* about interviewing Mrs. Atherton for her column. But the newspaper woman was reluctant to take on the novelist. Mrs. Atherton was a wonderful woman, she said, but an individual who had definite notions about what a columnist might print from their private conversations.[27] Liveright sent Miss Paterson's letter to Mrs. Atherton, whose reply was indignant:

> This is ridiculous. What has it to do with leaving my book out of the recommended Christmas list? Or mentioning it otherwise? Especially when historical novels are under discussion? If no personalities about myself were written until the day of doom that would not interest me one way or another.
>
> The truth of the matter is she wants to stand well with her running mates and they would suppress me altogether if they could. Please destroy this.[28]

Fortunately, Mrs. Atherton was a tremendous success in Boston when she spoke there. She wrote the publisher about her speech, its favorable reception, and the number of autographs she was called on to give. The only blemish on her complete triumph in Massachusetts was the review of her appearance written by Henry S. Canby. However, Mrs. Atherton was so pleased with herself that Canby's criticism provoked little comment. "That was a nasty slam by little Canby in his papers. But I expected nothing but. A mean little man."[29] The interviews the author had with writers for the Boston newspapers came off smoothly, too, with the sole exception of one questioner: "This Genn woman is a dumbbell. She used that horrible picture of me and never mentioned *The Jealous Gods.* She'll never get another interview from me. What does she imagine I wasted two hours on her for—to give her material for a seven page article?"[30]

Following her successful appearances in New York and Boston, Mrs. Atherton settled down to write a new novel. At first she intended to complete the *Immortal Marriage-Jealous Gods* trilogy with an historical novel she had begun about Creusa, the daughter of Priam and wife of Aeneas.[31] Then the American Classical League announced that Virgil would be its theme for 1929, so Mrs. Atherton decided to change her own subject to Dido instead.[32] In three months she had completed her manuscript. Either the novelist worked with the speed and perseverance of Trollope, or she simply changed the names in her partially completed Creusa work, for by May 1929 Liveright had read and was returning to her the major part of her manuscript.[33]

With the production of *Dido, Queen of Hearts* underway, correspondence between Liveright and his author became even more frequent; it sometimes appears that Mrs. Atherton sent her publisher daily directions. At first she was irritated about the book jacket, then the number and size of the proofs, and finally she wanted to argue about the retail price of the book. She bombarded Liveright with letters and telegrams until he assured her that "Abyssinia" had been changed to "Assyria" throughout the text.[34] At the same time she sent him all her good publicity notices, remarking on her embarrassment at such praises. When the publisher asked her opinion of getting Carl Van Doren to read her manuscript for Literary Guild consideration, Mrs. Atherton showed her ever-present business sense:

> I doubt if Canby or Van Doren would do anything to advantage me as I despise both of them as bootlicking time-servers and they know it.
>
> However their snobbishness might induce them to take *Dido*—as I wrote it at the request of the American Classical League. If they do—so much the better. I have no objection to making use of them.[35]

In the next letter she was furious about the picture on the book jacket and wanted her volume to have a yellow cover because she believed yellow sold better. Liveright answered:

I have never felt that the *Dido* jacket was anything but effective. I knew perfectly well that it might not be accurate historically. I am enclosing two other proofs that we discarded although they were I believe historically accurate, though they made Dido much too dark and semitic for sales effect.

The finished book won't be manufactured until every detail has your approval. I know perfectly well that you'll consider the sales end when you give your opinions.[36]

When Liveright suggested that the publication of *Dido* might better be postponed until the following spring to create more audience appeal by making her readers wait an extra year for her latest work (not to mention giving her publisher a respite from the barrage of letters and telegrams he had been receiving), he found that Mrs. Atherton was adamantly opposed. Moreover, she still was not pleased with the book jacket.

You have a gay fashion of doing anything you please without consulting the author—as witness that ridiculous jacket.
P.S. The Phoenicians had no helmets—as they never made war and were rarely attacked.
P.P.S. I wish you would suggest an idea for a modern novel.[37]

Dutifully Liveright denied irresponsibility on his part and replied that he prayed every night that they would get a contract from the Literary Guild.[38] While the Guild delayed making its decision, Liveright checked the final proof of *Dido*.

Please put your mind at ease about the jacket. It is very difficult to get up the right sort of jacket before one has read the manuscript of a book, and even then the jackets that we sometimes use on our dummies have to be very hurriedly made as I already told you. The jacket of *Dido* will be on a yellow background and the front of the jacket will have no illustration but merely well-chosen and arranged type. A new picture of you will be used on the back of the jacket and the text will be changed as you have directed.[39]

In August, he reported to Mrs. Atherton that the Guild had decided not to accept her novel. Moreover, the outlook for its sales was not encouraging:

It is probably not so rich in historical background and detail and perhaps, too, its subject matter is better known and for that reason the book may not be considered quite so unusual. But I stick to it that for me *Dido* possesses more charm than either *The Immortal Marriage* or *The Jealous Gods.* . . . It is only honest to tell you that our salesmen are not meeting with particularly favorable reactions from the book trade. The sellers want a novel since historical fiction is temporarily on the wane. The advance orders are not as good as hoped for.[40]

Liveright went on to say that he had made a few manuscript corrections. The problem which most concerned him was how the nobles who deserted Tyre could have gotten their possessions on board ship without Pygmalion's finding out about it. He asked the novelist to insert some sort of explanation. Mrs. Atherton answered that an explanation wasn't needed.

As to the nobles getting their possessions on board undetected, remember they only took their portable treasure—jewels and gold— and this could easily be done at night. The ancients all went to bed early. There was no night life.

I am sorry the advance orders are unsatisfactory, but perhaps the great Virgil celebration next year will help it. I hope so, not only for its own sake but because I want to write more "ancient" novels.

Why are people so mentally lazy? That is the secret of their antagonism to the historical novel.

I do wish you sent out proofs like those Houghton Mifflin sent me. . . . They were cut in strips of reasonable length and bound at the top. I spend half my time picking [your proofs] up off the floor and then sorting them out.[41]

The next month Mrs. Atherton wrote again from her home in San Francisco. She was coming east in order to take a ship to Europe, and she hoped to have a few advance copies of *Dido* to take along with her.

The days are beginning to drag, for I am quite ready, and anxious to get off. I carried your fan to the first night of the opera —in a box—and again it was the only one in the house, which was packed with the fashionable and rich. Odd, how long anything new takes to get out here. I wore my jade green chiffon embroidered with silver, so it was very effective.[42]

Dido was issued late in October 1929. The advance orders, amounting to about ten thousand copies, accounted for the major part of its sale. The reviews were consistently unfavorable, and a reading public alarmed by the Wall Street panic did not turn for comfort to Mrs. Atherton's *Queen of Hearts*. Liveright wrote her in Rome.

> The book has not done very well but I don't want to pretend that I think it's because of the collapse in the stock market and the general depression that really and truly does exist in most circles. I think the break in the stock market has put the country back on some sort of saner and more spiritual basis and that people are looking to books for comfort.
>
> In talking to the leading booksellers who I visited and to many in New York who drop into my office they tell me they think three historical novels of the ancient world from your pen so quickly in succession was ill-advised. I have told them that you didn't care whether it was ill-advised or not, that you wanted to write these books, that they were books that were not for a season, and that all in all we were both perfectly satisfied. With a few exceptions, too, the reviews are not kind to *Dido*. I hope you don't see some of them. The book has sold about 11,500 copies and I think almost entirely on your name. We advertised it well but in the last few weeks diverted our advertising expenditures and energies from the newspaper to posters and direct-by-mail work with the book-stores and lists of names particularly in scholastic circles.
>
> No particular books have sold sensationally this Fall. There were so many fairly good novels and works of non-fiction published in an avalanche that all suffered accordingly. . . . After being out of the National Association of Book Publishers ever since the censorship battle which you so valiantly helped me win, I finally persuaded myself to rejoin. I received such a highly flattering invitation to come back into the fold that conditions being what they are, I accepted it. With the numbers of new publishers, with the book-clubs, with the log-rolling and what not that has become worse and worse in the years I've been publishing books, I feel that I may be of some little influence at the various meetings and dinners the publishers give.[43]

The publication of *Dido, Queen of Hearts* was followed the next month by the first major work of new fiction by Theodore

Dreiser since *An American Tragedy*. Called *A Gallery of Women*, this two-volume collection of stories appeared on November 30, received limited praise, and had a disappointing first-year sale of only 13,653 copies.[44] It had been preceded in 1926 by a book of Dreiser's verse, *Moods, Cadenced and Declaimed*, which had proved an enormous loss to the house when only 922 copies were purchased initially; in 1927 by *Chains*, a volume of Dreiser's earlier short stories which fared much better on the market but still—with twelve thousand copies sold—represented a major falling off in the author's popularity; and in 1928 by *Dreiser Looks at Russia* which had a sale of only about four thousand copies.[45] As he almost invariably did when his books did not sell, Dreiser opened negotiations with other firms interested in acquiring him. This time they included the Cosmopolitan Book Corporation, Harper's, and Simon & Schuster.[46]

In the spring of 1929, Dreiser confronted Liveright to complain of lagging sales and the publisher's failure to produce the collected edition of the writer's works promised in the 1926 contract.[47] But by this time the era of collected editions was nearly over, and Liveright dared not risk the enormous expense of a Dreiser edition, especially since the author seemed unable to finish a best-selling novel to follow *An American Tragedy*. In order not to lose the author who had been with him the longest and whose prestige in the literary world was still great, Liveright met Dreiser's demands and then some. In return for the promise of the elusive new novel (a work that neither Liveright nor his firm was ever to see) and the writer's lesser efforts, the publisher promised him payments of $1200 each month, retroactive to January 1, 1929, and reaffirmed Dreiser's right to examine the firm's books at any time the suspicious author wished to commission an auditor to do so. (On February 11, 1929, Dreiser's auditor had reviewed the books.) And once again, Dreiser decided to stay with Liveright and signed a new contract on April 19, 1929.

Mrs. Atherton was a lady to be handled carefully, and Dreiser was so suspicious that he expected the worst at all times. With Bertrand Russell, however, Liveright maintained a cordial relationship that became fruitful for both. From the beginning of his association with the publisher in January 1925 the British writer was amenable to most suggestions Liveright made regarding the text, production, or promotion of Russell's work in America. The author rarely asked to see the proofs of his books after minor corrections had been made, and he generally took Liveright's advice on writing for the American market. Moreover, Russell never questioned the terms of his contract with Liveright, never demanded additional advances or royalties, and never looked for special treatment. This harmonious relationship between publisher and author figured in a growing audience and increasing royalties for Russell as well as larger profits and satisfaction for Liveright.

The first Russell volume Liveright published was *Education and the Good Life,* which appeared in 1926 and sold six thousand copies.[48] The following year the publisher signed a contract with the writer for a book tentatively called *Sex Freedom;* the terms of their agreement included a $2,000 advance and royalties of 15 per cent per volume. Liveright understood that the work would deal with three major topics:

1. The advocation of absolute sex freedom.
2. The hypothesis that some people are the better for promiscuity.
3. The belief that few men and women ought to be content with one partner for life.[49]

Russell's manuscript, retitled *Marriage and Morals,* finally arrived in New York two years later. In the meantime the publisher had entertained the writer during his speaking tour of the United States in 1927 and issued Russell's *The ABC of Relativity* in 1928.

Both Liveright and Russell were aware of the controversial nature of *Marriage and Morals.* After he had received the work, Liveright wrote Russell enthusiastically:

> What a wonderful book you have written in *Marriage and Morals!* I have read the manuscript twice and I want you to know that I consider it the most important book on our Fall list.
>
> I have already had the business manager of the Book-of-the-Month club read the manuscript and he telephoned me yesterday that while some modifications in the text might be in order should their six judges choose it as the book of the month, say for any month from November until February, he did not believe that the

spirit of the book or any principles involved should be changed at all. Please don't let me mislead you. All that this manager has done has been to recommend it to the judges for reading. I, personally, am rather close to two or three of the judges and will do everything in my power to bring it to their favorable attention. It does not strike me, though, that this organization or any other book club would dare to send this book to 70,000 middle class people throughout the country as their selection. It would be a most heartening sign of liberalism in this country if they did.

I am, of course, personally delighted with the book and assure you that there will be very few, if any, changes in certain rather strong sentences. There is one suggestion, or, I suppose, I should say request, that I would like to make of you. In two or three places in the book you speak about freedom of speech, of the press, censorship, etc., etc. In that the manuscript is now in the hands of the compositor, I can't exactly recall where you might do me the justice (if I do say this myself) of mentioning the active and successful campaign which I waged practically singlehanded in 1924 [sic] in defeating the most outrageous bit of censorship legislation ever proposed in the State of New York. . . . I think I can say without fear of denial that outside of the active officers of the Civil Liberties Union, I have for the past ten years in my publishing, in my speeches and in the amount of time and money I have expended done more to oppose all sorts of censorship than almost any one else in this country. If a reference to this is made in *Marriage and Morals*, it will be a lasting monument to me and to what I have done in this field. Naturally, my dear Russell, if you feel that a paragraph about this will be out of place don't hesitate to tell me so.[50]

Russell agreed to discuss Liveright's contributions in a footnote near the end of chapter eight in his book.[51] Later, Liveright suggested other small, but significant changes in the text.

May I make two or three suggestions, most of them minor ones? Can't you change the headings of the first three chapters? Introduction is a bad heading because most people refuse to read introductions, even though they are printed in the body of the text. However, this isn't as vital as the changing of the next two chapter headings, Matrilineal Societies and Patriarchal Systems. Several of the leading book-sellers with whom I have discussed the book at length say that these chapter headings sound pretty heavy and may hurt the sale of the book. I am sure you will be able to give us better headings that will be more popular.

On page 68 you say that I do not think it can be denied that women are on the average stupider than men, etc. You may be entirely correct in this, but maybe you can soften it. On the other hand, there might be a distinct advertising angle in leaving this in. I merely call it to your attention.

On the next page, 69, you say that almost all elderly gentlemen are so perverted, etc. I sincerely question this.

You will see that I have read the manuscript very carefully. The fact that I have found so remarkably little to question is the best tribute I can pay to your sound and fine volume.[52]

Marriage and Morals was published about the time the stock market crashed. Despite the season twenty-three thousand copies of the book were soon sold.[53] The next year Liveright accepted Russell's new work, *The Conquest of Happiness,* and gave the manuscript the same careful reading as well as offering the author suggestions about ways to improve it.[54] In his final letter to Russell before leaving the firm and New York, Liveright, in effect, announced the end of his publishing career:

Because of the book-war and many meetings which took place for about ten days after your manuscript arrived, I read it only yesterday or you would have had a cable from me before this. I believe that you have done in this your best book so far as any we have published is concerned. If it does not have a very wide sale it will only be because of terrible business conditions in general and the peculiar conditions attending book-publishing just now due to the fight between certain large publishers and the cutting of prices on so many of the new Fall books.

Let me reiterate that reading your book not only gave me one of the greatest intellectual pleasures that I have had in a long time, but I know it is going to give me a great deal to think about for a long time to come. It seems that I have all of the vices that make for unhappiness; envy, sense of sin, fear of public opinion, and what not. I haven't reached the stage of having a persecution complex.

I believe that it will interest you to know that I am going out to the Pacific Coast in two or three weeks to see two or three of our authors who are out there and who have been begging me for a long time to visit them and also to work on the filming of two or three books in which we are interested. I don't know exactly how long I'll be away, but in my absence everything will be in very good hands.[55]

Epilogue

Liveright's departure for Hollywood in the late summer of 1930 was brought on by a number of causes, all of them financial. First, the books he had published in 1929 and the first six months of 1930 had not sold, nor did he hold any hope of their ever catching on. Second, a book war among New York publishers which had begun in June 1930 threatened to ruin his firm.[1] Several companies—such as Farrar and Rinehart, and Doubleday—had issued volumes that retailed for a $1.00 per copy in an attempt to recapture a reading public that had been greatly reduced by the Depression. Liveright had refused to offer any $1.00 books in order to protect the prestige of his list of authors whose books retailed at from $2.00 to $5.00 per volume. Third, Liveright himself was bankrupt, because his losses in the theatre and more especially in the market had wiped him out. In Hollywood he hoped to sell to the film studios the movie rights to books he still had an interest in; his share in such sales might make him solvent again. The publisher explained his decision, or indirectly suggested the reasons for his new venture, in a parting letter to Eugene O'Neill, written in July 1930:

> What do you think of my going to Hollywood? No, I haven't sold myself down the river or anything like that, but due to Otto Kahn's connection with Paramount Publix Corporation, his firm being their bankers, I think I have worked out a plan which may be very profitable for my publishing firm and our authors. I am to spend two or three months in carefully going over our entire list of books from the time we started publishing and attempt to find two or three really outstanding publications for the talkies.
>
> I think the change in climate will do me good. This summer in New York has been frightful and after a strenuous trip abroad, and then the dollar book situation over here,—well the combination has run me down.[2]

Despite this apparent frankness with O'Neill, Liveright kept the really decisive reason for his removal to Hollywood from his friends and the public. He no longer controlled the publishing house that bore his name and had been forced by his former employees to leave the firm.[3]

It is possible to determine how but not exactly when Liveright was deposed and became only the figurehead president of Horace Liveright, Inc.; several surviving letters outline his downhill progress. Best-sellers seemed to have sustained him through 1928, but January of 1929 began the worst book-selling season he had ever known, and the failure of *The Dagger and the Rose*, his costly production that never reached Broadway, was all it took to put him further in debt. In June he wrote to Wallerstein at length:

> Suppose I sort of departmentalize this letter. (1), the publishing business: I'm pretty badly worried, Alfred, about our situation. We have always been undercapitalized and have made the mistake, when we have made money, of always drawing it out. So far this year, our sales are about $150,000. shy of last year's. This in spite of *Henry VIII* being a book-of-the-month book, and apart from that, the best selling book in the country for almost six weeks. Now *All Quiet on the Western Front* is about to take its place. We missed this book by only about six days and through no slip-up on our part. None of our fiction has sold at all to speak of, and none of our non-fiction for the Spring has gone well, but it is generally agreed in the trade that this is the worst season they have experienced in fifteen years. . . . This doesn't help our position, but it does make me feel that it hasn't been entirely because of a bad list. Our fall list is in very good shape. We are about a month ahead of last year on our catalogue and dummies, and I think we have a splendid fiction list, the best in a long while, but not as good a non-fiction list as we sometimes have. I am still looking around for two good non-fiction books to spring as surprises after the catalogue goes out. On and off I have worked most strenuously. Naturally while Julian is away, I will be absolutely on the waterwagon as though I had a play in rehearsal. This will mean a period of from seven to eight weeks, I think, and it will do me a lot of good. And when I work I thoroughly enjoy it, and would revel in it if I felt more confident of publishing as a permanent means of making a very good living without any educational or juvenile department or a

fine back-list (which we haven't go) and with such keen competition from new publishers and the book clubs to combat. I feel that the book clubs are getting to be a bigger menace every day. Of course, the booksellers are frantic about the situation. Naturally with sales falling off so badly and with no cut in overhead, our financial position is affected, but Arthur feels that with general business conditions good this Fall, book-business will be bound to pick up, and with our list as good as it is, we may recapture a part of our loss of $150,000. sales. The office is functioning wonderfully well.

(2), play business: *Dracula* has more or less disappointed us in Chicago, due I think to our getting in the wrong theatre which was nobody's fault as we booked through Erlanger and could only get the theatre we took blocks away from the Loop. . . . I have read hundreds of plays and have as yet found nothing of which I feel sure enough for the Fall. I've been to several rehearsals of plays I could buy into but worse than the manuscripts I have read. My one big mistake of last year was in turning down *Street Scene*, but so did The Theatre Guild. . . . It's a smash-hit.

There is nothing to report on *The Dagger and the Rose*. I've tried and tried to raise money on it. I, personally, would not put another cent into it because I don't think I know that game well enough to risk any more money. . . . My own hope now is that one of the motion picture concerns may buy the score for a talkie either backing the production of *The Dagger and the Rose* and getting those rights for practically nothing, or buying the score outright. . . . I feel that practically anything I can get out of *The Dagger and the Rose* is so much velvet. I doubt whether I'll get more than $3000. for the $30,000. worth of costumes. Naturally, I'm through with musical plays for the rest of my life.

We're putting out two *Dracula* companies this coming season of 1929–1930, having arranged all of the bookings. I should say that with business conditions normal throughout the country, these two companies should make at least $50,000 together, maybe more.

(3), the stock market: The less said about this the better. I still have my 2500 Mexican Seaboard which sold down as low as 37 last Friday (including the rights) and which closed today at 45¾ including the rights. Naturally, I had to put up more margin and luckily had $5700 of my own and Arthur Pell very kindly loaned me about $4000 worth of bank stock. He is a grand old scout. The more one knows him, the more one must appreciate his true worth and ability. In addition to Seaboard, I still have 1000 Stutz, 500

Butterick and 500 Transcontinental Oil. In other words, I don't believe my holdings have changed at all since you left. I get nothing but good news from Mexican Seaboard. . . . They say the stock will surely sell for $150. within a year's time. I am going to hold it if I possibly can. Last year in figuring out my income tax, Arthur found that I made about $40,000 on the market. If it hadn't been for the loss of approximately $90,000 on *The Dagger and the Rose*, I would be in pretty fine financial shape except for my worry regarding the future of the book business. But then you know, I've worried about this for twelve years and have in spite of this managed to make a pretty good living out of it.[4]

By the end of August 1929, two months before the Crash, Liveright realized the extent of his security losses. Turning to another friend for financial advice, he wrote:

The stock market has been disastrous for me. I'm a stubborn fool and realize it. I have nothing but Stutz and Mexican Seaboard and I'm out $100,000 on these two stocks when other people have been making fortunes on good ones. I assure you I'm not blaming fate but only myself.[5]

In February 1930 Liveright turned over what remained of his investment portfolio to a friend of Alfred Wallerstein's:

This will confirm our conversation of yesterday in which I agreed with you that Mr. Norman Toerge should be given full control in the handling of the purchase and sale of any and all stocks in my account which you took over in October. I thoroughly agree with you that he, as a complete outsider, is better able to make back part of my losses than either you or I would be. Naturally, if I have information from such people as Otto Kahn and Jesse Lilienthal, I will not hesitate to communicate it to you and then Mr. Toerge can act as he sees fit.[6]

At the same time, Wallerstein invested in Liveright's publishing firm and became a director of it. Both actions, though taken too late to save Liveright, were intelligent ones. They had, unfortunately, been preceded by the publisher's production of two plays, *Boolie of Broadway* and *Wound Stripe*. Both had gone the way of *The Dagger and the Rose* and closed out of town.[7] Naturally, Liveright lost large sums on each of these ventures.

For some time Liveright had felt the serious effects of his reversals in the theatre and the market on his private life. Two letters to Van Loon, the author of Liveright's first great success, written on June 8, 1929, and September 27, 1929, are revealing in this light. The façade and the bravado are present, but the humor and confidence of the past are missing. First:

> I'll be glad to see you when you get here in October. I'll be sort of lonely then with both my kids away at school. Herman as you know is away at the University of Wisconsin, and next fall Lucy goes to Boarding School. Speaking of Wisconsin, I was out in Madison a few weeks ago and had a 2½ hour lunch with Glenn Frank. Is anybody happy? There was Glenn Frank, President of a big University, getting $20,000 a year, a beautiful house, and the use of a beautiful car, and earning another $30,000 or $35,000 from his lectures and syndicate work. Yet all he could seem to think about at lunch was his new book and how he could make enuf [sic] money to give him some sense of financial security. Again I ask you, my dear friend, what's it all about? I am convinced that happiness comes almost exclusively through extraverted development. The counter-jumper who is passionately interested in whether or not the Yankees will win the pennant and who anticipates with real joy the game of checkers he is going to play every night in the week, can be happier on $20 a week than a millionaire who cannot get into the Union Club or the violinist who hasn't quite the excellence of Kreisler. They are thinking of themselves all the time. I may do the book on Everyday Philosophy myself.

And then later:

> I've been in the frightful throes of moving in the past few weeks. It's frightful because I'm giving up, temporarily at least, house-keeping, and I am moving around the corner to the Hotel Maurice on 58th Street. I finally came to the conclusion that having two extra bedrooms and baths and a good Japanese cook and plenty to eat and drink simply meant being one of the greatest suckers in the world. I always had non-paying lodgers and boarders; but what was worse, I rarely had a chance to entertain my own friends without some conflicting groups being there. I think I'll have a little more privacy at the hotel apartment where I won't put anyone up for the night except Lucy or Herman or someone I really want.

Book business is simply ghastly not only with us but with everyone. But you'll see from the Fall catalogue which I am sending you, separately, that we have a splendid list this Fall. Most of the good books on it are not out yet and Julian thinks our Fall season will end in a blaze of glory. The Bertrand Russell book promises to be a big seller. It's frightfully audacious and he has just arrived in The States for a lecture tour which will help. Otto Kahn is taking him and me out to dinner Monday night and then we're going to see Dorothy Peterson in her new play, *Subway Express*, which unfortunately I did not produce because it's a big hit.

At the close of each successful publishing season in the past, Liveright had drained his company of any substantial excess profits. Every Christmas each employee had received a generous bonus and a raise. But, for the first time, in 1929 there were neither bonuses nor raises.[8] With the advent of earlier financial crises, he had been able to preserve his control of the house, and, for that matter, the house itself, through the unexpected success of some book or by selling a share of the business to an enterprising newcomer. No best-seller appeared in the fall of 1929, and Liveright hastily directed Fred Hummel, a former author who had joined the firm as an associate, to find a partner.

> The general nature of your service is to raise $100,000 as working capital for the business, and to dispose of 50% of the stock in the business along the lines set forth between us, which are to be similar to the Friede contract which you have seen.
> We figure our business as being worth, including contracts with authors, plate values written off, and any other hidden values, to say nothing of good will, after the expenditure of about $1,000,000 in advertising during the course of the last twelve years, none of which items is shown on our books, . . . $400,000.[9]

But no welcome neophyte appeared to save the firm, and Liveright publications continued to fare poorly on the market, with the exception of *Henry VIII*. Moreover, when Sumner and the Vice Society threatened to draw Liveright into court early in January 1930 for the publication of an allegedly obscene work called *Josephine, the Great Lover*, the publisher capitulated immediately before his old enemy.[10] The days of battle were ending as Liveright quietly withdrew the volume from circulation and destroyed the plates and the remaining copies. The book wasn't selling well enough, he said, to justify the expense of defending it.

On March 14, 1930, Liveright sailed for Europe, ostensibly to meet with Mustapha Kemal, Mussolini, the former Kaiser, and Stalin who, he hoped, would provide him with several best-sellers.[11] While he was away, Hummel kept him informed of the firm's activities: $13,500 had come in from the Literary Guild, when the book club adopted Van Loon's *Rembrandt van Rijn* as one of its selections.[12] The house was able to pay O'Neill the $19,000 in royalties due him with the help of a $10,000 loan from Alfred Wallerstein, and Hummel had received an offer of $29,500 for the building that housed the firm.[13] The most ominous transaction that Hummel completed was the sale of the company's rights to Ludwig's *Napoleon* to the Star Publishing Company for $10,000. Giving up a best-selling work outright to a reprint house was a radical measure. It was, Hummel reminded his employer, an act which took them "a big stride along the path that leads . . . in the wrong direction for any publishing firm."[14] For his own part Liveright was unsuccessful in his dealings with the political leaders of Europe, and he returned home to find the publishing trade in the midst of a book war. On June 27, 1930, he wrote to a friend in England:

> Why haven't I cabled or written you? My dear friend, if you had met with my experience when you landed in New York, you would have jumped into the river. I knew, of course, that general business had been rotten and that this included the publishing business to an alarming extent. But on the morning of the docking of the Aquitania, I woke up at eight o'clock, rang for my breakfast and with it came the ship-newspaper, containing the cute little item which I saw immediately, that four important New York publishers including Doubleday Doran, the biggest of them all, were immediately reducing prices of all new fiction to $1.00, and announcing a cut of prices of non-fiction for the Fall by about 40%. I haven't time nor energy to tell you what this all means except that none of the booksellers are buying anything, bills are coming in, and few books are going out. This doesn't hurt the concerns with big text-book departments or with cheap lists which they can reduce in price if they want to. But by and large we have a highbrow list of authors who are worth from $2.50 to $5.00 and we won't make a cut.

The Paramount people have asked me to shoot a few pictures, supervise them or something like that, and inasmuch as I have to go to California . . . I'm likely to accept their proposition which is rather handsome so far as remuneration is concerned, unless I feel that I'm too badly needed right here.

My address of course will always be 61 West 48th Street no matter where I happen to be temporarily.[15]

The book war continued the rest of the year, but Liveright's most pressing concern was finding money to pay the accounts due his writers. One of the largest was Dreiser's $1200 monthly stipend in addition to a costly weekly advertising campaign—much of it in the *New York Times*—for the novelist's *A Gallery of Women*.[16] Then, in June 1930 an unforeseen calamity occurred. Augustin Duncan, the brother of Isadora Duncan, appeared with a court order directing the publisher to pay him the royalties which had accrued from the sale of his deceased sister's very successful autobiography. In a memorandum to his treasurer, Pell, Liveright asked: "Was this money for royalties put in escrow or is this another blow?" Pell replied: "Sorry—just another blow."[17]

To still another friend, this one Otto Theis, his firm's London representative, Liveright suggested something of the state of his business and announced his plans.

I know, Otto, that since I have gotten back to New York I have not kept you very thoroughly posted, but, after all, there hasn't been a hell of a lot to post you about. Things have been in such a condition of flux that from day to day none of us has known just where we stand. You speak about not knowing what Fall books are coming out. Our catalogues are at least a month late because of the book-war. We couldn't make the statement that we did prefacing our list of books until we had weeded out a lot of books that might properly have been called $1.00 books. Then when we wanted to weed out certain books it took days to make arrangements with the authors. Believe me, it has been a mad, mad time.

The book club proposition isn't nearly as profitable as it was when I was in England. The Book-of-the-Month Club adoption used to net a publisher around $18,000 to $20,000. Now the Book-of-the-Month Club has met the Literary Guild competition and it only means about $7000 to the publisher. I don't blame the Book-of-the-

Month club at all. It's a mystery to me why they didn't fight the Literary Guild with their own weapons long ago.

I have a piece of interesting news to give you now which I must ask you to hold in strictest confidence until the news breaks generally which I don't suppose will be very long, and, of course, when it appears in print, it will be greatly garbled and our competitors will, of course, do their best to use it against us. The facts are these: Due to the book-war and my prognostication that it will last a long time and may cut into the profits of houses like ourselves, Knopf, Harcourt, Cape and Smith and, of course, more deeply into the profits of the lesser fry, I saw the necessity for making some capital readjustment in the business, and in spite of the stock market being at practically the lowest point in several years and the general business depression, I have been successful in putting things in very good shape through selling a certain amount of my own stock. This, however, does not mean that I am not actively interested in the business, although I am going to Hollywood in two or three weeks to be there for several months (if not longer) working in conjunction with the Paramount Publix Corporation on such a loose and fantastic basis that it would be impossible for me to tell you just what my activities are going to be. All I can say is that they have wanted me very much and are paying me high. And this in turn is relieving my book activities of considerable overhead expense. Of course people will say that Liveright has gone theatre, or Liveright has gone movie. To a certain extent this is true, but that doesn't mean that I don't have considerable stock interest here and a very active editorial interest. When things are a little more definite, I will write you again to tell you just with whom you will be corresponding in this office, etc., etc. This will in no way affect our arrangements with you. I don't think that anyone who takes my seat at this desk will expect you to do any very brilliant things this year with conditions as they have been.[18]

On July 18, 1930, Liveright announced to the press that he was temporarily withdrawing from the publishing firm which bore his name to make an extended business trip to Hollywood, where he planned to take up new duties as an associate of the production department of Paramount Publix Corporation.[19] He was not quitting publishing and would, in fact, continue as a director and chairman of the executive committee of Horace Liveright, Inc. The publisher did not tell reporters that he was going to the West Coast because he was no longer president of the firm. Of the twenty-one hundred and fifty shares of stock in the company, Liveright's holdings had dwindled to a mere fifty. Having lost control of the firm through continual borrowing on his majority share, he was forced to leave. He simply made his departure as respectable as he could. Following Liveright's departure to the Coast, Arthur Pell became a partner in the company and soon head of the business, since he owned the most stock.[20]

The aura of success and the glamour which had surrounded Liveright throughout the flush Twenties years, even when he was bordering on bankruptcy, soon disappeared altogether. In Hollywood, he found himself dependent upon Paramount for a salary, drinking more and more heavily, and, most important, bereft of the celebrity he had enjoyed in the East. He was no longer the boss of a company or the host of the party; rather, he was simply another employee with an all but meaningless title and, of course, very little knowledge of film production. He was unsuccessful in negotiating the sale of movie rights for any of the books he had selected, and he was without any real power. In 1931, his contract at Paramount was not renewed, and he returned to New York jobless, broken in spirit, but nevertheless announcing grand new schemes, mostly involving Broadway plays, that he believed would restore his solvency and catapult him back into prominence. The necessary financial backing for the plays did not materialize, however, and soon Liveright was simply haunting the scenes of his former glories. Again and again he was, quite naturally, drawn to his old publishing friends and associates at Horace Liveright, Inc. But the firm had moved. As an economy measure, Pell had cut salaries, sold the West Forty-eighth Street brownstone, and relocated the house in considerably smaller, less elegant quarters at 31 West Forty-seventh Street.[21]

The removal of Liveright from his firm had little effect on the fortunes of the house. In 1933 it became Liveright, Inc., but it was never able to regain its former standing. Later that year, on May 4, 1933, an involuntary petition in bankruptcy was filed against the company. It was signed by three creditors with claims totaling

$3500.[22] The Liveright balance sheet at this time included advance royalties of nearly $120,000 as well as a total deficit of over $30,000.[23] In an effort to satisfy the firm's debts and prevent receivership, the owners at first agreed to turn over their holdings for assignment to creditors, but apparently as a consequence of Pell's decision the next month not to give up his stock to the creditors' committee, the final adjudication in bankruptcy was ordered for the house on June 12.[24] The following July 25 the entire assets of Liveright, Inc., were sold to Victor Gold for $18,100.[25] Pell later took over the firm and called it the Liveright Publishing Corporation. He retained the Black and Gold library, as well as the reprint rights to works by Van Loon, Mrs. Atherton, Bodenheim, Freud, Moore, and some others, while the rights to the earlier works of many other major writers were sold to rival houses. During the confusion of the bankruptcy proceedings, the sale of two significant volumes suffered considerably; the first was Anderson's collection of short stories, *Death in the Woods*, and the second was Nathanael West's important novel, *Miss Lonelyhearts*.

On December 8, 1931, Liveright had married Elise Bartlett Porter, an actress who had appeared in several Broadway plays and movies and who had formerly been the wife of the actor Joseph Schildkraut.[26] The marriage was a brief, unhappy one that ended early in 1932.[27] Aside from the newspaper announcements of his marriage and divorce, the only public attention Liveright received came in January 1933 when the "former publisher," as he was called, was first reported hospitalized for pneumonia and then emphysema.[28]

Finally, on September 24, 1933, at 7 A.M., Liveright died of pneumonia at his home in a hotel-apartment at 33 West Fifty-first Street.[29] He was forty-six, nearly penniless, sick, and alone. New York papers noted his meteoric rise to fame as a publisher, the number of famous authors he had discovered and promoted, along with his single-handed, almost constant battle against censorship. The obituary notices also mentioned that at the time of his death Liveright had a play, *Hotel Alimony*, awaiting Broadway production and was writing his autobiography, *The Turbulent Years*, to be published by Simon & Schuster. But the play was just another desperate scheme and so, more or less, was the book. Funeral services were held on September 26 at the Universal Chapel, 597 Lexington Avenue, and the publisher was buried in Mount Sinai Cemetery in Philadelphia.

Shortly thereafter Bennett Cerf, a former partner who gained greatly from his association with Liveright, wrote for *Publishers' Weekly* this estimation of Liveright's importance to the world of letters:

A straggling handful of people gathered in the Universal Chapel yesterday morning while Upton Sinclair, fearfully embarrassed, mumbled inadequate nothings over the last remains of Horace Liveright, dead at 49 [sic]. Most of the authors he had started on the road to success, and the friends for whom he had neglected his business when it needed him most, were far too busy to pay him a last tribute. It was a dismal last curtain to a spectacular career—and to a publisher whose like will never be seen again.

There has been much talk to the effect that Liveright failed in publishing only when he began to neglect it. This is not so. A man who conducted his publishing business as Liveright did was doomed by changes in the book world over which he had no control. Intensified competition, the rise of young men who breathed fresh life into doddering, but financially impregnable, old houses, and, above all, the spectre of diminishing outlets and narrower profit margins, left no chance for a madhouse like Liveright's. His excursions into the theatrical business and his ill-starred splurges in the stock market (the Wall Street overlord who gave him all those magnificent tips didn't turn up at the funeral services, either) undoubtedly hastened his downfall, but the foundations were crumbling long before he stepped out. The famous Liveright "flair"—it came through too often to be set down as just a series of incredibly lucky breaks—staved off the inevitable time and again, but it simply could not hold out forever.

When I went to work for Horace Liveright in 1924, his list included Dreiser, O'Neill, Anderson, George Moore, Atherton, Lewisohn, Jeffers, Van Loon, Rose Macaulay, Sigmund Freud, and Sarah Millin—and for good measure he had the Modern Library, which, although almost completely neglected, was already selling over three hundred thousand copies a year. What a list for a one-man publishing house! That was the year Liveright did a business of over a million dollars, and on the first of January did not have a red cent in the bank. Seven men in the organization had authority to turn in bills for "entertainment." Authors in the waiting room were often outnumbered by bootleggers. One of the big executives had a bottle of whisky in every drawer of his desk, the top of which was piled inches high with weeks-old communications of the greatest importance. The head bookkeeper (the only real business man in the place, as he proved so convincingly by winding up at the last as the sole owner of the entire outfit) had to show a perpetual deficit in his daily reports to the president, because if there ever *was* a cash balance it was gone by nightfall. . . . The editorial meetings, which [Liveright] assembled occasionally with much fanfare and ceremony, were one-man shows, with little patience wasted on anyone who dared dispute his edicts. And yet he had an amazing faculty for winning the unquestioning loyalty of a great number of fine men and women. They love him still. They probably always will. Underneath all his sham and pretense, they saw a rather helpless person, craving affection and admiration, with a rare love of life and a reckless generosity they could not resist.

Other publishers—particularly in London—were continually outraged by Liveright's methods, and amazed that he could continue in the wild, reckless manner that he pursued. Of course, they were right in the end. "The Story of Mankind" fell from Heaven to end one crisis, and "Black Oxen" averted another. Then came a succession of young men who wanted to learn the publishing business— and had some money to invest. But finally there came a day when the whole house of cards began to tumble about his ears. Liveright, always more of a gambler than a publisher, played out his string like a gentleman, and proved infinitely more gallant and more admirable when he was taking it on the chin than he did in his heyday. A poseur to the last, he could be found tapping his long cigarette holder nervously at a table at the Algonquin, a mere shadow of his former jaunty self, announcing ambitious theatrical projects to all the critics, a few weeks before he died, although everybody knew that he was playing through a heartbreaking farce. . . . One of the many successful authors whom Liveright befriended when he didn't have a dime could repay his debt by . . . telling of some of the genuinely important accomplishments to Horace Liveright's credit— by bringing out the underlying charm of personality that he could turn on at will with such devastating effect; by emphasizing an incredible streak of generosity that piled up over a hundred and fifty thousand dollars of unearned advances before he stepped down from control!

A few months ago Liveright happened into the publishing office he had founded, to visit an old friend. He looked tired and worn. His friend was out. Liveright waited and waited. Then—in the presence of at least three employees—one of the new directors (Liveright had given him his first job there) said gruffly, "Better leave, Horace. I don't think it looks well to have you seen hanging around here!" Liveright didn't even answer. To those of us who knew the old Horace, charlatan and poseur, if you will, but alive, on the move, bursting with vigor and supreme confidence in himself, that is one of the saddest anecdotes we have ever heard.[30]

Though members of his family were on hand, very few of the publisher's friends and associates paid their final respects by attending his funeral. One exception was Sherwood Anderson. Anderson had been out of touch with Liveright for three years, but his regard and affection for his publisher had not diminished. In his *Memoirs*, issued nearly ten years later in 1942, Anderson wrote a brief but significant tribute to Liveright:

It was all rather crazy, rather splendid. Horace was a gambler and if he believed in you would gamble on you. I have always thought, since the man's death, that too much emphasis has been put on the reckless splendor of the man rather than on his never-ending generosity and his real belief in men of talent.[31]

Notes

All letters—indicated by the form "HL to EP, June 4, 1920"—and all unpublished documents including letters to the publisher are, except as otherwise noted, among the Liveright papers in the Charles Patterson Van Pelt Library at the University of Pennsylvania. The single exception is the "Statement of Operations" for the firm, dated December 31, 1930, which is in private hands. Letters from Dreiser to Liveright and other material relating to Dreiser are in the Dreiser Collection, which is also at the University of Pennsylvania. All correspondence between Liveright and Sherwood Anderson, as well as documents relating to their association are among the Anderson papers at Newberry Library. The location of smaller collections is cited in the notes.

With the exception of fewer than a dozen typographical errors and misspellings, which have been corrected, Liveright's letters and the extracts from them have been printed as they appeared in carbon copies among his papers. When circumstances seemed appropriate, I have quoted letters in their entirety (without the complimentary close or the signature) ; more often, however, the context seemed only to require portions of Liveright's correspondence. In this case, for the sake of smoother reading, I have not always indicated elisons in the quotations, but in following this practice I have attempted to keep the meaning of Liveright's remarks intact.

Boni & Liveright

1. Interview with Albert Boni, November 3, 1962.
2. *New York Herald Tribune*, September 25, 1933 (obit.) ; see also *New York Times*, September 25, 1933, p. 15:1 (obit.) .
3. *Publishers' Weekly*, September 30, 1933, p. 1141.
4. Boni interview.
5. Alfred Kreymborg, *Troubadour* (New York, 1925) , pp. 205–211.

6. Boni interview; see also Kreymborg, *Troubadour*, pp. 208–211.

7. Boni interview; see also Charles Lee, *The Hidden Public, The Story of the Book of the Month Club* (New York, 1958), pp. 22–24.

8. Lawrence Langner, *The Magic Curtain* (New York, 1951), pp. 67–73, 75–76; see also Gorham Munson, "Greenwich Village That Was: Seedbed of the Nineteen Twenties," *The Literary Review*, V (Spring, 1962), pp. 323–325.

9. Boni interview; see also Langner, *The Magic Curtain*, pp. 90–95; Arthur and Barbara Gelb, *O'Neill* (New York, 1962), pp. 304–306.

10. Boni interview.

11. Boni interview; see also Charles A. Madison, *Book Publishing in America* (New York, 1966), p. 330; the Gelbs, *O'Neill*, pp. 395–396.

12. The first B & L advertisement appears in *Publishers' Weekly*, June 23, 1917, p. 1977. Early references to the firm in *PW* include June 2, 1917, pp. 1797, 1871. Unless otherwise noted material in the following paragraphs about the publishing milieu is based on the following interviews: Louis Greene, November 6, 1962; Aaron Sussman, November 12, 1962; Henry Simon, November 5, 1962; Malcolm Cowley, November 13, 1962; Ken McCormick, June 14, 1962; Louis Kronenberger, November 3, 1962; Lewis Galantière, November 6, 1962; Manuel Komroff, November 11, 1962; and B. W. Huebsch, November 7, 1962.

13. Robert E. Knoll, *McAlmon and the Lost Generation: A Self Portrait* (Lincoln, Neb., 1962), p. 25.

14. Frank Luther Mott, *Golden Multitudes* (New York, 1947), pp. 312–313; see also Alice Payne Hackett, *Fifty Years of Best Sellers, 1895–1945* (New York, 1945), pp. 105–113.

15. Frederick J. Hoffman, Charles Allen, and Carolyn F. Ulrich, *The Little Magazine* (Princeton, N.J., 1947), pp. 250–251. The demise of *The Seven Arts* occurred when its financial backer withdrew support because of its editors' anti-war position.

16. Charles A. Madison, "Jews in Publishing," *The Chicago Jewish Forum*, XXVI (Summer, 1968), p. 282.

17. *Ibid.*, pp. 282–283; see also Knoll, *McAlmon and the Lost Generation*, p. 26.

18. Galantière interview.

19. Boni interview; see also *Publishers' Weekly*, August 4, 1917, p. 405 for B & L advertisement.

20. Greene interview.

21. Boni interview; see also *Publishers' Weekly*, July 21, 1917, p. 175.

22. Boni interview; see also B & L announcements and advertisements in *Publishers' Weekly*, June 2, 1917, p. 1797; June 23, 1917, pp. 1977, 1995; and August 4, 1917, p. 405.
23. Boni interview; see also W. A. Swanberg, *Dreiser* (New York, 1965), pp. 222–224, and Robert H. Elias, *Theodore Dreiser: Apostle of Nature* (New York, 1949), p. 208.
24. Swanberg, *Dreiser*, pp. 215, 219, and Elias, *Theodore Dreiser*, pp. 202-203.
25. See Jack Salzmann, "The Publication of *Sister Carrie*: Fact and Fiction," *Library Chronicle of the University of Pennsylvania*, XXXIII (Spring, 1967), pp. 119–133.
26. Swanberg, *Dreiser*, p. 117.
27. *Ibid.*, pp. 123, 129.
28. *Ibid.*, p. 138.
29. *Ibid.*, p. 150.
30. *Ibid.*, pp. 166–167.
31. *Ibid.*, p. 172; see also Elias, *Theodore Dreiser*, p. 174.
32. Swanberg, *Dreiser*, p. 173; see also Elias, *Theodore Dreiser*, pp. 174–175.
33. Swanberg, *Dreiser*, pp. 203–205.
34. *Ibid.*, pp. 204–205.
35. Elias, *Theodore Dreiser*, p. 203.
36. Undated card in the Dreiser Collection at the University of Pennsylvania.
37. Swanberg, *Dreiser*, p.222.
38. See HL to TD, September 7, 1917, September 26, 1917, and November 11, 1917.
39. Boni interview; see also *Publishers' Weekly*, August 4, 1917, p. 405.
40. Elias, *Theodore Dreiser*, pp. 209–210, and Swanberg, *Dreiser*, pp. 226–227.
41. Swanberg, *Dreiser*, p. 226.
42. *Ibid.*, p. 235.
43. HL to TD, December 10, 1918.
44. HL to TD, January 1, 1919, and February 7, 1919; see also Elias, *Theodore Dreiser*, pp. 210–211.
45. HL to TD, February 9, 1920; see also Swanberg, *Dreiser*, p. 244.
46. Boni interview.
47. For advertisements see *Publishers' Weekly*, January 12, 1918, pp. 122–123; March 2, 1918, p. 611; and May 25, 1918, p. 1593.
48. *Publishers' Weekly*, January 25, 1919, p. 232.

49. HL to AL, August 14, 1918. See also *Publishers' Weekly*, August 3, 1918, pp. 393, 396. In a letter to George Creel, August 27, 1918, printed in James R. Mock, *Censorship, 1917* (Princeton, 1941), p. 156, Liveright asserted that military intelligence officers had kept the firm under surveillance to maintain the ban. See Paul S. Boyer, *Purity in Print* (New York, 1968), p. 59.
50. Mott, *Golden Multitudes*, pp. 241, 325.
51. HL to AL, June 11, 1919.
52. HL to AL, July 27, 1920.
53. Mott, *Golden Multitudes*, pp. 241, 325, 329.
54. Boni interview.
55. Boni & Liveright catalogues for Fall, 1918 and Fall, 1919.
56. Boni interview.
57. *Ibid.* See also *Publishers' Weekly*, August 3, 1918, p. 379.
58. Boni interview. See also *New York Times*, November 25, 1920, p. 17:7.
59. Boni interview. See also HL to Dreiser, July 3, 1919, and July 8, 1920.

The Radical Writers

1. Floyd Dell, *Homecoming* (New York, 1933), 246–247.
2. Interviews with Boni, Komroff, and Kronenberger.
3. Boni interview.
4. *Ibid.* See also Granville Hicks, *John Reed, The Making of a Revolutionary* (New York, 1936).
5. Hicks, *John Reed*, pp. 325–326, 353. For the naming of Reed's book see Arthur Garfield Hays, *City Lawyer* (New York, 1942), p. 239.
6. Hicks, *John Reed*, p. 382. Reed's letter was dated May 13, 1920.
7. Interviews with Boni and Komroff.
8. Interviews with Gorham Munson, June 16, 1962.
9. A memorandum from Arthur Pell to Liveright dated August 18, 1927, gives the following figures on Frank's books:

	Loss	Gross Gain
Our America		$597.82
Chalk Face	$ 570.00	
Dark Mother	888.06	
Holiday	374.84	
Rahab	819.44	
Salvos	462.93	

Unwelcome Man	406.81	
Virgin Spring		338.25
	$3522.08	$936.07
	936.07	
Loss to date	$2586.01	

Overhead and selling charge of $7200—making total loss on his books of $9786.01.

10. Frederick J. Hoffman, _The Twenties_ (New York, 1955), pp. 12–13.

11. According to the "Statement of Operations" for the firm in 1930, 4,011 copies of _Our America_ had been sold between its publication in 1919 and December 31, 1930.

12. _The Moon of the Caribbees_ was first performed in the Village on December 20, 1918. According to an undated memorandum concerning O'Neill publications, this play was published in April, 1919. See also Arthur and Barbara Gelb, _O'Neill_ (New York, 1962), p. 388.

13. The Gelbs, _O'Neill_, p. 395.

14. According to an undated memorandum this play was issued in March, 1920. See also the Gelbs, _O'Neill_, p. 406.

15. The Gelbs, _O'Neill_, p. 339.

16. Interviews with Boni and Komroff. See also HL to Mike Gold, September 19, 1929: "Our policy on plays with almost no exceptions is to wait to see if they make a hit and then try to buy them for publication."

17. Harry Hansen, "The First Reader," _New York World-Telegram_, September 26, 1933, and Hansen interview, June 5, 1969.

18. Interviews with Boni and Komroff for the paragraph.

19. Interviews with Boni, Komroff, Kronenberger, Sussman, Huebsch, and Cowley.

20. Edward Bernays, _Biography of an Idea: Memoirs of a Public Relations Counsel_ (New York, 1966), pp. 277, 284.

21. _Ibid._, pp. 278–282, for the remainder of the paragraph.

22. _Ibid._, pp. 280–281, for the paragraph.

23. B & L catalogue for Fall, 1921, for the material in this paragraph. In a letter to the editor of _The Independent_ (February 18, 1922, p. 163), Liveright wrote: "Not one of [the Modern Library volumes] ever pretended to be a best-seller or a lure for the tired business man. It is my opinion that book, magazine, and newspaper publishers, and the producers of plays and motion pictures, should begin to realize that the _average_ woman and man of the twentieth century are eager

to support what is truly fine instead of what merely purports to be fine."

24. Bernays, *Memoirs*, pp. 252–255, 265–266, 275, for the paragraph.
25. Interviews with Hansen and Komroff for the paragraph.
26. Komroff interview and the B & L catalogue for Fall, 1921, for the paragraph.
27. JGH to TRS, April 22, 1919. All Huneker documents cited are on deposit in the Baker Library, Dartmouth College, Hanover, New Hampshire.
28. JGH to TRS, June 17, 1919.
29. Memorandum of Agreement between Boni and Liveright, Inc., and James Huneker, September 11, 1920. This contract called for the author to receive $1.50 royalty on each copy sold.
30. Arnold T. Schwab, *James Gibbons Huneker, Critic of the Seven Arts* (Stanford, California, 1963), p. 294.
31. Komroff interview and the B & L catalogue for Fall, 1921.
32. Forrest Read, *Pound/Joyce, The Letters of Ezra Pound to James Joyce with Pound's Essays on Joyce* (New York, 1967), pp. 155–156, 181, 185.
33. *Ibid.*, pp. 181, 185. See also Richard Ellmann, *James Joyce* (New York, 1959), p. 512.
34. John Edwards, *The Writings of Ezra Pound* (New Haven, Conn., 1953), p. 6.
35. According to the Statement of Operations for the firm in 1930, 591 copies of *Instigations* and 593 copies of *Poems: 1918–1921* had been sold between publication and December 31, 1930.
36. Charles Norman, *Ezra Pound* (New York, 1960), p. 253. The duration of this agreement was, apparently, brief. Only one book, Edouard Estaunie's *The Call of the Road,* was translated by the poet and published by Liveright in 1923.
37. Fall, 1921 catalogue for this and the next paragraph.
38. Material in this paragraph is from the Komroff interview and Edith Stern, "The Man Who Was Unafraid," *Saturday Review of Literature,* June 28, 1941, pp. 10, 14.
39. Fall, 1921 catalogue, p. 13, for the paragraph.
40. Frant Luther Mott, *Golden Multitudes* (New York, 1947), p. 313.
41. Komroff interview for the paragraph.
42. Interviews with Henry Simon and Malcolm Cowley.
43. According to the Statement of Operations for the firm, 112,663 copies of *The Story of Mankind* were sold between its publication and

December 31, 1930. See also, Burton Rascoe, *We Were Interrupted* (New York, 1947), pp. 90–91.

44. Komroff interview for this and the next two paragraphs. See also the B & L catalogue for Fall, 1922. According to the Statement of Operations for the firm, 73,611 copies of *Flaming Youth* and 17,588 copies of *Gargoyles* were sold between their publication and December 31, 1930.

45. 12,700 copies of *Tramping on Life* were sold between publication and December 31, 1930, according to the Statement of Operations for the firm.

46. Komroff interview and the Fall, 1922 catalogue for the paragraph.

47. The Cummings material is based on the Komroff interview and Charles Norman, *The Magic-Maker, E. E. Cummings* (New York, 1958), pp. 111–113, 122–124.

48. From *Contempo*, April 5, 1933, as quoted in Norman, *E. E. Cummings*, p. 123. According to the Statement of Operations for the firm in 1930, 2,454 copies of *The Enormous Room* were sold between its publication and December 31, 1930.

49. Komroff interview and the Fall, 1922 catalogue for the paragraph.

50. The 1930 Statement of Operations shows that 32,973 copies of *Replenishing Jessica* had been sold.

51. Komroff interview.

52. Interview with Gilbert Seldes, June 2, 1969.

53. *Ibid.* See also Rascoe, *We Were Interrupted*, pp. 156–157.

54. According to the 1930 Statement of Operations, 2,579 copies of *The Waste Land* had been sold. The remainder of the paragraph is based on the Komroff interview. The catalogue announcement of the book described Eliot as "a man to be reckoned with, now, and hereafter, among the few unique talents of the times."

Theodore Dreiser

1. W. A. Swanberg, *Dreiser* (New York, 1965), p. 232.

2. *Ibid.*, pp. 235–236.

3. *Ibid.*, p. 247.

4. HL to TD, March 22, 1920.

5. Swanberg, *Dreiser*, p. 244.

6. HL to TD, June 4, 1920.

7. HL to TD, June 28, 1920.

8. HL to TD, June 4, 1920.

9. HL to TD, July 8, 1920.

10. Swanberg, *Dreiser*, pp. 249–250.
11. HL to TD, October 4, 1920.
12. TD to HLM, August 27, 1920, printed in full in the *Letters of Theodore Dreiser*, ed. Robert H. Elias (Philadelphia, 1959) , I, pp. 275–276.
13. *Ibid.*, p. 275.
14. Swanberg, *Dreiser*, p. 249.
15. TD to HL, December 10, 1920, printed in full in the *Letters*, I, pp. 309–311.
16. HL to TD, December 10, 1920.
17. *Letters*, I, p. 320.
18. TD to HL, December 21, 1920, printed in full in the *Letters*, I, pp. 320–323.
19. HL to TD, January 1, 1921.
20. HL to TD, January 6, 1921.
21. Swanberg, *Dreiser*, pp. 257–258.
22. HL to TD, February 7, 1921.
23. William H. Briggs to TD, January 4, 1921, see the *Letters*, I, p. 356.
24. Printed in full in the *Letters*, I, pp. 356–358.
25. TD to HL, April 20, 1921, printed in full in the *Letters*, I, pp. 367–369.
26. Swanberg, *Dreiser*, p. 259; see also TD to Arthur Carter Hume, March 30, 1922,, printed in the *Letters*, II, pp. 391–395.
27. Swanberg, *Dreiser*, p. 259; see also TD to ACH, April 18, 1922, printed in the *Letters*, II, pp. 396–398.
28. TD to ACH, March 30, 1922; see the *Letters*, II, p. 394.
29. TD to HLM, March 22, 1922, reprinted in Swanberg, *Dreiser*, p. 259.
30. HL to TD, March 18, 1922.
31. HL to TD, June 28, 1922.
32. HL to TD, July 24, 1922.
33. Swanberg, *Dreiser*, p. 275.
34. *Ibid.*, pp. 275, 277–278.
35. Undated advertisement in the Liveright Collection at the University of Pennsylvania.
36. HL to TD, August 7, 1923.
37. HL to TD, March 18, 1922, and November 25, 1922.
38. Swanberg, *Dreiser*, p. 281. According to the Statement of Operations for the firm, 47,353 copies of *The "Genius"* were sold between publication and December 31, 1930.
39. Messner to TD, July 25, 1923.
40. Swanberg, *Dreiser*, p. 281.

John Sumner's Vice Society

1. Robert H. Elias, *Theodore Dreiser: Apostle of Nature* (New York, 1949), p. 195; see also Paul S. Boyer, *Purity in Print* (New York, 1968), p. 5.
2. Floyd Dell, *Homecoming* (New York, 1933), p. 278. Dell misdates the year of Comstock's death as 1916.
3. Elias, *Theodore Dreiser*, pp. 201–202.
4. Interviews with Albert Boni, Manuel Komroff, and Louis Kronenberger.
5. B & L Catalogue for Fall, 1921, pp. 24–25.
6. Interviews with B. W. Huebsch, Manuel Komroff, and Louis Kronenberger.
7. Komroff interview for the paragraph.
8. *Ibid.*
9. *New York Times*, March 23, 1920, p. 4:3; see also *Times*, March 28, 1920, II, p. 2:3.
10. Allen Churchill, *The Improper Bohemians* (New York, 1959), p. 44.
11. *New York Times*, March 23, 1920, p. 4:3; see also *Publishers' Weekly*, March 27, 1920, p. 1033.
12. *New York Times*, April 21, 1920, p. 8:4; see also *Publishers' Weekly*, April 17, 1920, p. 1232, and April 24, 1920, p. 1324.
13. *New York Times*, March 28, 1920, II, p. 2:3, and "Literary Bootlegging," *New York Times*, August 6, 1922, III, p. 1:1 for facts in this and the next paragraph.
14. *New York Times*, July 12, 1922, p. 32:2.
15. Undated memorandum from T. R. Smith to Liveright.
16. Interviews with Huebsch, Komroff, and Donald Friede, November 6, 1962; see also Boyer, *Purity in Print*, pp. 78–79, 83. Apparently Sumner and the Vice Society were particularly interested in Jewish publishers. Boyer reproduces a page of the New York Vice Society record book in which the age, occupation, nationality, and religion of the "offenders" are carefully recorded. In addition, see pp. 95–96 and 142–143 of this work.
17. *New York Times*, July 21, 1922, p. 10:5.
18. *Ibid.*, August 4, 1922, p. 1:6.
19. *Ibid.*, August 5, 1922, p. 20:2.
20. *Ibid.*, August 6, 1922, II, p. 1:1.
21. *Ibid.*, August 7, 1922, p. 6:1.
22. *Ibid.*, September 13, 1922, p. 23:1, and September 17, 1922, II, p. 1:3.

23. *Ibid.*, September 28, 1922, p. 11:1; see also *Publishers' Weekly*, August 12, 1922, p. 526.
24. *New York Times*, September 28, 1922, p. 11:1.
25. *Ibid.*, September 29, 1922, pp. 18:6, 9:1; see also October 1, 1922, p. 14:3.
26. *Ibid.*, September 29, 1922, p. 9:1.
27. *Ibid.*, October 15, 1922, II, p. 1:2.
28. *Ibid.*, October 17, 1922, p. 12:1, for Banton's announcement and the remainder of the paragraph as well.
29. *Ibid.*, October 22, 1922, II, p. 1:4.
30. *Ibid.*, October 20, 1922, p. 3:2.
31. *Ibid.*, November 2, 1922, p. 19:3.
32. Succeeding catalogues show that this edition was soon sold out. A one-volume, expurgated *Satyricon* was issued in 1927.
33. *New York Times*, November 18, 1922, p. 19:3.
34. Boyer, *Purity in Print*, pp. 89–91.
35. *New York Times*, February 6, 1923, p. 23:4 for the entire paragraph.
36. *Ibid.*, February 7, 1923, p. 19:3.
37. *Ibid.*, February 11, 1923, p. 18:1.
38. *Ibid.*, February 25, 1923, p. 1:4 for the paragraph.
39. *Ibid.*, February 27, 1923, p. 18:4.
40. *Ibid.*, March 9, 1923, p. 17:5.
41. *Ibid.*, March 18, 1923, VIII, p. 2:1.
42. *Ibid.*, April 18, 1923, p. 20:4.
43. *Ibid.*, March 20, 1923, p. 20:5.
44. *Ibid.*, April 18, 1923, p. 20:4.
45. *Ibid.*, March 23, 1923, p. 2:2.
46. *Ibid.*, April 19, 1923, pp. 1, 4.
47. *Ibid.*, April 18, 1923, p. 7:2.
48. *Ibid.*, April 19, 1923, pp. 1, 4.
49. Komroff interview; see also *New York Times*, June 15, 1923, p. 6:2.
50. Boyer, *Purity in Print*, p. 108.
51. *New York Times*, April 23, 1923, p. 14:5.
52. Komroff interview.
53. CX (March 17, 1923), pp. 192–193.
54. Komroff interview and Boyer, *Purity in Print*, pp. 106–108.
55. *New York Times*, April 19, 1923, pp. 1, 4.
56. Komroff interview; see also Boyer, *Purity in Print*, pp. 117–119, and Charles A. Madison, *Book Publishing in America* (New York, 1966), p. 333.

57. *New York Times*, April 19, 1923, pp. 1, 4 for the paragraph.
58. *Ibid.*
59. *Ibid.*
60. *Publishers' Weekly*, April 21, 1923, p. 1262.
61. Komroff interview for the paragraph.
62. *New York Times*, April 21, 1963, p. 6:2; see also April 24, 1923, p. 3:5.
63. *Publishers' Weekly*, April 28, 1923, pp. 1323–1324; see also Boyer, *Purity in Print*, pp. 108–109.
64. *New York Times*, April 22, 1923, p. 19:5.
65. *Ibid.*, May 3, 1923, pp. 1, 5.
66. *Ibid.*, p. 5.
67. *Ibid.*, May 4, 1923, p. 16:4.
68. *Ibid.*, May 14, 1923, p. 6:3 and May 18, 1923, p. 15:1.
69. For later defeats of the Clean Books Bill see *New York Times*, April 11, 1924, p. 2:2 and March 19, 1925, p. 6:6.
70. *New York Times*, June 15, 1923, p. 6:2; see also *Publishers' Weekly*, June 16, 1923, p. 1826.
71. Undated dinner announcement in the Liveright Collection at the University of Pennsylvania.
72. *New York Times*, June 15, 1923, p. 6:2; see also *Publishers' Weekly*, June 16, 1923, p. 1826.
73. HL to FH, May 19, 1923. For still another version see Dreiser to Rex Beach, May 5, 1923, *Letters of Theodore Dreiser,* ed. Robert H. Elias (Philadelphia, 1959), II, pp. 408–410, and Dreiser to Gelett Burgess, between May 19 and June 2, 1923, in the same work, II, pp. 410–417.

The B & L Offices

1. Unless otherwise noted, material in this chapter describing the firm is based on the following interviews: Manuel Komroff, November 3, 1962, and November 9, 1962; Louis Kronenberger, November 3, 1962; Aaron Sussman, November 5, 1962; Manuel Siwek, November 9, 1962; Donald Friede, November 6, 1962; Bennett Cerf, June 2, 1969; and Edith Stern, June 9, 1969.
2. HL to Francis Hackett, May 19, 1923; see also *Publishers' Weekly*, August 18, 1923, p. 547.
3. See TD to Onorio Ruotolo, April 6, 1932, reprinted in the *Letters of Theodore Dreiser*, ed. Robert H. Elias (Philadelphia, 1959), II, p. 578.
4. Friede interview and *The Mechanical Angel* (New York, 1948), pp. 29–30.

5. Komroff interview.
6. See, for example, Lillian Hellman, *An Unfinished Woman* (Boston, 1969) , pp. 36–37.
7. Interviews with Bennett Cerf, Donald Friede, Louis Kronenberger, and Manuel Komroff; see also Louis Kronenberger, "Gambler in Publishing: Horace Liveright," *Atlantic Monthly*, CCXV (January, 1965) , pp. 98–99.
8. "The House of Boni and Liveright," *Literary Digest International Book Review*, II (August, 1924) , pp. 686–687.
9. Edith Stern, "The Man Who Was Unafraid," *Saturday Review of Literature*, June 28, 1941, p. 14.
10. According to the Statement of Operations for the firm in 1930, 251,715 copies of *Napoleon* were sold between 1927 and December 31, 1930.
11. Stern interview.
12. Kronenberger interview.
13. Kronenberger, "Gambler in Publishing," p. 95.
14. Cerf interview. For the sale of the Modern Library to Cerf see the *New York Times*, July 13, 1925, p. 12:3.
15. Komroff interview for this and the following paragraphs.
16. Material in this and the following two paragraphs, except where otherwise noted, is from interviews with Aaron Sussman and Manuel Siwek.
17. Friede, *The Mechanical Angel*, p. 17.
18. Kronenberger, "Gambler in Publishing," p. 99.
19. Hellman, *An Unfinished Woman*, p. 38.
20. Sussman and Siwek interviews.
21. *Ibid.*
22. Kronenberger, "Gambler in Publishing," p. 97.
23. Cerf interview for this and next paragraph.
24. Friede interview for this and the next paragraph; see also *The Mechanical Angel*, pp. 16–17.
25. *The Mechanical Angel*, pp. 30–31.
26. *Ibid.*, pp. 44–61.
27. Kronenberger interview; see also "Gambler in Publishing," p. 97.
28. *Ibid.*; see also "Gambler in Publishing," p. 95.
29. Stern, "The Man Who Was Unafraid," pp. 10, 14.

New Writers and New Ventures

1. Material in this paragraph from interviews with Bennett Cerf, Manuel Komroff, and Louis Kronenberger.

2. B & L catalogues, Fall, 1923, and Fall, 1924.

3. Komroff interview.

4. *Ibid.* Miss Bowen's work, *Ann Lee's and Other Stories,* was issued by the firm in 1926.

5. *Ibid.*

6. See the *Letters of Edna St. Vincent Millay,* ed. Allan Ross Macdougall (New York, 1952), p. 1965.

7. Francis Hackett to HL, August 29, 1929.

8. *New York Times Book Review,* January 19, 1969, p. 3.

9. *Ibid.* See also *Dark Symphony,* eds. James A. Emanuel and Theodore L. Gross (New York, 1968), pp. 95–98.

10. *New York Times Book Review,* January 19, 1969, p. 3.

11. Komroff interview; see also Bennett Cerf, "Horace Liveright, An Unedited Obituary," *Publishers' Weekly,* October 7, 1933, p. 1230.

12. Mrs. Atherton's change from Stokes to B & L was announced in *Publishers' Weekly,* September 9, 1922, p. 763.

13. Burton Rascoe, *A Bookman's Day Book* (New York, 1929), pp. 45–46.

14. Frank Luther Mott, *Golden Multitudes* (New York, 1947), p. 330, and Alice Payne Hackett, *Fifty Years of Best Sellers, 1895–1945* (New York, 1945), pp. 47–48. According to the Statement of Operation for the firm, 115,391 copies of *Black Oxen* were sold between its publication and December 31, 1930.

15. B & L catalogues for Fall, 1923, and Fall, 1924, for the paragraph.

16. *Ibid;* see also the *New York Times,* December 3, 1923, p. 6:1.

17. Komroff interview for the remainder of the paragraph.

18. B & L catalogues for Fall, 1923, and Fall, 1924, for the paragraph.

19. *Ibid.* Gorham Munson has a statement showing that 500 copies of his work were printed. Of these volumes 242 were sold at $1.50 a copy. Liveright spent $298.29 on advertising for an average cost of $1.23 per book. This far exceeds a normal budget of 10%. The total loss to the firm on *Waldo Frank: A Study* was $452.50.

20. B & L catalogues for Fall, 1923, and Fall, 1924. Samuel Ornitz was an editor at Macfadden Publications and a noted welfare worker in New York. In his "autobiography" he attacked capitalistic society through the ironic rise and revelations of his unheroic protagonist—Walter B. Rideout, *The Radical Novel in the United States* (Cambridge, Mass., 1956), pp. 117–118; Elizabeth Marbury was one of the founders of the American Play Company; Samuel Harden Church was president of the Carnegie Institute.

21. Liveright's Nobel Prize winners were O'Neill, 1936; du Gard, 1937;

Eliot, 1948; Faulkner, 1949; Russell, 1950; Mauriac, 1952; and Hemingway, 1954.

22. Donald Friede, *The Mechanical Angel* (New York, 1948), p. 27.
23. B & L catalogues for Fall, 1925, and Fall, 1926.
24. *New York Times*, July 16, 1924, p. 20:4.
25. *The Best Plays of 1924–1925*, ed. Burns Mantle (New York, 1925), pp. 473, 606.
26. *New York Times*, September 21, 1925, p. 16:1.
27. *The Best Plays of 1925–1926*, ed. Burns Mantle (New York, 1926), pp. 491, 607.
28. *New York Times*, March 23, 1928, p. 3:3; see also May 29, 1928, p. 11:1. Mrs. Liveright's divorce was granted on May 28, 1928. Extant letters suggest that Liveright and his wife separated sometime during the first six months of 1926. See, for example, HL to Fred Hummel, July 21, 1926, and HL to Fred Hummel, September 2, 1926.
29. This conclusion is supported by many of the people I interviewed.
30. Cerf interview.
31. See the *New York Times*, July 13, 1925, p. 12:3, for announcement of the sale.
32. Interview with Anita Loos, November 12, 1962. Miss Loos recalled that after H. L. Mencken had read her manuscript, he remarked: "Little girl, you're making fun of sex, and that's never been done before in the United States." See also Anita Loos, *A Girl Like I* (New York, 1966), pp. 265–270.
33. Loos and Komroff interviews.
34. Rascoe, *A Bookman Day Book*, pp. 199–200.
35. Loos interview; see also *A Girl Like I*, p. 272.
36. Mott, *Golden Multitudes*, p. 326, and Hackett *Fifty Years of Best Sellers*, p. 53.
37. Material in this paragraph is based on interviews with Anita Loos, Manuel Komroff, and Donald Friede. According to the Statement of Operations for the firm in 1930, 187,298 copies of *Gentlemen Prefer Blondes* had been sold. See also Friede, *The Mechanical Angel*, pp. 18–19.

Sherwood Anderson

1. James Schevill, *Sherwood Anderson* (Denver, 1951), p. 80.
2. *Ibid.*, pp. 72–73. See also Irving Howe, *Sherwood Anderson* (New York, 1951), pp. 56, 76.
3. *Sherwood Anderson's Memoirs* (New York, 1942), p. 334. See also

Theodore Dreiser to HL, December 3, 1920, in the *Letters of Theodore Dreiser*, ed. Robert H. Elias (Philadelphia, 1959), I, p. 331.

4. Schevill, *Sherwood Anderson*, p. 91, and Howe, *Sherwood Anderson*, pp. 83, 88.
5. Howe, *Sherwood Anderson*, p. 88.
6. Schevill, *Sherwood Anderson*, pp. 81, 111, 151.
7. SA to Trigant Burrow, September 15, 1919, printed in full in the *Letters of Sherwood Anderson*, eds. Howard Mumford Jones and Walter B. Rideout (Boston, 1953), pp. 48–49.
8. Howe, *Sherwood Anderson*, p. 112.
9. Schevill, *Sherwood Anderson*, pp. 126, 152; Howe, *Sherwood Anderson*, pp. 134–135.
10. Schevill, *Sherwood Anderson*, pp. 152–153.
11. SA to Trigant Burrow, October 12, 1921, printed in full in the *Letters*, pp. 74–75.
12. Schevill, *Sherwood Anderson*, pp. 174–176, and Howe, *Sherwood Anderson*, p. 142. In a letter to Lucile Blum, July 1, 1923, Anderson said that magazines were reluctant to accept his stories as a result of the *Many Marriages* trouble—*Letters*, p. 101.
13. Huebsch's letter appears in Schevill's *Anderson*, p. 177.
14. SA to Roger Sergel, December 18, 1923, printed in full in the *Letters*, pp. 116–118.
15. Komroff interview; see also Schevill, *Sherwood Anderson*, p. 196, and SA to Alfred Stieglitz, July 12, 1924, printed in the *Letters*, p. 127.
16. Howe, *Sherwood Anderson*, p. 134.
17. Schevill, *Sherwood Anderson*, p. 185. See also T. R. Smith to SA, August 15, 1923, HL to SA, February 11, 1924, and HL to SA, February 25, 1924.
18. Komroff interview.
19. Otto Liveright to SA, May 26, 1924.
20. *Sherwood Anderson's Memoirs*, p. 352.
21. Schevill, *Sherwood Anderson*, p. 196.
22. Komroff interview.
23. Howe, *Sherwood Anderson*, p. 146; see also Schevill, *Sherwood Anderson*, p. 204.
24. HL to SA, November 18, 1924.
25. SA to HL, after November 22, 1924.
26. SA to Paul Rosenfeld, December (?), 1924, printed in the *Letters*, p. 133.
27. *Sherwood Anderson's Memoirs*, pp. 354–355. See also the *Memoirs*,

ed. Ray Lewis White (Chapel Hill, N.C., 1969), pp. 491–492.

28. Huebsch interview.
29. See also Schevill, *Sherwood Anderson*, pp. 205–206.
30. HL to SA, April 11, 1925.
31. SA to JE, April 5, 1925.
32. SA to OL, April 5, 1925.
33. Huebsch and Komroff interviews. See also Schevill, *Sherwood Anderson*, p. 206.
34. SA to BH, April 15, 1925.
35. SA to HL, April 15, 1925.
36. SA to HL, April 18, 1925, printed in full in the *Letters*, pp. 141–143.
37. SA to HL, May 6, 1925, printed in full in the *Letters*, p. 143.
38. TRS to HL, May 23, 1925. See also HL to SA, May 26, 1925.
39. HL to SA, September 12, 1925. See also Schevill, *Sherwood Anderson*, p. 206.
40. HL to SA, September 19, 1925. See also Schevill, *Sherwood Anderson*, pp. 206–207.
41. See also Schevill, *Sherwood Anderson*, pp. 206–207. According to the Statement of Operations for the firm, by December 31, 1930, 29,240 copies of *Dark Laughter* had been sold.
42. SA to Alfred Stieglitz, December 31, 1925, printed in the *Letters*, p. 151.
43. SA to Konrad Bercovici, September (?), 1925.
44. Schevill, *Sherwood Anderson*, pp. 224–225.
45. SA to HL, August 17, 1926. For Liveright's small profit of *Dark Laughter* see HL to SA, March 9, 1926.
46. Schevill, *Sherwood Anderson*, p. 231.
47. SA to Ralph Church, September 28, 1927, printed in full in the *Letters*, pp. 174–176.
48. *Sherwood Anderson's Memoirs*, pp. 365–366. See also the *Memoirs*, ed. Ray Lewis White, pp. 493–495.
49. HL to SA, March 2, 1929.
50. SA to HL, March 5, 1929.
51. SA to HL, July 8, 1929, July 29, 1929, and November 11, 1929.
52. SA to HL, December 16, 1929, printed in full in the *Letters*, pp. 200–201.
53. HL to SA, December 16, 1929.
54. Schevill, *Sherwood Anderson*, pp. 266–268. See also Howe, *Sherwood Anderson*, pp. 212–213.
55. SA to HL, December 27, 1929.
56. HL to SA, December 30, 1929. See also HL to SA, January 2, 1930.

Hemingway, Faulkner, Jeffers, and Crane

1. Carlos Baker, *Hemingway, The Writer as Artist* (Princeton, 1963), pp. 349–350.
2. Carlos Baker, *Ernest Hemingway: A Life Story* (New York, 1969), p. 133.
3. *Ibid.*, p. 139.
4. *Ibid.*, p. 133.
5. *Ibid.*, pp. 133, 139.
6. Baker, *Hemingway, The Writer as Artist*, pp. 29–30, 350.
7. Interviews with Stern and Komroff.
8. Baker, *Ernest Hemingway: A Life Story*, pp. 147, 588. See also James Schevill, *Sherwood Anderson* (Denver, 1951), p. 207.
9. Baker, *Ernest Hemingway: A Life Story*, pp. 140–141.
10. EH to HL, March 31, 1925. This letter and all the other Liveright-Hemingway correspondence cited in this chapter are in the Clifton Waller Barrett Library of the University of Virginia.
11. Baker, *Ernest Hemingway: A Life Story*, p. 144.
12. FSF to MP, circa April 22, 1925, printed in *The Letters of F. Scott Fitzgerald*, ed. Andrew Turnbull (New York, 1963), p. 179.
13. EH to HL, June 21, 1925.
14. *Ibid.*
15. Baker, *Ernest Hemingway: A Life Story*, p. 158. According to the Statement of Operations for the firm in 1930, 1942 copies of *In Our Time* were sold between 1925 and 1930.
16. EH to HL, December 7, 1925.
17. EH to FSF, December 31, 1925, see Baker, *Hemingway, The Writer as Artist,* p. 38.
18. *Ibid.* See also Fitzgerald to Perkins, circa December 30, 1925, and circa January 19, 1926, printed in *The Letters of F. Scott Fitzgerald*, pp. 195–196, 197–198.
19. Baker, *Ernest Hemingway: A Life Story*, p. 162.
20. HL to EH, December 30, 1925.
21. Baker, *Ernest Hemingway: A Life Story*, p. 162.
22. FSF to MP, circa January 19, 1926, printed in *The Letters of F. Scott Fitzgerald*, p. 198.
23. Interviews with Friede and Stern.
24. Baker, *Ernest Hemingway: A Life Story*, p. 164.
25. Friede interview. See also Baker, *Ernest Hemingway: A Life Story*, p. 184.

26. Schevill, *Sherwood Anderson*, pp. 194–195, 207. See also Irving Howe, *Sherwood Anderson* (New York, 1951), pp. 144–145.

27. William Faulkner, "Sherwood Anderson: An Appreciation," *The Achievement of Sherwood Anderson*, ed. Ray Lewis White (Chapel Hill, N.C., 1966), p. 199.

28. SA to Phil Stone, August 17, 1925, printed in the *Letters of Sherwood Anderson*, eds. Howard Mumford Jones and Walter B. Rideout (Boston, 1953), pp. 145–146. See also SA to HL, June 1, 1925, and HL to SA, June 5, 1925.

29. HL to SA, June 12, 1925. See also SA to HL, August 28, 1925, printed in the *Letters*, p. 146, and Schevill, *Sherwood Anderson*, p. 207.

30. SA to HL, April 19, 1926, printed in full in the *Letters*, *pp.* 154–155.

31. HL to SA, April 26, 1926.

32. The Statement of Operations for the firm shows that 2,193 copies of *Soldiers' Pay* were sold between publication and December 31, 1930.

33. The Statement of Operations for the firm shows that 1,793 copies of *Mosquitoes* were sold between publication and December 31, 1930.

34. Kronenberger interview. See also Louis Kronenberger, "Gambler in Publishing: Horace Liveright," *Atlantic Monthly* CCXV (January, 1965), p. 100.

35. Melba Berry Bennett, *The Stone Mason of Tor House: The Life and Work of Robinson Jeffers* (The Ward Ritchie Press, 1966), p. 103.

36. *Ibid.*, pp. 103–106, and Friede interview.

37. Bennett, *Robinson Jeffers*, p. 106.

38. RJ to George Sterling, August 8, 1925, RJ to GS, November 3, 1925, and RJ to Donald Friede, November 25, 1925, all printed in *The Selected Letters of Robinson Jeffers, 1897–1962*, ed. Ann N. Ridgeway (Baltimore, 1968), pp. 44, 50, 52.

39. Friede interview. See also *The Selected Letters*.

40. According to the Statement of Operations for the firm, 5,201 copies of *Roan Stallion, Tamar, and Other Poems*, 2,919 copies of *The Women at Point Sur*, and 3,070 copies of *Dear Judas and Other Poems* were sold between the publication of these volumes and December 31, 1930.

41. RJ to Donald Friede, August 20, 1931, printed in *The Selected Letters*, p. 180.

42. Cerf interview. See also Bennett, *Robinson Jeffers*, p. 154.

43. Interviews with Komroff and Friede.

44. Interviews with Komroff and Kronenberger.

45. Brom Weber, *Hart Crane* (New York, 1948), p. 3.

46. *Ibid.*, p. 33.

47. Philip Horton, *Hart Crane, The Life of an American Poet* (New York, 1937), p. 64.

48. Munson interview.

49. HC to Grace Hart Crane, June 10, 1923, printed in full in *The Letters of Hart Crane, 1916-1932,* ed. Brom Weber (New York, 1952), pp. 135-136.

50. HC to Grace Hart Crane, January 24, 1924, printed in *The Letters,* p. 171.

51. HC to GHC, March 28, 1925, p. 201.

52. HC to Thomas Seltzer, May 4, 1925, and HC to Waldo Frank, July (?), 1925, both printed in *The Letters,* pp. 202-203, and 212-213.

53. HC to William Sommer, October 27, 1925, printed in full in *The Letters,* pp. 218-219.

54. Horton, *Hart Crane,* p. 191. See also HC to Waldo Frank, June 19, 1926, printed in *The Letters,* pp. 258-260.

55. Horton, *Hart Crane,* p. 192. See also HC to Otto Kahn, December 9, 1925, and March 18, 1926, printed in *The Letters,* pp. 222-224, and 240-242.

56. John Unterecker, *Voyager, A Life of Hart Crane* (New York, 1969), pp. 427-428.

57. HC to WF, June 19, 1926, printed in full in *The Letters,* pp. 258-260.

58. HC to WF, July 3, 1926, printed in full in *The Letters,* pp. 262-263. In his letter Crane quotes Sue Jenkins' account.

59. HC to Grace Hart Crane, July 30, 1926, printed in full in *The Letters,* pp. 269-270.

60. Horton, *Hart Crane,* p. 221.

61. HC to Waldo Frank, January 28, 1927, and HC to Allen Tate, March 30, 1927, printed in *The Letters,* pp. 285-286 and 294-295.

62. HL to HC, March 25, 1929. See also HC to Isidor Schneider, May 1, 1929, printed in *The Letters,* pp. 340-342.

63. Memorandum from Messner to Liveright, April 10, 1929.

64. *Ibid.*

65. During 1930, 712 copies of *The Bridge* were sold, according to the Statement of Operations for the firm dated December 31, 1930. See also HL to HC, January 13, 1930, and HC to HL, February 21, 1930. A limited edition of *The Bridge* was issued by the Black Sun Press just prior to its publication by Liveright.

66. TRS to Grace Hart Crane, May 26, 1932. This letter is in the Special Collections Department of the Columbia University Library in New York.

An American Tragedy

1. HL to TD, September 1, 1922.
2. TRS to TD, June 3, 1925.
3. HL to TD, May 6, 1924.
4. Komroff interview.
5. Komroff interview for the paragraph.
6. W. A. Swanberg, *Dreiser* (New York, 1965), pp. 295–296.
7. *Ibid.*, p. 297.
8. TRS to TD, January 9, 1926.
9. Swanberg, *Dreiser*, p. 318.
10. *Ibid.*, pp. 310–311, 318. According to the Statement of Operations for the firm, 77,398 copies of *An American Tragedy* were sold between its publication and December 31, 1930.
11. Swanberg, *Dreiser*, p. 369.
12. *Ibid.*, p. 318.
13. *The Best Plays of 1925–1926*, ed. Burns Mantle (New York, 1926), pp. 472, 608.
14. HL to TD, March 8, 1926.
15. HL to TD, March 11, 1926.
16. Different versions of this incident appear in several places. The most thorough account is in Swanberg, *Dreiser*, pp. 305–308; others include Helen Dreiser, *My Life with Dreiser* (New York, 1951), pp. 121–123; Donald Friede, *The Mechanical Angel* (New York, 1948), p. 42; Robert H. Elias, *Theodore Dreiser: Apostle of Nature* (New York, 1949), p. 226; and Bennett Cerf, "As Publisher Sees Author," *Variety* (January 9, 1963), p. 12.
17. TD to HL, March 23, 1926.
18. The contract was dated June 2, 1926.
19. *The Best Plays of 1926–1927*, ed. Burns Mantle (New York, 1927), pp. 399–400.
20. Swanberg, *Dreiser*, p. 315.
21. Friede, *The Mechanical Angel*, pp. 42–43.
22. HL to FH, July 9, 1926.
23. *New York Times*, July 24, 1926, p. 9:2.
24. HL to FH, September 2, 1926.
25. *The Best Plays of 1926–1927*, ed. Burns Mantle (New York, 1927), p. 395. See also the *New York Times*, July 10, 1926, p. 5:2.
26. Friede, *The Mechanical Angel*, pp. 39–40.
27. HL to Betsy Wallerstein, February 24, 1927.

28. Alfred Wallerstein to HL, February 24, 1927.
29. HL to Julie Lasdun, July 7, 1927.
30. HL to Alfred Wallerstein, August 3, 1927. Dorothy Peterson was an actress on Broadway during the Twenties. Later she went to Hollywood and appeared in supporting roles in many films.

Two Censorship Trials

1. Material in this paragraph is based on the *New York Times*, March 9, 1928, p. 8:2; March 20, 1928, p. 18:2, and March 21, 1928, p. 28:1.
2. *Ibid.*, July 1, 1925, p. 3:4; see also *Publishers' Weekly*, July 4, 1925, p. 32.
3. Arthur Garfield Hays, *Let Freedom Ring* (New York, 1928), p. 266. Hays was a director of the American Civil Liberties Union in New York. Throughout his career as a lawyer he was involved in numerous cases dealing with civil liberties. For example, he was active in opening up closed towns during the Pennsylvania coal strikes of 1922; he took part in the Scopes trial (1925); the Sweet case in Detroit involving segregation (1925); the *American Mercury* censorship case in Boston (1926); and the Sacco-Vanzetti case (1927).
4. *New York Times*, February 10, 1927, p. 1:8.
5. *The Best Plays of 1926–1927*, ed. Burns Mantle (New York, 1927), pp. vi-vii, 390. *The Captive* was chosen one of the ten best plays of the season by New York drama critics.
6. *New York Times*, February 16, 1927, p. 1:5 and February 17, 1927, pp. 1:6, 20:1, for the paragraph.
7. *Ibid.*, February 17, 1927, p. 1:6.
8. Details about Liveright's activities appear in the *Times*, February 19, 1927, p. 32:2; February 20, 1927, p. 1:2; February 26, 1927, p. 15:1; March 1, 1927, p. 21:2; and March 3, 1927, p. 25:3. See also Hays, *Let Freedom Ring*, pp. 252–258.
9. *New York Times*, March 9, 1927, p. 27:1. See also Hays, *Let Freedom Ring*, pp. 257–264.
10. Hays, *Let Freedom Ring*, pp. 226–266.
11. *New York Times*, March 20, 1928, p. 18:2. See also the *New York Evening Telegram*, March 20, 1928, in the Liveright Collection at the University of Pennsylvania.
12. *New York Times*, March 21, 1928, p. 28:1.
13. *Ibid.*
14. This group of newspaper clippings concerning the trial is in the Liveright Collection at the University of Pennsylvania.

15. *Ibid.*
16. *Ibid.* See also the *Times*, March 23, 1928, p. 14:6.
17. Hays, *Let Freedom Ring*, p. 266. See also the *New York Times*, March 24, 1928, p. 30:6, and *Publishers' Weekly*, March 31, 1928, p. 1449.
18. According to the Statement of Operations for the firm dated December 31, 1930, 32,973 copies of *Replenishing Jessica* had been sold.
19. March 27, 1928.
20. A complete list of jurors and their replies are in the Liveright Collection at the University of Pennsylvania.
21. Louise Heald to HL, November 11, 1929.
22. MB to HL, August 18, 1927.
23. Liveright wrote across the bottom of Bodenheim's letter, "I gave him $75.00."
24. MB to JM, March 27, 1928.
25. HL to MB, March 29, 1928.
26. MB to HL, March (?), 1928. Liveright's check was dated April 2, 1928.
27. MB to HL, June 25, 1928.
28. MB to JM, August 24, 1928.
29. HL to MB, August 28, 1928.
30. Hays, *Let Freedom Ring*, p. 165.
31. Edward Weeks, "The Practice of Censorship," *Atlantic Monthly*, CVL (January, 1930), pp. 22–23.
32. *New York Times*, July 3, 1927, II, p. 2:6, for material in this paragraph. See also Boyer, *Purity in Print*, pp. 171–172; Hays, *Let Freedom Ring*, p. 165; and Weeks, "The Practice of Censorship," pp. 22–23.
33. Hays, *Let Freedom Ring*, pp. 166–168, and Boyer, *Purity in Print*, pp. 176–178.
34. *New York Times*, March 12, 1927, p. 1:4. See also Boyer, *Purity in Print*, pp. 181–183, and Hays, *Let Freedom Ring*, p. 185.
35. *New York Times*, March 13, 1927, p. 2:5.
36. *Ibid.*, March 14, 1927, p. 14:7.
37. *Ibid.*, March 12, 1927, p. 1:4.
38. *Ibid.*, April 13. 1927, p. 16:5. See also Boyer, *Purity in Print*, p. 185.
39. *New York Times*, April 14, 1927, p. 20:3. See also *Publishers' Weekly*, April 16, 1927, pp. 1569–1571.
40. *Ibid.*
41. Friede interview and DF to HL, April 15, 1927. See also *The*

Mechanical Angel, pp. 137–138, and Hays, *Let Freedom Ring,* p. 189.

42. *New York Times,* April 17, 1927, p. 23:7. See also Hays, *Let Freedom Ring,* p. 190, and Boyer, *Purity in Print,* pp. 185–186.
43. *New York Times,* April 23, 1927, p. 14:5, and *Publishers' Weekly,* April 30, 1927, p. 1712. See also Friede, *The Mechanical Angel,* pp. 137–138, and Boyer, *Purity in Print,* p. 186.
44. Hays, *Let Freedom Ring,* pp. 190–191.
45. Hays to Edward Weeks, December 12, 1929, in the Liveright Collection at the University of Pennsylvania.
46. *New York Times,* May 28, 1927, p. 15:6, and June 13, 1927, p. 19:3. See also Hays, *Let Freedom Ring,* pp. 191–192.
47. *New York Times,* June 23, 1927, p. 23:2. See also Boyer, *Purity in Print,* pp. 186–187.
48. *New York Times,* January 22, 1928, III, p. 1:6, for the paragraph.
49. *Ibid.,* April 17, 1929, p. 14:2.
50. *Transcript* of the trial, pp. 3–4. Material having to do with the *American Tragedy* case, both in 1927 and 1929, is located in the Theodore Dreiser Collection, Department of Special Collections, The University Library, University of California, Los Angeles, California.
51. *Ibid.,* pp. 37–38.
52. *Ibid.,* p. 83.
53. *Ibid.,* p. 84.
54. *Ibid.,* p. 90.
55. *New York Times,* April 17, 1929, p. 12:3. See also Boyer, *Purity in Print,* pp. 193–194.
56. Boyer, *Purity in Print,* p. 194.
57. *Transcript,* pp. 119–120.
58. *New York Times,* April 18, 1929, p. 2:3.
59. *Ibid.*
60. *Transcript,* p. 153.
61. *Ibid.,* p. 146.
62. *New York Times,* April 19, 1929, p. 1:5.
63. AGH to HL, April 18, 1929.
64. Donald Friede to HL, April 18, 1929. See also the *New York Times,* April 19, 1929, p. 1:5, and *Publishers' Weekly,* April 20, 1929, p. 1906.
65. *New York Times,* April 28, 1929, III, p. 1:6.
66. *Ibid.,* April 19, 1929, p. 1:5, and December 5, 1929, p. 13:5. See Friede's version of the trial in *The Mechanical Angel,* pp. 142–148, and *Publishers' Weekly,* December 7, 1929, p. 2676.

67. Arthur Garfield Hays to Edward Weeks, December 12, 1929.

68. Material in this and the next paragraph is based on Hays' appeal brief, which, along with the transcript of the trial, is located in the Dreiser Collection at the University of California. Hays' argument is specifically set forth on pages 1–5. See also the *New York Times*, April 1, 1930, p. 24:4–5.

69. Appeal brief, p. 15.

70. *Publishers' Weekly*, June 7, 1930, p. 2826. Eventually Friede paid the fine. See the *New York Times*, August 5, 1930, p. 14:5, and August 12, 1930, p. 24:6.

71. Edward Weeks, "The Practice of Censorship," p. 24.

72. Boyer, *Purity in Print*, pp. 201, 205.

73. Anne Lyon Haight, *Banned Books* (New York, 1955), pp. 78, 101–102.

74. *Ibid.* See *Commonwealth vs. Isenstadt* (318 Mass. 543).

75. Haight, *Banned Books*, pp.113–114.

76. Charles Rembar, The End of Obscenity (New York, 1968) pp. 193–194.

Eugene O'Neill

1. All of the following letters written by O'Neill are deposited in the Baker Library, Dartmouth College, Hanover, New Hampshire. Those written by Liveright are in the Liveright Collection at the University of Pennsylvania.

2. Undated memorandum in the Liveright Collection at the University of Pennsylvania.

3. Arthur and Barbara Gelb, *O'Neill* (New York, 1962), p. 651.

4. *Ibid.*

5. Komroff interview and the Gelbs, *O'Neill*, pp. 574–575, for the remainder of the paragraph.

6. Komroff interview for the paragraph. See also the Gelbs, *O'Neill*, pp. 651–652.

7. Gelbs, *O'Neill*, pp. 703–704. See also Lawrence Langner, *The Magic Curtain* (New York, 1951), p. 276.

8. AP to HL, September 27, 1925.

9. HL to AP, October 8, 1925.

10. AP to HL, June 29, 1926.

11. AP to HL, August 27, 1929.

12. HL to AP, September 28, 1929.

13. AP to HL, October 7, 1929.
14. HL to AP, October 17, 1929.
15. AP to HL, October 25, 1929.
16. Gelbs, *O'Neill*, pp. 703–704, for the paragraph.
17. O'N to HL, June 14, 1929, printed in the Gelbs, *O'Neill*, p. 704.
18. HL to O'N, June 25, 1929.
19. Gelbs, *O'Neill*, p. 730. See also the *New York Times*, July 28, 1929, p. 20:1.
20. Gelbs, *O'Neill*, pp. 654, 742, 885.
21. *Ibid.*, p. 674. According to the Statement of Operations for the firm dated December 31, 1930 107,474 copies of *Strange Interlude* had been sold.
22. *Dynamo* opened on February 11, 1929. See the Gelbs, *O'Neill*, p. 687.
23. HL to O'N, February 28, 1929.
24. O'N to HL, February 17, 1929. See also the Gelbs, *O'Neill*, pp. 688–689.
25. HL to O'N, February 28, 1929.
26. Gelbs, *O'Neill*, pp. 688–689.
27. HL to O'N, March 20, 1929.
28. Gelbs, *O'Neill*, p. 689.
29. HL to O'N, April 3, 1929.
30. HL to O'N, June 25, 1929.
31. O'N to HL, June 14, 1929 and July 26, 1929 for the paragraph.
32. HL to O'N, August 12, 1929.
33. HL to O'N, June 19, 1930.
34. HL to O'N, July 28, 1930.
35. *New York Times*, March 12, 1931, p. 23:1. See also the Gelbs, *O'Neill*, pp. 730–733, and Langner, *The Magic Curtain*, p. 276.
36. *New York Times*, March 13, 1931, p. 48:2, and March 14, 1931, p. 23:1.
37. Gelbs, *O'Neill*, pp. 730, 733. See also Langner, *The Magic Curtain*, p. 276.
38. Cerf interview.

Horace Liveright, Inc.

1. Komroff and Kronenberger interviews for the paragraph. See also the B & L catalogue for Fall, 1927 and Fall, 1928, as well as the *New York Times*, November 19, 1928, p. 9:1, for the Judd Gray book.
2. Undated memoranda. Mrs. Hall was arrested in 1927 for the murders

of Reverend Edward Wheeler Hall and Mrs. Eleanor Mills five years before.

3. The Black and Gold Library is still in existence, as one of the publications of the Liveright Publishing Corporation.

4. Interviews with Komroff, Sussman, and Siwek.

5. Liveright advertisements at this time cite a report of the *Retail Bookseller*, a publication of the Baker and Taylor Company, "the world's largest wholesale book jobbers." The works specifically referred to in the ads were: *Strange Interlude, Sunset Gun, Unforbidden Fruit, Poems in Praise of Practically Nothing, Georgie May,* and *But—Gentlemen Marry Brunettes.*

6. Komroff interview. According to the Statement of Operations for the firm, for example, 85,383 copies of *Revelry*, 41,606 copies of *Enough Rope*, 23,228 copies of *Georgie May*, 36,496 copies of *The Crystal Cup*, 33,216 copies of *My Life*, and 18,332 of *Meet General Grant* were sold between the dates of their publication and December 31, 1930.

7. See *The Letters of Frances Newman*, ed. Hansell Baugh (New York, 1929), for material about Miss Newman.

8. Other members of the Round Table who were published by Liveright included: Marc Connelly, George S. Kaufman, Herman Manckiewicz, John Peter Toohey, and, occasionally, Burton Rascoe and Lawrence Langner.

9. Fall, 1927 catalogue, and Fall, 1928 catalogue.

10. *Ibid.*

11. Kronenberger interview.

12. KAP to HL, June 10, 1929.

13. HL to KAP, June 14, 1929.

14. KAP to HL, June 29, 1929.

15. HL to KAP, September 4, 1929.

16. KAP to HL, December 8, 1929.

17. HL to KAP, December 10, 1929.

18. Portions of *The Devil and Cotton Mather* appeared as follows: "Affection of Praehimincies," *Accent*, II (Spring, 1942), 131–138, and (Summer, 1942), 226–232; "A Bright Particular Faith," *Hound and Horn*, VII (January, 1934), 246–247; and "A Goat for Azazel," *Partisan Review*, VII (May-June, 1940), 188–199—Edward Schwartz, *Katherine Anne Porter: A Critical Bibliography* (New York, 1953), p. 27.

19. 5,238 copies were sold between publication and Dceember 31, 1930, according to the Statement of Operations for the firm.

20. Komroff and Kronenberger interviews.
21. Wasserman joined B & L through the efforts of Ludwig Lewisohn. See LL to HL, October 8, 1924. Wassermann's royalty statement for the six months ending June 30, 1928, showed the author's credits amounted to $334.42.
22. JW to HL, November 14, 1928.
23. HL to EL, January 21, 1927.
24. By December 31, 1920, 251,715 copies of *Napoleon* had been sold, according to the Statement of Operations for the firm.
25. HL to EL, February 25, 1927.
26. EL to HL, April 6, 1927.
27. EL to HL, August 19, 1927.
28. HL to EL, November 16, 1927.
29. EL to HL, November 30, 1927.
30. HL to EL, January 19, 1928.
31. EL to HL, April 25, 1928; EL to HL, April 29, 1928; HL to EL, April 30, 1928; EL to HL, May 1, 1928; and HL to EL, May 2, 1928.
32. HL to EL, June 25, 1928.
33. HL to EL, October 3, 1928.
34. EL to HL, August 13, 1928.
35. August 21, 1928.
36. HL to ER, June 26, 1929.
37. Friede interview. Mauriac was taken over by Covici-Friede, which issued *Destinies* and *The Desert of Love* in 1929 and *The Family* in 1930.
38. Friede interview. See also Donald Friede, *The Mechanical Angel* (New York, 1948), pp. 70–73, and Richard Ellmann, *James Joyce* (New York, 1959), p. 599.
39. *Ibid.*
40. *Ibid.* See also the *Letters of James Joyce,* ed. Stuart Gilbert (New York, 1966), I, p. 253, for Joyce's letter to Harriet Shaw Weaver, May 20, 1927.
41. See, for example, the following memoranda: HL to DF, June 20, 1927; DF to HL, June 22, 1927; DF to HL, July 5, 1927; and HL to DF, July 11, 1927.
42. Apparently Liveright was never able to buy back all of Friede's stock. According to an examination of the firm's books made in December, 1932, Friede held nearly half the preferred stock in Liveright, Inc.
43. HL to Julie Lasdun, February 6, 1928.
44. HL to Julie Lasdun, April 16, 1928.

45. *The Best Plays of 1927–1928*, ed. Burns Mantle (New York, 1928), pp. 422–424. See also the *New York Times*, August 1, 1927, p. 25:5.
46. HL to AW, July 26, 1928.
47. House publicity release, August, 1928. See also HL to Rose Macaulay, January 18, 1928.

1929–1930

1. HL to Rose Macaulay, December 17, 1928, and Curtis Brown to HL, December 20, 1928.
2. In a letter to Joel Spingarn on August 31, 1927, Mumford said he was looking for a "respectable" house, and in March, 1928, he signed with Harcourt. Mumford's letters to Spingarn are deposited in the Manuscripts Division of the New York Public Library.
3. See Adams to HL, January 9, 1930. For Dreiser, see HL to Arthur Garfield Hays, February 11, 1929, and W. A. Swanberg, *Dreiser* (New York, 1965), pp. 349–351.
4. HL to FH, January 4, 1923.
5. HL to FH, February 8, 1923.
6. HL to FH, September 5, 1923.
7. HL to FH, October 4, 1924.
8. *Ibid.*
9. HL to FH, May 20, 1925.
10. HL to Emory Buckner, February 16, 1929.
11. Alice Payne Hackett, *Fifty Years of Best Sellers, 1895–1945* (New York, 1945), p. 59. See also Frank Luther Mott, *Golden Multitudes* (New York, 1947), p. 326. According to the Statement of Operations for the firm, 159,158 copies of *Henry VIII* were sold between its publication and December 31, 1930.
12. FH to HL, August 6, 1929.
13. HL to FH, June 3, 1929.
14. HL to FH, September 10, 1929.
15. FH to HL, December 4, 1929.
16. HL to FH, January 8, 1930.
17. According to the Statement of Operations for the firm, 16,352 copies of *Peter Arno's Parade* and 19,305 copies of *Hullabaloo* were sold between publication and December 31, 1930.
18. HL to MG, August 9, 1928. See also MG to HL, July (?), 1928.
19. 13,370 according to the Statement of Operations for the firm.
20. EP to HL, March 24, 1929.

21. HL to EP, April 19, 1929.
22. Komroff and Kronenberger interviews.
23. GA to HL, October 11, 1928.
24. AS to HL, October 14, 1928.
25. NH to HL, October 18, 1928.
26. NH to HL, January 3, 1929, and AS to HL, January 8, 1929.
27. IP to HL, January 9, 1929.
28. GA to HL, January (?), 1929.
29. GA to HL, January 27, 1929.
30. GA to HL, February 16, 1929.
31. HL to GA, February 18, 1929.
32. GA to HL, February 19, 1929.
33. HL to GA, May 27, 1929.
34. HL to GA, June 4, 1929.
35. GA to HL, June 29, 1929.
36. HL to GA, July 11, 1929.
37. GA to HL, July 16, 1929.
38. HL to GA, July 18, 1929.
39. HL to GA, July 30, 1929.
40. HL to GA, August 6, 1929.
41. GA to HL, August 13, 1929.
42. GA to HL, September 21, 1929.
43. HL to GA, December 16, 1929.
44. Swanberg, *Dreiser*, pp. 359, 379.
45. *Ibid.*, pp. 340, 349, 379.
46. *Ibid.*, p. 343.
47. Dreiser's contract, April 19, 1929, and the minutes of the Board of Directors Meeting of Horace Liveright, Inc., February 11, 1929 for the paragraph. See also Swanberg, *Dreiser*, pp. 349–350.
48. Memorandum on Russell's work dated September, 1926.
49. Contract dated July 28, 1927. See also BR to HL, February 9, 1926.
50. HL to BR, July 9, 1929.
51. A paragraph on Liveright appears on page 114 of the first edition.
52. HL to BR, July 31, 1929.
53. According to the Statement of Operations for the firm, 23,136 copies of *Marriage and Morals* were sold between its publication and December 1, 1930.
54. HL to BR, April 5, 1930.
55. HL to BR, July 7, 1930.

1. For example, see the *New York Times*, May 23, 1930, pp. 22:3, 25:1; May 24, 1930, p. 8:1; May 26, 1930, p. 7:6; and May 29, 1930, p. 39:7.
2. HL to O'N, July 28, 1930.
3. Interviews with Komroff, Siwek, and Sussman. See also Bennett Cerf, "Horace Liveright, An Unedited Obituary," *Publishers' Weekly*, October 7, 1933, pp. 1229–1230.
4. HL to AW, June 5, 1929.
5. HL to Leon Amster, August 29, 1929.
6. HL to AW, February 6, 1930.
7. Louis Cline to Gilmer, December 8, 1961.
8. Kronenberger interview.
9. HL to FH, September 6, 1929.
10. *New York Times*, January 10, 1930, p. 11:1; see also *Publishers' Weekly*, January 18, 1930, p. 311.
11. *New York Times*, March 15, 1930, p. 24:2.
12. FH to HL, March 20, 1930, and April 7, 1930.
13. FH to HL, April 7, 1930.
14. *Ibid.*
15. HL to Charles Gordon.
16. Dreiser's contract also guaranteed the author a 20 per cent royalty on each copy of any new work written by him that Liveright sold.
17. June 20, 1930.
18. July 7, 1930.
19. *New York Times*, July 19, 1930, p. 6:1. See also *Publishers' Weekly*, July 23, 1930.
20. According to an examination of the firm's books executed by Adolf Hirschfield in December, 1932, Arthur Pell and Donald Friede owned most of the preferred stock in Horace Liveright, Inc. Pell owned well over two thirds of the common stock, and Alfred Wallerstein was president of the corporation. Of the 2,150 shares in the company, Pell owned 1,055, Friede, 841, and eight others owned the remaining 254.
21. *Publishers' Weekly*, June 20, 1931, p. 2867. See also Louis Kronenberger, "Gambler in Publishing: Horace Liveright," *Atlantic Monthly*, CCXV (January, 1965), pp. 102–104.
22. *New York Times*, May 5, 1933, p. 16:3. See also May 6, 1933, p. 14:1, and *Publishers' Weekly*, May 13, 1933.

23. The Statement of Operations for the firm in 1932 shows $115,601.56 in royalties advanced; $38,555.97 in royalties payable (including $4,871.32 owed O'Neill); and a total deficit of $30,515.28.

24. *Publishers' Weekly*, June 17, 1933, p. 1544.

25. *Ibid.*, July 29, 1933, p. 278.

26. *New York Times*, December 9, 1931, p. 33:6.

27. *Ibid.*, June 18, 1932, p. 14:5.

28. *Ibid.*, January 30, 1933, p. 9:6.

29. *Ibid.*, September 25, 1933, p. 15:1. See also September 27, 1933, p. 21:2.

30. *Publishers' Weekly*, October 7, 1933, pp. 1229–1230.

31. *Sherwood Anderson's Memoirs* (New York, 1942), p. 357. See also the *Memoirs*, ed. Ray Lewis White (Chapel Hill, N.C., 1969), p. 518.

Index

Laforgue, Jules, 197
Langner, Lawrence, 3, 20, 79, 99, 184
Lansbury, George, 28
Lasky, Jesse L., 84, 136, 139, 140, 141, 142, 143, 144
Latzko, Andreas, 16, 17–18, 85
Lavelle, Thomas D., 172
Lawrence, D. H., 9, 19, 64, 65, 69
Lawrence, T. E., 36, 99
Lazarus Laughed, 175
Leech, Margaret, 188
Le Gallienne Anthology of English Poetry, The, 31
Le Gallienne, Richard, 31, 127
Leighton, Isabel, 199
Lengel, William, 41, 45
Lenin, Nikolai, 21
Let Freedom Ring, 189
Lewis, Sinclair, 43, 84
Lewisohn, Ludwig, 18, 27, 34, 85, 97, 100, 101, 235
Lewys, Gladys "Georges," 177, 178, 179, 182, 184
Liberal Club, 3, 20, 31, 83
Liberalism in the United States, 22
Light, James, 131
Lilienthal, Jesse, 227
Liliom, 31
Lincoln, Joseph C., 52
Lindsay, Benjamin, 90, 101
Literary Guild, 190, 208, 215, 216, 230, 231, 232
Literature of Ecstasy, The, 31
Little, Brown and Company, 5, 195
Little Leather Library, 3, 4
Little Review, The, 7, 30, 34, 107, 197
Little Shepherd of Kingdom Come, The, 7

Liveright, Henrietta Fleisher, 1
Liveright, Henry, 1
Liveright, Herman, 228
Liveright, Horace, life prior to entering publishing, 1–2, 4; begins publishing with Albert Boni, 1, 4–5; and Lucile Elsas Liveright, 2, 103; and Alfred Wallerstein, 4, 225–226, 227; early publications, 10–11, 16–18; as a publisher, 10, 19, 20, 23–24, 29, 41, 81, 83–86, 90, 93–95, 96, 100–102, 112, 151, 185, 200, 201, 224, 225, 229–230, 231–233, 235–237; and Theodore Dreiser, 12, 14–16, 39–59, 134–148, 219; and Andreas Latzko, 17–18; takes over Boni & Liveright, 18–19; and John Reed, 21; and Waldo Frank, 22; and Eugene O'Neill, 22–23, 175–184, 224; and T. R. Smith, 24; and Edward Bernays, 25; and Rose Macaulay, 28; and James G. Huneker, 29; and Ezra Pound, 30, 211–213; and Hendrick Willem Van Loon, 31–33; 228–229; and Harry Kemp, 34; and E. E. Cummings, 35–36; and John S. Sumner, 35, 53, 57, 58, 61–68, 73–74, 76–78, 153–154, 155, 159, 229–230; and T. S. Eliot, 37–38; and *The Story of a Lover,* 63; and *The Satyricon,* 64–68; and John Ford, 73–74, 76–78, 79–80; and the Clean Books Bill, 73–74, 76–78, 79–80; "The Absurdity of Censorship," 74–76; and Bennett Cerf, 91, 103, 235–237; and the Modern Library, 91, 103, 187; and Donald Friede, 91–92, 198;

and Gertrude Atherton, 97–98; and the theatre, 102, 148–152, 153–154, 198–199, 225, 226, 227; and the Stock Market, 102–103, 150–152, 198–200, 201, 226–227; and Anita Loos, 103–105; and Sherwood Anderson, 106, 108–119, 237; and Ernest Hemingway, 120–125; and William Faulkner, 125–127; and Robinson Jeffers, 127–128; and Hart Crane, 129–133; receives award from French government, 149; and Maxwell Bodenheim, 153, 158–162; and the *Replenishing Jessica* case, 153–154, 155–157; and the *American Tragedy* case, 164–165, 167, 172–174; and Katherine Anne Porter, 189–191; and Jakob Wassermann, 191–192; and Emil Ludwig, 192–197; and Francis Hackett, 202–211; and Michael Gold, 211; and Gertrude Atherton, 213–218; and Bertrand Russell, 219–223; and Hollywood, 222–223, 224, 225, 231, 232, 233; and Elise Bartlett Porter, 234; death, 234

Liveright, Inc., 233

Liveright, Lucile Elsas, 2, 103, 111, 151

Liveright, Lucy, 228

Liveright, Otto, 22, 109, 110, 112

Liveright Publishing Corporation, 234

Lives of the Saints, The, 207

Loeb, Harold, 120, 121

London, Jack, 6

Londres, Albert, 185

Long Voyage Home, The, 23

Longfellow, Henry Wadsworth, 5

Longmans, Green and Company, 78

Loos, Anita, 28, 101, 104–105, 159, 187

Loose Ladies, 167

Louys, Pierre, 62

Lowell, Amy, 2

Lowell, James Russell, 5

Lowie, Robert H., 31

Lucienne, 102

Ludwig, Emil, 28, 86, 187, 192–197, 201, 230

Lugosi, Bela, 199

Macaulay, Rose, 27, 28, 31, 35, 84, 96, 97, 101, 188, 201, 235

Macgowan, Kenneth, 20, 31

MacKaye, James, 18

MacKaye, Percy, 188–189

Macmillan Company, 6, 7, 41, 42, 86, 97, 127

Macrea, John, 80

Macy, John, 27, 100

Mad Professor, The, 191

Madden, Richard, 22

Mademoiselle Fifi and Other Stories, 11

Maeterlinck, Maurice, 11

Main Currents of Nineteenth Century Literature, 100

Man Nobody Knows, The, 104–105

Man, the Miracle Maker, 188

Man's Man, A, 137

Mandel, Frank, 102

Manhattan Transfer, 168

Mann, Klaus, 92

Mann, Thomas, 10, 92, 192

Mansfield, Katherine, 10

Manual of Philosophy, 211, 212

Many Marriages, 108

Virgin Man, 154
Virgin Spain, 101
Vorse, Mary Heaton, 3, 20, 23, 28, 188

Wagner, Richard, 30
Waldo Frank: A Study, 100
Walker, James J., 76, 77, 78–79, 84, 153
Walker, June, 137, 138, 148
Wallace, James G., 155, 156
Wallerstein, Alfred, 4, 150, 151, 200, 225, 227, 230
Walling, William English, 3
Walrond, Eric, 92
Wanger, Walter, 139, 140, 142, 143, 144
War in the Air, 11
Washington Square Book Shop, 2, 3, 4, 11-12, 21, 83
Washington Square Players, 3, 20
Wassermann, Jakob, 191, 192, 193
Waste Land, The, 37–38
Watch and Ward Society, 60, 162, 163, 165, 167, 170
Way of All Flesh, The, 11
We and Our Government, 85
Wedekind, Frank, 3
Wedlock, 191
Weeks, Edward A., viii, 87, 173, 174
Weinberger, Harry, 179, 183
Welded, 99, 175
Wells, H. G., 9, 11, 32, 152
West, Mae, 154
West, Nathanael, 234
Wharton, Edith, 6, 98
What I Believe, 167
What I Saw in Russia, 28
What Is the German Nation Dying For?, 18

When a Man's a Man, 8
Where the Cross is Made, 23
White Buildings, 129–133
White Wings, 188
Whitman, Walt, 27
Whittier, John Greenleaf, 5
Whose Body?, 97
Why Religion?, 188
Wiggin, Kate Douglas, 7
Wilde, Oscar, 11
Wilder, Thornton, 19
Williams, Albert Rhys, 31, 85
Williams, William Carlos, 2
Wilson, Edmund, 38, 100
Wilson, Katherine, 148
Windy McPherson's Son, 106
Winesburg, Ohio, 9, 31, 107, 109
Wister, Owen, 7
Wolfe, Thomas, 84
Women at Point Sur, The, 128
Women in Love, 64, 69, 70
Wong, Anna May, 84
Woodward, W. E., 187, 188
Woolsey, John M., 184
Work in Progress, 198
World's End, 191
Wound Stripe, 227
Wright, Harold Bell, 8, 52
Wright, Willard Huntington, 27
Wylie, Elinor, 84

Year In, You're Out, 201
Years of Indiscretion, The, vii
Yeats, William Butler, 27
Young, Art, 8, 20, 188
Young Girl's Diary, A, 64, 70
Young, Stark, 101
Youth, (Dawn), 55

Zugsmith, Leane, viii, 89